"The Government of God"

"THE GOVERNMENT OF GOD"—
Iran's Islamic Republic

Cheryl Benard *and* Zalmay Khalilzad

New York COLUMBIA UNIVERSITY PRESS

Institute of War and Peace Studies
of the School of International Affairs
of Columbia University
and
The Modern Middle East Series
No. 15
Sponsored by
The Middle East Institute
Columbia University, New York
and
The Ludwig Boltzmann Gesellschaft
Vienna, Austria

Library of Congress Cataloging in Publication Data

Benard, Cheryl, 1953–
"The government of God."

(The modern Middle East series; no. 15)
Includes bibliographical references and index.
1. Iran—Politics and government—1979– .
I. Khalilzad, Zalmay. II. Title. III. Series: Modern
Middle East series (Columbia University. Middle East
Institute); no. 15.
DS318.8.B46 1984   955′.054   83-20880
ISBN 0-231-05376-2 (alk. paper)
ISBN 0-231-05377-0   (pbk)

Columbia University Press
New York   Guildford, Surrey

For Alexander

CONTENTS

PREFACE

Our early preoccupation with the phenomenon of contemporary Iran began with a series of random events. In Hamburg during Christmas of 1977, the festively decorated inner city became a battlefield, obliging us to take refuge in a department store while heavily equipped riot police combated German students shouting for the overthrow of the Shah with the slogan "Der Schah ist, ein Mörder und Faschist." By the following Christmas, the situation looked substantially different, and when we visited Khomeini in his Parisian suburb headquarters on New Year's Eve we did not need to know the address. One merely had to follow the stream of well-wishers who all got off at the usually deserted little stop of Neauphle-le-Château. There, in a room decorated only with Persian carpets and with the cuckoo clock the former French tenants had apparently left behind, a constant crowd awaited a glimpse of the leader, engaged in heated debates with clerics, and fantasized about the future. Ibrahim Yazdi was there to instruct the Imam's followers on the proper mode of interacting with Western press: "be sure to stress three points," he told them. "The rights of minorities, the rights of women, and the holding of elections." Representatives of the Iranian left were there, and Communists, and feminists; everyone was of good cheer, and the tedious question of whether or not to wear a scarf in honor of the ayatollah was painlessly resolved, for female guests, by the below-freezing temperatures.

In 1982, we were again visiting Paris suburbs, but this time it was a different suburb and a different Iranian: Auvers-sur-Oise, historic home of Vincent Van Gogh, Abol Hasan Bani-Sadr, and Masoud Rajavi. The monarchists were ensconced in villas in Paris, and many of the formerly prominent were dead, disgraced, or imprisoned. In Westwood, California, prosperous Iranians sought a touch of home in the falafel shops, and in universities in Europe and the United States baffled Iranians of various political tendencies tried to rally their energies and to understand what had happened. And so did we.

This book represents our effort to apply social science concepts to the crisis in Iran. We would like to thank several colleagues for their comments and advice: William T. R. Fox, Joseph Rothschild, Richard Bulliet, Douglas Chalmers, Robert Jervis, John Ruggie, and J. C. Hurewitz of Columbia University; Roberta and Albert Wohlstetter of Pan Heuristics; William Griffith of MIT. Karen Mitchell and Bernard Gronert of Columbia University Press were helpful and patient with the editing and publication, and Anna Hohri of the Columbia University Institute of War and Peace Studies supervised the logistics of typing and reproducing the manuscript with her usual exemplary efficiency. We would like to thank the Ford Foundation, especially Enid Schoettle, for funding a trip to the region.

INTRODUCTION

It is common, in academic books and articles, to begin by announcing that everyone else has been wrong, or has at least missed one particularly relevant angle. Iran is an instance where no justification is needed to explain one's interest, and where at the same time claims of comprehensive analysis would be ill placed. The final word on the Iranian "revolution"—perhaps including the judgment whether it really was a revolution—will not be spoken for some time to come. Our intention, in this book, is to bring some order into the kinds of questions raised by contemporary Iranian events. Iranian students, Iranian leftists, the Shah, the U. S. government, the CIA, European activists, and the world media were not the only ones overtaken by events in Iran; the academic world, too, found itself at a loss. Its previous work on Iran had tended to express some convictions about the future of Iran that were now revealed to have been quite unfounded. What was left was a set of questions and controversies. The purpose of this book is to deal with some of them. And from the viewpoint of political science, one central concern must be the question why our discipline so seriously misjudged the situation in Iran, neglecting to register what was happening until the very last moment. In our first chapter, "Crisis in Iran, Crisis in Development Theory," we have undertaken to formulate this question in a broad context and have, for this purpose, reviewed the main directions of Western development theories from the 1950s. Our purpose is not to present a critique of these earlier theories, many of which have been exhaustively debated within the discipline already, or to assemble a collection of the errors of esteemed colleagues, since those who made incorrect predictions about Iran are certainly in the best of company. Our purpose, rather, is to trace the evolution of social science's dealings with Iran up to the present time. Such a review, we believe, elicits not only what was wrong but also what was right about modernization theory, and in the conclusion of the chapter we offer some comments on a possible synthesis of divergent strands within these theories.

What surprised the analysts, besides the overthrow of the Shah, was the fact that this overthrow had taken place by a broad-based movement under the auspices of Islamic fundamentalists (our use of this terminology is explained in the text). In chapter 2, "Why Islam?" we seek to identify the factors that gave the crisis its Islamic imprint and led to the dominance—at least for a time—of radical Islamic actors. In order to analyze Iranian events and determine whether they represent an aberration in the context of the Islamic world or are part of a political setting which determines the condition of many states besides Iran, we review the changing configuration of responses adopted by political actors in the region. These responses, we believe, can be categorized into a set of four broad ideological and tactical approaches, and the second section of the chapter tries to explain why, in Iran, the fundamentalist sector assumed such a dominant role in the overthrow of the Shah.

Chapter 3 ("Iran—What Happened?") turns to the issue of conceptually characterizing the unfolding events. In scholarly texts as well as in common usage, the overthrow of the Shah and the establishment of an Islamic Republic are generally referred to as a revolution. In contrast to this general consensus, we argue that what distinguishes a revolution from other forms of violent and rapid change is its subsequent accomplishment of lasting social transformations, so that the judgment on whether a revolution has occurred or not must ultimately be a retroactive one. Without denying the possibility that Iran may indeed be in the process of experiencing a revolution, we refer also to other explanatory categories, such as peasant rebellions, millennialist movements and the function of charisma, and totalitarian democracy.

Chapter 4, "Prejudice as a Cultural Weapon: Orientalism vs. Occidentalism," explores the role of mutual images and perceptions as a distorting factor and as a conflictual tool in Western-Muslim interaction. Defining prejudice as part of the offensive and defensive arsenal of national actors, we juxtapose the Western image of "the East" and the Eastern image of "the West" as articulated in popular stereotypes and in the attitudes of policymakers. These images had a dual effect. On the one hand, they served to simplify dealings with the other side by offering a blanket explanation (the "Oriental mind," "Western decadence," etc.); on the other hand, they made revisions of judgment difficult. One section of the chapter illustrates the distorting role of their Persia image on the behavior of American diplomats and policymakers; another explores some aspects of Iran's image of the West in order to elicit some generalities about the phenomenon of cultural prejudice in political interactions.

Chapter 5, "The Islamic Republicans in Power," studies the political process in Iran after the overthrow of the Shah, through a review of the phases that the Islamic Republic experienced—the phase of shared power between fundamentalists and others, the rule of Bazargan and then Bani-Sadr—before the culminating domination of the state apparatus by the fundamentalists. After examining the reasons for the fundamentalists' triumph, we sketch their efforts at consolidation. The policies adopted in the course of these efforts show a striking conformity with totalitarian systems during analogous phases of their establishment. At the same time, an analysis of the ruling party reveals some basic conflicts over central policy issues that point to a significant crisis potential for the future.

The ideology of Islamic Republicanism has as one of its core elements a particular and distinct view of the international system. Chapter 6, "The Islamic Republicans and the World," examines the confrontation of this ideology with real politics by reviewing the actual policies pursued. The combination of an absolutist world view, the deliberate maintenance of conditions of external stress, nonconformity with established norms of international behavior, glorification of struggle, and a belief in the inevitability of one's victory with a sometimes paradoxical degree of tactical pragmatism is characteristic of totalitarian systems in their consolidation phase, and describes the foreign policy behavior of the Islamic Republic to date. As in regard to domestic policy, the ruling party is divided over some important foreign policy issues as well; differences that could under some circumstances become greatly exacerbated and give a different direction to Iran's political development.

The final chapter evaluates the prospects for Iran's future from the vantage point of 1983. The aim here is not to make long-term and specific prognoses—to try again where far more prominent colleagues have failed would be not only immodest but also rash—but to extrapolate some plausible trends on the basis of current configurations.

Regardless of what the ultimate outcome will be—and it remains uncertain whether the Islamic Republic will turn out to be an economically, politically, and socially viable system—the contemporary Iranian experience was one of the pivotal events of our time. It may, in retrospect, turn out to have set in motion a genuine revolution; it may simply consolidate itself into a totalitarian regime motivated by Islamic fundamentalist ideology; it may fail or be overturned. But whatever the outcome, the Islamic Republic has been one of the significant political experiments of our age.

"The Government of God"

CHAPTER ONE

Crisis in Iran, Crisis in Development Theory

In 1921, Balfour gave his evaluation of Persia, one of the trouble spots of his time. He wrote:

> There are apparently three possibilities. That things will continue much as at present, that another revolution will take place, or that a general breakup will occur. In a more highly organized country the chances in favor of one of the two latter alternatives would be considerable, but we cannot apply European standards of conduct to Persia with any expectation that they will furnish a reliable gauge of action.[1]

More than six decades later, many analysts would still—or again—describe their projection of Iran's future along Balfour's three lines of possibility. We are all still looking for "reliable gauges of action," and many authors are still wondering more about why European standards of conduct have not been met than about why they should be.

To the academic community no less than to U. S. policymakers, the ascent of Khomeini at the head of a mass-based movement was a startling departure from the anticipated course of events. Certain expectations were reflected in the analyses of social scientists in the U. S., and there were elements that authors of different ideological and methodological persuasions held in common. In spite of their differences on a number of substantive points, they nevertheless shared an approach that was highly partisan in favor of the Western present, ideal or archetypal: this bias made and continues to make events in other parts of the world difficult to assess adequately.

Theories of Development: Basic Premises

Modern Western social science, dating back to its origins in Positivism, has generally approached other societies with two parallel sets of assumptions. The first was a belief in universal progress, and the conviction that all societies are moving, sometimes gradually and sometimes in revolutionary surges, toward a common model of being, following the Western industrial states who formed the vanguard of this movement. The second belief held that "other" societies (whether that otherness be defined as heathen, traditional, underdeveloped, non-Western) are inherently different from the West. While apparently contradictory, these two beliefs have often represented a kind of "division of labor," proving very functional to the active politics of the West during the last several centuries. Expansionism and incursions into other societies were justified on the grounds that Enlightenment, Christianity, and the Modern Age were being brought to the Backward, who were part of the one and indivisible human race. At the same time, the oppression and enslavement of portions of this brotherhood of man could be explained through the need for tutelage and through the civilizing mandate of the superior West.

Social science mirrored this dual world view. In their most current version, Huntington has described the two beliefs as the "Grand Process of Modernization" and the "Great Dichotomy," respectively,[2] and identified them as important strains in development literature. Going a step further, one can define them as the two most essential components of the current paradigm in development theory. Together, they make possible the integration of new events into the orthodox world view of Western civilization, a world view described by the Grand Process and rescued by the Great Dichotomy whenever reality threatens to falsify it.

The Grand Process of Modernization: The Mainstream Version

The predominant view from industrial Europe and later the United States has long included the conviction that civilization and modernity were being transported eastward and southward through their standard-bearer, the modern West. The white man's burden, the civilizing mission, the eventual unity of mankind, all these were components of a world view that accommodated colonialism, the occupation and administration of other societies through military and bureaucratic means, and at times the destruction of religious and cultural values of other groups. The continuity of some of these beliefs through time and their influence on efforts to study political modernization have been noted by many authors.[3] Exactly how much difference, how much cultural pluralism, the eventual universality of the modern world could encompass remained unclear. A fundamental ambiguity between the terms "modern" and "Western" was inevitable in this thinking. Modernity was universal: "The modern man," authors of this direction argued, was a "cross-national, trans-cultural type who can be identified by our scales whatever the distinctive attitudes with which his culture may otherwise have endowed him."[4] At the same time modernity was Western: "The political scientist who wishes to study political modernization in the non-Western area will have to master the model of the modern which in turn can only be derived from the most careful empirical and formal analysis of the modern Western polities."[5] The developing countries differed from the "first wave" of industrialization—a historic moment that had passed them by—in two regards. First, they were faced with a growing gap between themselves and the modern world, and required aid; and second, they were spared the necessity of having to develop, through trial and error, a modern political system, modern technology, etc., since the model already existed.

The basic pattern was assumed to be the same, and the essential elements of its composition were described by a few central concepts, namely, "industrialization in economics, secularization in thought and social and legal organization,"[6] urbanization, the acquisition of modern patterns of behavior, personality, and communication ("cosmopolitan attitudes"),[7] democratization in the political sphere, and integration into the "world culture."[8] Modernizing institutions, according to this tradition, were to be implanted in Third World societies and left to have their effect on the population; the introduction of new values through the media, of new models for behavior, work, and everyday life, new patterns for the relationship between individuals and groups, would bring about new societies. In the traditional literature and up to the present time, modernization theories continued to study the impact of radios, movies, newspapers, and journals as indices of growing modernity.[9] Discussion focused on the "two pillars" of modernity: the "modern mentality" and the "modern social system." Authors like Lerner, Almond, Powell, Eisenstadt, Smelser, and Shils opposed the traditional, authoritarian, "non-empathetic," static social model to the "secular political culture." This latter was defined as "multi-valued," "rational-calculating," "bargaining and experimenting," dynamic, innovative, and integrated.[10]

To test for the presence, absence, or degree of the desired pattern of behavior and personality, one popular methodological approach was the country case study using interviews to determine the level of "empathy"[11] displayed and the progress made in the "modernity syndrome."[12] In fact, the extent to which the work of analysts favoring this approach remained the same over time demonstrates the high level of stability achieved by the basic paradigm. Lerner's approach of the 1950s, for example, was duplicated both methodologically and theoretically by a study carried out in the 1970s by Alex Inkeles and David Smith.[13] The critical prerequisite for modern societies, Inkeles and Smith argue, is a population that possesses certain behavior forms, desires, and values, and it is primarily these personal properties and attitudes that make up modernity, not the institutions that function on their basis. Like Lerner, Inkeles and Smith defined modernity as a "state of mind."

Unanimity never existed as to these beliefs, and it would be unfair to neglect mentioning the ambivalences and cautions that went along with mainstream expectations. Significantly, the most ambivalent reports came from authors—particularly anthropologists—dealing directly with other cultures and personally living within them for a period of time. Through the focus of their questions, which differed from those of political science development research, and through their personal circumstances, they tended to view other cultures as actors rather than units to be explained and divergences to be "solved." Cultural anthropologists, historians, comparative sociologists, and practitioners involved in the management of colonial regions often gained a more realistic picture of the dynamics of social change going on in the Third World than many modernization theorists. Anthropologists like Clifford Geertz or Sylvia Thrupp, authors like David Apter or Bernard Lewis[14] consistently warned against some of the "Gleichmachung" going on in development theory and stressed the neglected variables of political religion, the forgotten dimension of leadership, the militant sentiments arising from a consistent devaluation of cultural and political identity.

Within orthodox development literature, too, criticism arose. Most of it was a response to manifest difficulties the models and theories were experiencing in the face of unpredicted events in Third World societies. Such experiences were frequent, both in the case of individual countries and in broader contexts. Nations that had been classified as stable and placed in a leadership role for the modernization efforts of their region experienced breakdowns of government, violent coups, and popular revivalist movements. Turkey, Lebanon, and a host of African regimes were the subject of optimistic country studies, only to collapse shortly after the publication of the research results. Not just specific case studies but whole theories experienced such setbacks. In the 1950s and early 1960s, the nation-building school predominant at the time suffered serious losses when many of the newly erected "democratic" governments broke down or were overthrown by military coups. The school rallied and responded in a dual way. First, a military elite would be integrated into the model of modernization, classified as an NMC, a "new middle class," and declared to be a characteristically Third World agent of modernization; second, a developing country would be explained to have characteristic political forms at variance with those of Europe and the United States, a "non-Western political process."[15] Theory had been unable to predict what would occur in developing societies, authors concluded, because the political process there was different; more irrational, more spontaneous, more combustible.

In the late 1960s and early 1970s, more substantive criticism and revision were undertaken, this time in response to the long-term failure of the "Third World" generally to progress in the expected directions. Increasing dissatisfaction with mainstream models began to be articulated by prominent authors such as Samuel P. Huntington,[16] Reinhard Bendix,[17] Lloyd and Suzanne Rudolph,[18] Joseph Gusfield,[19] and S. N. Eisenstadt.[20] They criticized the modernization theorists for regarding traditional societies as homogeneous; for failing to distinguish between westernization and modernization; for regarding tradition as static; for treating modernity and tradition as mutually exclusive; and for approaching modernization as a singular, unilinear process.

Huntington's "The Change to Change," perhaps the most thorough and encompassing critical review of the current assumptions of development theory, identified two problems as lying at the root of the theoretical inadequacy. These were first, the inability to come to terms with social change, and second, the unquestioned orientation on a Western example. Ultimately, his own conclusion does not depart very greatly from the approaches he criticized. Citing illustrations for models he considers promising, for example, he refers to the "12 equation Brunner-Brewer approach." However, he writes, this model "was limited by the degree of discontinuity in the political system"—it could predict with some usefulness the consequences of governmental policy changes, but it could not predict such events as "a military coup bringing to power a radical, nationalist junta of officers."[21] Continuing to view events in Third World societies as "discontinuities," as annoying disturbances of academic models, does not really reflect a new attitude toward change. And the focus on the internal political processes of Third World countries in an effort to chart the variables and set them in relation to each other continues another major flaw of mainstream development theory: the tendency to regard the countries of that region as units developing modernity the way a seed may grow into a plant and being hindered in the effort by their own internal problems. Rarely did the analytic approach focus on their place in the international system, or view them as polities engaged in conflict and interaction with the other actors of this system.[22] Hence it was not recognized that the crises and problems they were experiencing might partially stem from just this interaction and not from domestic characteristics alone.

Most of the criticism that ultimately gained acceptance was the kind that we have characterized as belonging to the "Great Dichotomy" category. Differing from its traditional antecedents in its conviction that, with all the cultural differences, "the twain" eventually *would* meet in some form of convergence, intellectually these efforts served as a form of crisis management for thwarted hypotheses. One recalled the "fundamental differences" to explain the failure of predictions to materialize. In the initial response of theory to events in Iran, this was particularly evident.

The Grand Process of Modernization: The Version of the Left

At first glance, the dependence school of development theories—and the other neo-Marxist schools with which it stands in (sometimes hostile) association—seemed to avoid two basic errors of mainstream theory. Where the mainstream regarded change as anathema, the left placed it at the center of every study. Where the mainstream neglected the historic and current international interaction as a factor determining the condition of Third World societies, dependence theory viewed it as the primary cause. The underdevelopment or distorted development of certain regions of the world, dependence theory holds, was always the necessary accompaniment of the development and prosperity of the industrialized *metropolis;* as Europe and the United States modernized, they systematically robbed and impoverished the *periphery,* crippling its economy, perverting its social and political systems, and drawing it into a fatal dependence on the *center.*

Once the school moved out of the stage of critique of the mainstream and into description of alternative explanatory models, a key word in the recommendations became the concept of *dissociation.*[23] The poverty and the deformed economic structure of Third World countries were the result of continued unequal exchange, of economic, military, and cultural dependence on and exploitation by the industrial metropoles and multinational companies.[24] Therefore the solution lay not in attempting to follow in the footsteps of the industrialized states but in breaking, wherever possible, the "stranglehold" of the metropolis and attempting some form of autonomous development, optimally in cooperation with other periphery populations. Ties with the industrialized center brought debts, a cycle of subordination to the needs of other economies and dependence on them for the basics one could not (any longer) supply for oneself;[25] the profits and the gain, the control and the initiative remained with the center, with some share going to subordinate elites of the periphery.

As long as Third World societies were caught within this circle, the gap between rich and poor and the structural inequalities were bound to remain.[26] The arguments of dependence theory against mainstream models have remained essentially the same since the 1960s. Basically, they argue that neither the traditional behavior and attitude structure of the "underdeveloped" individual nor any other quality of the Third World nation itself, but rather the structures of international trade and production, the interests of the industrial powers and their industrial giants, preserve the weakness of Third World countries as a structural necessity of their own strength and profits. Any development program initiated by the industrial world has, according to the dependence school, to be viewed not just with cynicism[27] but with analytic suspicion. It is either a meaningless gesture of symbolic charity or an attempt to cement still more firmly the unequal relationship between rich and poor.[28] The changes introduced by Western domination, dependence authors argued, were not a question of "states of mind." Structural relationships determined by unequal economic exchange implied alienation in cultural norms and subjection to the goals of the metropolis. The "colonial mind" was a necessity of imperial domination.

The subsequent attempts to "modernize" the individual inhabitants of Third World countries by familiarizing them with modern values had the purpose, in this view, of making them into consumers for the products of the industrial world, of weakening or destroying traditional ties and turning the population into a group of isolated and thus more easily governable individuals, alienated from their culture and from the possibility of resistance. On the other hand, if the industrial world supported an authoritarian regime under the pretext that it was modernizing from above, then the real reason was likely to be that the regime was composed of the alienated and dependent elite within the periphery, acting as an agent of the industrial power or at least acceding to some of its most central interests.

There was a great deal of truth to many of these observations. However, the model soon acquired independence from its subject. It no longer considered the cases of particular countries with particular histories, social systems, and conditions; this was not deemed necessary, since conditions in any developing country were thought to be explainable through reference to the imbalances in the global system and to imperialist influence. If a country was poor then it had been *made* poor (by a colonial power, by a foreign industry, mining concern, or plantation system); if its government was corrupt and its social system fragmented, then it had been bought off, set up, or destroyed by a superpower or a multinational concern. Tony Smith has criticized this neglect of national histories in favor of global explanations.[29] Authors such as Paul Baran, he points out, ascribe every evil in Indian society to the British administration, while other authors of the school explain tribalism in Africa as the product of colonialism.[30]

In part, this approach was a theoretical overreaction to the tendency in orthodox theory to assign all the "responsibility" for poverty and under-development to the countries themselves: to their backward social and political order, to their lack of innovative skills, military competence, and technical ingenuity. Dependence theory, initially the voice of authors from developing countries, had responded to this ethnocentrism and some-times racism by reversing the explanation: the rich countries were rich not because they were necessarily superior but because they were more ruthless, because they had concentrated their cultural and economic ener-gies on warfare and expansionism, because they had robbed others. However, as this polemical counterargument solidified into a theoretical school, it had the paradoxical effect of consigning the Third World to a role of passive victim. Short of breaking all ties with the international system and proceeding with an indigenous and autonomous socialist rev-olution, there was little for Third World countries to do.

The determining role, the decision-making, and the trend-setting were all controlled exclusively by the elites within the industrialized center. On the question of where this autonomy and this socialist revolution were going to come from, and on the basis of what social cohesiveness the populations were going to mobilize, dependence theory remained and re-mains ambivalent. Traditional social forms and institutions are generally defined, cautiously and with a knowledge of the precariousness of the terminology, as feudalist. In order to resolve or at least avoid trouble-some questions, dependence authors often do, ironically, precisely that thing that they most severely criticize in orthodox theory:[31] they date the history of Third World countries with a colonialist calendar beginning with the day Africa, Latin America, or Asia was "discovered" by invaders from Europe,[32] and see salvation in a modified Marxism, a turning to Western thought made acceptable for Third World use by the link to anti-imperialism.

The theoretical responses to current events in the Third World on the part of the left followed a pattern analogous to that of the mainstream and are characterized by a similar dualism. Original Marxist thinking postulated a unified path to socialism and followed the same tutelary ap-proach to non-European cultures that colonial theory propounded. The writings of Marx contain numerous racist observations[33] and sometimes commend colonialism for bringing Western discipline to the decadent and stagnant East. At the same time, a recognition of the Great Dichotomy, of fundamental differences, was contained in such concepts as that of the "Asian mode of production." The Great Dichotomy served to explain the absence of an authentic socialist revolution. Lin Biao's theory of the "villages and the cities"[34] was adopted partially to introduce the category of the peasantry in a role more central than that granted it by the orthodox Marxist model. The "third way" to socialism finally emerged as a means of reconciling disparate events with socialist theories.

At the same time, leftist theories, particularly as developed by European and U. S. authors, tended to retain a strong Western leaning. This was not so evident as in the case of the mainstream because of the postulated "solidarity with the Third World" and the "oneness of the struggle against imperialism,"[35] but it found a clear expression in the fact that authors often used the Third World to prove a point they wanted to make about Europe or about other ideological groups inside and outside the left. The Third World was a way of striking at the established academic community in America and also at the Maoists, Trotskyites, pro-Soviet Marxists, etc. As a result, much of the discussion on the left has included bitter infighting. Concern for the societies being studied receded as the ideological struggle took precedence. Stylistically, where the mainstream tended to be imposingly axiomatic, the writings of the left tended to border on the sentimentally proletarian and the intellectually romantic.

In the journal *The Insurgent Sociologist,* a publication featuring woodcuts of resolute workers raising rifles behind barbed wire fences and of women guerrilla fighters clutching babies and machine guns to their breasts, authors such as Wallerstein, Amin, Palloux, and Poulantzas are the *eminences grises* and the scholarly debate is conducted in lengthy sections of "replies," in fact vitriolic accusations employing moral and methodological ridicule to discipline straying comrades. Platform issues often take priority over analysis, as the question of whether Lenin was right or wrong on some particular point attracts more attention than the study of the country or region purportedly under analysis. It is frequently possible in this school to discuss developments in a Third World country without mentioning that country except in the title: a study of capital formation in, for example, Poland or England will tell us all we need to know. Wallerstein anticipates our criticism by arguing that "to be historically specific is not to fail to be analytically universal . . . just as in cosmology the only road to a theory of laws governing the universe is through the concrete analysis of the historical evolution of this same universe."[36] Since, according to the leftist position, developments in the Third World are merely part of a process going on globally and initiated in Europe, a detailed and basic study of Third World politics is not really necessary, and would, in fact, be misleading, since it might neglect the complete picture, that of the "future demise" of capitalism.

The conviction that other cultures would essentially follow the model of Western socialist revolution as it existed in theory if not in reality led leftist authors to subsume new occurrences under old headings. Revolutionary elites taking over political control were classified as "national bourgeoisies," and analysts of the left were ever watchful for any group that might qualify as a nascent proletariat.

Correspondingly, we read that "The large landowners [of Iran] converted themselves into a bourgeoisie";[37] "military regimes have emerged in some of the peripheral formations to carry out the task of accumulation and reproduction . . .";[38] and "our task is to work towards socialist revolution, not to support progressive bourgeoisies."[39] The terminology reflects a quixotic defense of an aprioristic, ideological paradigm against the onslaughts of political reality. The social and historical factors motivating behavior and constraining developments in other societies are neglected in favor of a mythical cast of actors who obligingly "convert themselves" into bourgeoisies and devote themselves to "accumulation" like obedient marionettes on the stage of a postulated "capitalist world system." Religious movements, charismatic groups, these cannot be more than the distracting apparitions of other cultures, exotic equivalents of the British factory owner, the Lancaster proletariat, the class war.

Dependence theory, originally a protest against the cooptation of the Third World into the ideological and theoretical grip of the dominant industrial world, was resisted by orthodox left authors (to whom it presented a greater threat than to the mainstream, which could simply reject dependence theory on the basis of the fundamental incompatibility of its tenets). Robert Brenner, one of the most eminent authors of the left, devotes an extensive article to a rebuttal of the dependence school. In the concluding paragraphs, it becomes clear what he means by the "serious logical and historical problems" of that school. Its main danger, he writes, is that it "opens the way to third-worldist ideology. From the conclusion that development occurred only in the absence of links with the accumulating capitalism in the metropolis, it can only be a short step to the strategy of semi-autarkic socialist development."[40] Such a "problem," of course, is less an analytic than an ideological one; it challenges the Marxist view of what lies ahead for the world.[41]

Mainstream Theory and the Shah's Iran

Given their theoretical framework, the emergence of an Islamic Republic in Iran was "unthinkable" for most modernization theorists. Popular uprisings, virulent anti-Western sentiments and the ascent of the clergy, the ousting of the Shah, these were developments not at all in line with either orthodox or neo-Marxist theory; for if there ever was a country that apparently conformed to the expected orthodox course of modernization, it was Iran, and if there was ever a country whose proletariat and peasantry were bound to be politicized by the left against all the traditional forms of oppression (by king, landowners, imperialists, and clergy), surely it was Iran.

Mainstream texts often cited the progress made by Iran in building a modern nation. In many accepted indicators of development, Iran occupied a leading position within the Third World. Literacy figures, urbanization, leadership in relation to its neighbors, growth of GNP, infrastructure, communications, and industrialization (indicators which according to Daniel Lerner and many others were indivisibly linked with secularization) were substantially higher than Third World averages. The Shah had even announced a plan to catch up with France economically and militarily by 1993.

Under the Shah, dramatic economic and social changes took place. Iran's GNP had grown by more than 50 percent in constant dollars between 1973 and 1976;[42] per capita income had reached a Third World record of $2,000; the urban population doubled between 1956 and 1966 (growing from 5 to 10 million) and was expected to reach 20 million by 1980, making about 50 percent of Iran's population "urban"; there was a total student population (elementary school to university) of 10 million, including 100,000 university and 500,000 secondary school students; 3 million peasant families were allotted 75 percent of Iran's arable land; the educated middle class had doubled in size between 1956 and

1976, growing from 6 to 13 percent of the total employed population—if merchants and businessmen were included in the figures, the middle class constituted 25 percent of the population;[43] and the number of industrial plants of various sizes increased from less than 1,400 in 1953 to more than 8,000 in 1978.[44]

Beyond the statistics, the understanding of social conditions in Iran displayed by many social scientists sometimes remained superficial. The popular uprising in Iran was interpreted by many as a "rejection of modernity." A more critical look at the indicators social science accepted as showing the progress of modernization in Iran suggests two questions: first, were the changes really classifiable as modernization, or were wrong labels attached to them? (For example, was the creation of large urban slums classifiable as a form of "urbanization"?) And second, was it modernity that the population was rebelling against or the manner in which it was being imposed?[45] Rural poverty was severe, infant mortality rates in urban slums and the countryside were high, unemployment created a class of impoverished displaced peasants on the outskirts of the cities, and finding food for their families was the primary concern of a large number of Iranian men and women. The writing of some U. S. analysts, however, conveyed the impression that "the population" of Iran was synonymous with the modernizing urban sector. Marvin Zonis, for example, wrote that: "the automobile represents a tremendous democratizing force, removing the power and status considerations otherwise operative in the social structure. Once behind the wheel, more Iranians are more nearly equal."[46] It is understandable that such statements generated hostility on the part of critical Iranians who were more concerned with the extreme inequities and the growing gap between a small class of westernized elites and a large population facing poverty than with explaining the anarchic traffic conditions in Tehran.

While there was a measure of criticism of some of the authoritarian means and repressive measures employed by the Shah, he was often depicted by development analysts as a successful guarantor of national stability—the precondition, for many theoreticians, of the gradual growth of integrated democratic forms. On the basis of these indicators, many political leaders and social scientists viewed Iran as a promising model case of planned growth. As late as August 1978, the CIA stated in its proposed National Intelligence Estimate that Iran could not even be considered a prerevolutionary society, and that "those who are in opposition, both violent and non-violent, do not have the capacity to be more than troublesome. . . . There is dissatisfaction with the Shah's tight control of the political process, but this does not threaten the government."[47]

A prominent author who inclined toward this position was Leonard Binder. In a paper published by the Rand Corporation in October 1969, he wrote of the "high level of domestic tranquillity under the political supremacy of the Shah" and of the Shah's success in "winning over" crucial sections of the ulama. From his analysis of the first 28 years of the Shah's reign, and the political measures for consolidating his position that he had taken during that time, Binder concluded that Iran seemed "clearly on its way to becoming a prosperous, stable, modernizing autocracy."[48]

Binder went on to list the reasons for this expectation; the juxtaposition of variables is, in retrospect, interesting.

> In less than 10 years . . . a large measure of domestic political stability has been achieved, important economic advances have been made, organized, legitimate domestic political opposition has collapsed, the religious authorities have been driven into disarray, and the queen has produced an heir to the throne.[49]

Binder reviewed and all but dismissed the likelihood of serious future threats to the Shah's rule in Iran.[50]

He ascribed little significance to the continuing opposition, but felt that the mass of the population could be described as either apathetic or loyal. There was in fact a great deal of substantiation for most of Binder's appraisal. His most serious misjudgment, however, related to the religious opposition. He did not believe that the "Qum school" of clergy had much chance of finding a following in Tehran, and he did not see a good possibility for any one person to gain leadership within the Shiʻi ulama. Specifically, he dismissed the chances of Khomeini in this capacity; the successful suppression by the Shah of the 1963 disturbances, Binder believed, had also eliminated Khomeini's leadership bid. Above all, Binder considered the economic program and the land reform to be successful and to be regarded as such by the population.

Binder was fairly certain, in 1969, that profound and lasting changes had taken place or were well on their way in Iran under the firm rule of the Shah. And he quoted, by way of substantiation, a similar appraisal made by Marvin Zonis in an MIT paper. In 1968, Zonis had written that "now, at last, the throne appears secure. Organized internal opposition has been decimated, while even the expression of anti-regime sentiment is absent. . . . With a firm grasp over the political process, the Shah has devoted himself and Iran's continually increasing oil income to internal development."[51]

Reading the work of such prominent authors raises two questions: if their observations were right, what imperatives of the model led them to interpret them incorrectly? If their observations were wrong, on the basis of which questions were they made? Retrospectively, it is clear that the authors of such studies were wrong on several counts: they failed to note the continuing social and political role of the religious leaders;[52] they overestimated the popular support given to the Shah's rule; they underestimated the continuing and in some regards even growing social problems.[53] Their view of the Shah and his policies was fundamentally approving, and this distorted their reporting of the situation.[54] Almost up until his ousting, American authors continued to hold certain beliefs about the Shah and about Iran. These included the belief that the ulama had been eliminated as serious rivals;[55] that rule of a "strong authority" was needed to integrate the country and that the Shah represented such an authority; and that in terms of secularization, growth, and progress, Iran was in a unique leadership position.

The 1971 *Area Handbook for Iran*[56] stated that the "remaining radical, inflammatory critics of the early 1950s had been removed from the scene or . . . had become ineffective"; that "the prevailing clerical attitude" was one of "supporting, or at least not opposing, the government"; their prognosis for the 1970s was the enthusiasm for and legitimacy of the monarchy. A symposium of leading U. S. and Iranian scholars held in Washington in October 1977 radiated optimism. At the same time, it was clearly the U. S.-Iran connection that stood in the forefront of attention. Iran's regional role as a supplier of oil to Israel, as a counter to Iraq, as a "bulwark" and a force against Communism, and the Shah's function as a guarantor of these, defined the participants' attitude. For example, Richard Foster, to whom the anti-Soviet nature of Iran was the ultimate good, said that "we are now witnessing an elite transforming their state in the name of and for the people, rather than in the name of and for a class."[57] Human rights or political repression were not mentioned in the symposium. There were authors who issued warnings. Rouhollah Ramazani warned in 1974 that unrest threatened if the disequilibrium brought about by economic growth and Iran's role in international affairs were not met by genuine political responsiveness and democratization internally.[58] Other authors pointed out that the Shah in fact did not really devote Iran's continually increasing oil income to internal development, unless one means thereby the internal development of the military. Over half of the annual oil revenues were devoted, as a matter of policy, to military purchases; military spending was indulged to such an extent that despite the favorable economic situation, Iran had to borrow from Europe to meet its expenses.[59]

Why did the more central studies of Iranian society disregard the available information about these tensions and misallocations of funds? Two possibilities exist: first, mainstream theory may have been excessively influenced by the official U. S. stance, which was one of approval toward the Shah and his military policy. At the Washington symposium, several U. S. participants defended U. S. foreign policy vis-à-vis Iran, taking the stand for the Shah's military ambitions on the grounds that they were necessary "transitional" steps; Richard Foster, for example, urged that "we keep up our arms supply," quoting Truman's statement that "if you are going to build a Garden of Eden, build a fence around it."[60] Second, mainstream theory was not looking for problems, disparities, inequities, and destabilizing factors. It was looking for a modernizing elite, successful modernization programs, and increasing secularization.

Iran and the Left

To the left no less than to the mainstream, Iran was a prize example of the accuracy of their analysis. The Shah and his entourage were archetypes of alienated agents of Western imperialism. The Shah's system of expenditures illustrated perfectly the deformation of dependent systems: luxury imports and enormous weapons purchases along with increasing dependence on the import of food staples, inflation, and poverty. U. S. support for a repressive regime was viewed as evidence of the center's effort to establish dependent satellites under the control of compliant rulers. The agitation against the Shah abroad was conducted mainly by students and mainly in the more familiar vocabulary of the left; this contributed, of course, to the surprise over subsequent developments in Iran, since the left and not any religious popular uprising was the visible and obvious challenger to the rule of the Shah.

An example is the book published by Monthly Review Press in 1969, *Iran: The New Imperialism in Action*. The author, Bahman Nirumand, begins his work with kowtows to the monopoly capital and dependence schools, lauding Paul Baran and Paul Sweezy as those "representing the better, the just part of the United States."[61] The book goes on to list the areas in which Iran represents a model case of U. S. policy toward dependent developing countries: economic exploitation particularly in the area of oil, the fostering of consumer desires in order to gain another market for U. S. products, cultural alienation created by Western movies, life styles, and morals, the sabotaging of the political process through CIA interventions, the bolstering of a repressive monarch who favored U. S. interests, the impoverishment of the peasants and workers, the duplicity of "aid" programs, etc. Hans Magnus Enzensberger, a prominent leftist author in Europe, wrote the afterword, in which he ruled out the possibilities of popular uprisings, politicization of the population or even the "working class," or a religiously based opposition. "Iranian Islam," Enzensberger states definitively, "is unable to release revolutionary energies." The only possibility for political change that Enzensberger could envision was from the military. "The one determinant factor left inside the country is the army," he wrote. "It would seem that a change of conditions in Iran by force could come only from this group."[62]

Crisis in Theory

On the subject of Iran, many authors of both ideological directions were tending to become somewhat complacent. To the left, Iran had become a symbol of imperialism and tyranny, and an occasion to discuss the problems of politicization in Third World countries. To the mainstream authors, the debate circled around familiar questions: evaluating the land reform, discussing the nature of the Shah's regime and the possibilities for a somewhat broader political base, analyzing the economic and strategy implications of U. S.-Iranian relations for the region, for the balance of power, and for the global scene. The religiously based popular uprising of 1978–79 burst into this placidly ongoing symposium with truly revolutionary impact. Western authors responded with confused flurries of prognostic energy: the riots could not possibly sustain themselves; the Shah would put them down forcefully as he had done on previous occasions; it was a CIA-inspired action to intimidate the Shah into greater subservience to U. S. interests; it was a Soviet-inspired takeover merely using camouflaged socialists in the guise of religious fanatics to distract the United States; the Iranian military would launch a coup; Bakhtiar would gain control of the situation; monarchists would tolerate the ousting of the Shah but would summon his son to be the nominal leader, etc.

The outcome—an Islamic Republic under the guidance of an 80-year-old, exiled religious scholar from Qum, encouraged by sporadic but enthusiastic popular demonstrations in the formerly (reports had asserted) cosmopolitan Tehran—dealt a resounding blow to many well-regarded theories. It was, clearly, an occurrence that had to be explained. One option was to try to salvage the paradigm.

Mainstream Theory

For orthodox theory, the restatement of the paradigm in such a way as to include a disturbance, a contradictory and unexpected event, can take place in either of two ways. One can try to argue that the disturbance is a temporary and, in the long run, insignificant deviation from a chain of events which remains as the model has predicted. The apparent revival of Islam, this line of argument would assert, is merely a brief fluctuation, one of the minor air pockets en route to the secularized society. Or, one can argue that the event is not a contradiction of the model at all but, on the contrary, exactly in accord with it. Only the form it has taken seemed momentarily unexpected, the authors explain; closer examination reveals that what happened was perfectly in accord with the theory. Both types of responses have already been made.

Some have tried to trivialize Khomeini, to reinterpret the influence of Islam as in fact being an expression of some entirely different political or social sentiment, to present Iran as a particularly unstable society that deviates from the models, eventually to return. The reassertion of the paradigm, the restatement of belief (in progress, growth, a pattern of development) takes the place of a substantive analysis of events. Y. Armajani, for example, wrote in May 1979 that "even religious leaders cannot set the clock back."[63]

There are also many signs of the second line of defense as authors try to argue that the Shah's rule was at best a superficial westernization attempt and that the reassertion of cultural values under the leadership of a religious movement (merely the circumstantial form that political repression has forced upon the active opposition in Iran) represented not a reversal of modernization but the necessary step for initiating a *genuine* modernization process that would include the population.

The term "revolution" was used generously but by no means uniformly. Richard Dekmejian argued that the "Iranian revolution of 1979 was a true revolution in the classical sense"; Aryeh Shmuelevitz, on the other hand, saw it as a "repeat performance of the classic Iranian conflict" that had been going on for 100 years; Theda Skocpol felt that it was both similar to classic revolutions and anomalous and hastened to describe it—in 1982, when the consolidation effort of the fundamentalist clerics was still far from complete—as having already been "thoroughly transformative of basic sociocultural and soioeconomic relationships in Iran."[64] Richard Falk, for example, described Khomeini as a virtuous and beneficent philosopher-statesman free of corrupting power drives or personal ambitions, leading a spartan life, a cross between a Muslim Gandhi and a nationalist Plato. In an article considering such issues as women's rights, minorities, and the consequences of rigorous application of Shariah law, Falk portrayed Khomeini as nonviolent and even speculated that "Iran may yet provide us with a desperately-needed model of humane governance for a Third World country."[65] In their—as subsequent events showed—overly hasty appraisals of Khomeini, many commentators understandably reacted against the general tendency to downgrade everything that is not Western and secular, or at least Christian. From a belief that Islam is backward, many authors plunged directly into the hypothesis that political Islam as symbolized by Khomeini is revolutionary and just.[66]

Religion, with the ability to mobilize far more of the population than did the Shah's essentially elitist approach, would in fact prepare the way for modernity: this appraisal tended to be just as assertive as the prior valuation of secularization. The phenomenon of Khomeini, another popular line of argument contended, was bound to be transitory. The "real" political groups would soon emerge, enabling a classification of the nature of the conflict and its possible outcome.

The Left

Marxist and dependence authors responded to the turmoil in Iran with a prompt effort to integrate the events into their theoretical models. While previously Iran had always been considered a solid bastion of tyranny in the firm grip of the "worldwide empire" of the United States, leftist authors now wrote as if they had expected its overthrow all along.[67] The religious aspect of the uprising was downplayed and attention focused on the strike by oil workers in order to locate the upheaval within a proletarian framework. In February 1979, the editors of *Monthly Review* wrote in their appraisal of the Iranian situation that "there have been few spectacles in recent history so inspiring and heartwarming as that of 70,000 oil workers, far and away the best paid and most privileged segment of the working class, bringing to a complete halt the huge production and refining complex which is the Iranian oil industry, and doing it . . . in support of the quintessentially political demand of the whole Iranian people that the Shah and what he stands for must go."[68]

The fact that the popular movement was unquestionably and impressively led by the religious opposition did not fit the model of socialist revolution, but valiant attempts were undertaken to make it do. The authors predicted that once the Shah had been overthrown, "questions of class" would come to the forefront and Khomeini's popularity would decline;[69] they identified a "basis for a cross-class alliance including workers, students, intellectuals, Bazaaris, technicians and religious leaders"; above all, however, they undertook to classify Iranian society. In the uprising itself, they saw the "emergence of the Iranian proletariat, led by the oil workers," and they defined the Iranian population in accordance with the expected class model.[70] This, in a society like Iran, is no mean task, and it took some effort: the elite with its wealth stemming from "finance, industry and real estate" was fairly easy to define as "high bourgeoisie";

the upper stratum of the Bazaaris required a somewhat more hazardous casting feat as it was assigned the role of "national bourgeoisie"; and the "working class" was cautiously left vague but placed under the leadership of the oil workers.[71]

That the model here dominates the social reality is evidenced by the fact that the peasantry hardly figures in the classification.[72] Displaced agricultural peasants, urban slum dwellers, and ethnic minorities are generally ignored by leftist authors, since they do not allow a class assignment. The participation of women on a large scale in the mass demonstrations finds brief mention, and then usually with a didactic purpose, namely to reproach the women in their own ranks who have strayed to the bourgeois aberration of feminism instead of subordinating themselves to solidarity as the truly revolutionary Iranian women do.[73]

Even where the articles themselves display some awareness of the complexities of the socal situation in Iran, the ultimate prognosis is a reaffirmation of the paradigm in its left version. Peter Waterman, after outlining how the process of change in Third World societies follows a "strikingly different pattern" from that of industrializing Europe in past centuries, and stressing that the "working class," where the term applies at all, can refer only to a small minority, nevertheless goes on to state that "despite complexity and ambiguity, I see a determinate process arising in the Third World. This is the development of the one *necessary* modernizing class"[74] (emphasis in the original). The necessity is provided by the model outlining the way world developments are to proceed.

Similarly, Ervand Abrahamian first describes the central role played by religion and religious leadership in Iran over time. Next, he attempts to integrate it into the historiography of European social development and industrialization by comparing contemporary Shi'ism to "Methodism in 19th-century England" and postulates that, since the situation is analogous, the role played by Khomeini is equivalent to that played by John Wesley.[75] And finally, without giving any substantiation for such an expectation and employing prescriptive terminology to describe the political actors involved, he concludes with the prognosis that "It is likely that the religious reactionaries will soon begin to lose their hold over the labor movement. The left will then have an easy entry into an arena that includes more than two and a half million wage earners and forms the single largest urban class in contemporary Iran."[76] Even at the time

Abrahamian wrote this, before the elimination of the Tudeh leadership and the party's banning by the fundamentalists, it was hard to see how a leftist triumph could have been achieved "easily"; the reference to a single "urban class" of wage earners readily susceptible to leftist leadership is hardly tenable in the face of the events of the last few years, and understandable only as the ideological defense of a paradigm.

In retrospect, it is easy to point out what was wrong in development theory's view of Iran. It may therefore seem paradoxical to conclude, as we would like to now, that development theory was largely right. If the Grand Process and the Great Dichotomy had not been viewed as mutually exclusive, it would have been easier to recognize that the situation contained elements of both. The essential tasks of modernization and the kinds of social and economic tensions resulting from it can be universal without the outcome being predestined and a local version of Western modernity being in the offing. Important structural differences can be present and can have the potential to affect the outcome significantly. Development theory contained the analytic elements and the information to deal with both these aspects of the problem. However, the theory underwent two distortions: the Western lens through which it persisted in viewing the concept of modernity led it to a number of incorrect projections; and the ideological controversy between the schools and factions precluded some important insights that could have been achieved through a constructive dialogue between them.

Much of mainstream theory correctly identified the elements and processes crucial to modernization: the process of state-building and integration; the process of economic development and the establishment of corresponding political change, including provisions for articulating demands and for controlled transformations in participatory structures; the creation of a new infrastructure and of institutions capable of managing these changes. Some of these functions appear in fact to be universal—more universal even than much of mainstream theory would credit. The extension of the center's authority, the integration of the population through such socializing institutions as schools and the military, efforts to impose a common language and to control other socially authoritative institutions, including religious institutions—these are among the tasks which great civilizations have faced historically, and which have historically been fraught with stress. Mainstream theory has tended to endow these processes with too many of the specific features they happened to assume in the case of the industrializing West.

Dependence theory could have rectified this distortion. It identified the links between processes going on in the Third World and the international power balance and recognized the deformation of the political process in many Third World countries by the coercive presence of outside powers in their economies, their social values, and their politics. Brought together with mainstream theory, it could have illuminated the two most important distinctions of development in the Third World:

1. That in Europe, these processes took place in a relatively "organic" or autonomous way, while the Third World is faced with an already existing and dominant foreign "modernity" seeking to affect almost every aspect of its national and international life;

2. That this difference transforms the constellation of actors, values, and sequences, giving the process a new dynamic. It may also give it a different outcome.

One aspect of modernization involves the conflict between old elites, with prestige, status, and power, and new productive forces with resources, ambitions, and potential that cannot be asserted under the old conditions. From this conflict, which takes a long time, frequently involves a great deal of violence, and features many shifts in the power relationship, the new forces ultimately emerge as the victors. In Europe, the religious values and elites were among those traditional forces blocking the way of the new forces; the conflict therefore ultimately involved what we term secularization.[77] Religion as traditionally practiced is also a blocking factor in Islamic societies, and parts of the intelligentsia, the entrepreneurs, and part of the urban sector feel that it should be "reformed" or assigned a less prominent place in society. However, in Iran there were critical differences from Western revolutionary societies. Religion was part of the beleaguered national culture. It was also, along with the intelligentsia, the entrepreneurs, the modernizing urban sector, and the poor, being thwarted in its goals by a secularistic government. Revolution and national independence were joint aims, and the secular West featured in a dual role as a model and as an opponent dominating one's culture. In the European revolutionary context, to be oppositional meant to oppose the established institutions and to rebel against one's own solidified culture, including the church. In an anticolonial context where "the church" was under attack by domestic power-holders with strong ties to a foreign power, religion could play a part in nationalism. To modernize while at the same time rebelling against a dominant Western modernity involves a new set of complexities. It also offers possible affiliations, coalitions, and settings that did not exist for European actors during their own period of modernization.

Giving in to an impulse to fit Iranian events into a framework with an assumed outcome, in which, so to speak, only the middle part was blank and needed to be filled in by history, many authors became distracted from the task of analysis. Assumptions about the ultimate destiny of the political world have often had such a distorting effect on theory. A modern and integrated world order, socialist or Western-democratic, may or may not ultimately come about. Proceeding from the ex post facto assumption that its installation is inevitable has seriously biased the analysis of political change. It may be better to aim for the middle road between Grand Theory and the Great Dichotomy, identifying structural patterns while avoiding determinisms in favor of the unique specifics of each case.

CHAPTER TWO

Why Islam?

In Western analysis, the danger of disregarding Islam as a factor is in the process now of giving way to a new danger, that of exaggerating Islam, of regarding it as an explanatory variable in and of itself.[1] It may be more useful to begin by defining the conditions and pressures inherent in the position Islamic polities occupy in the international system, and to identify the influences that form the boundaries and the framework of their ideological responses. We can visualize this position as being subject to four major impacts, which may be thought of as a kind of fracture line, bisecting each of the groups at different points on different issues. The setting in which political actors in Islamic Third World countries generally must operate is characterized by four overlapping conflicts:

1. The North-South conflict, in its material (economic, military, diplomatic) and ideological aspects;

2. The superpower or East-West conflict and the constraints it places on weaker countries, particularly those who occupy a "strategic" location as defined by these outside powers;

3. The conflict between traditional and new values and actors; and

4. The conflict of ideologies.

These broad categories represent no more than the "divisive minimum." Added to them are a variety of other divisive issues, and the political actors will respond to them in different ways at different times as other lines of division (such as the ethnic) come into play or as their assessment of priorities and means changes. Even before going into the subject in greater depth, however, we can observe that Islam has a useful role within each of the conflict dimensions. In the North-South split, it provides the Third World country with a positive identity framework and a link, at least in the abstract, with other countries and societies within that framework as well as with a history that predates colonialism. In the East-West conflict, Islam is an alternate source of identification. In the splits between tradition and modernity and between leftist and conservative ideology, it gives the society a continuity that transcends the new rifts. However, the ways in which actors in the polity will respond to this "Islamic factor," or, to use Mohammed Ayoob's term, the ways in which they will "operationalize Islam," and with what success, will show some important differences. These differences fall into a pattern which it is the purpose of this chapter to describe. First, however, we would like to introduce three conditions in the setting of Third World countries today that seem especially striking.

1. *The Radicalization of Tradition.* Much of modernization literature had expected that "anachronistic" sources of identity and conflict such as ethnicity, sectarianism, and political religion[2] would gradually be displaced and become depoliticized, making way for the new structures and conflicts of the modern nation-state. This assumption overlooked the fact that traditional lines of cleavage were at the same time identity structures and interest groups, and that the influx of new influences would act on existing structures in a way that in some cases did make them anachronistic but in other cases revived them. Thus, leftist ideology could combine with ethnic nationalism; a modern secular education could provide tribal groups with a leadership generation that had access to entirely new means of conflict; nationalism could combine with religion; and some kinds of old interest groups, long slumbering in inactivity, could feel themselves threatened by the changes and rouse themselves to new vigor, or else take on new life by assuming a new form, as in the case of traditional families reappearing in the shape of political parties.

2. *The Internationalization of Internal Conflicts and the Internalization of International Conflicts.* Given the nature of the international system today and the position of Third World countries vis-à-vis the superpowers, conflicts in these countries will rarely be, and even more rarely remain, purely domestic. Especially in those regions most vital to superpower in-

terests, such as the Middle East, domestic events and problems acquire international significance. They also take on a cumulative character. After the fall of the Shah, for example, President Reagan announced that the U. S. would not "allow Saudi Arabia to be another Iran," implying that there is a regional quota on revolutions.[3] Foreign involvement in domestic conflicts takes many forms. The converse is also true: domestic actors are involved in international or external affairs in a variety of ways. There are possibilities for outside support and risks of outside intervention that were not faced by European states during their classic phase of modernization.

3. *The Multiplication of Conflicts.* Much less than in the European past can transformations of modernization now be dealt with in a sequential fashion. Nasser expressed his awareness of this when he spoke of the three simultaneous revolutions facing Arab society.[4] This situation is exacerbated by the fact that some of the transformations may require contradictory responses, that consensus on the best response does not exist, and that agreement on one of the issues (leading to a coalition) does not necessarily imply agreement on the others. The history of the Middle East in modern times is sufficiently known that we do not have to cite illustrations for the degree and the extent to which this region has been the object of great power politics. To the actors in the region, and speaking very generally, four things followed from this situation.

1. They had to try to survive the aggressive or at any rate the encroaching interests of these outside powers.

2. They could try to make use of the foreign presence and enter into alignments with foreign forces that might further their domestic or international interests.

3. They could make use of the foreign threat or presence in internal disputes. (The employment of Palestine as an irredenta by various Arab governments and movements is a good example.)[5]

4. They could employ the foreign presence as a catalyst and a definition point for internal affiliations, in order to unite with each other and/or to play different foreign powers off against each other.[6]

The involvement of superior foreign forces brought an era of political defeat and domination, but beyond that it also offered room for political activity. A foreign power could supply you with guns and money; it could proceed forcefully against those traditional rivals you had been wanting to eliminate for a long time without success; it could help you onto your throne or help to overthrow your king. Existing conflicts, some old, some new, adapted themselves to the new environment. An ethnic minority could acquire the added dimension of leftist ideology and enter into negotiations with other leftist groups or with the Soviet Union. In some countries, such as Libya, a nationalist, modernist military leader was able to come to power on an antimonarchist, anticolonialist, antiforeign platform and establish an authoritarian rule while getting assistance from Communist countries and doing business with the West. In Afghanistan, on the other hand, the monarchy was followed by a series of secularist modernizers who failed to manage either the internal or the external dimensions of their problem. The introduction of a powerful set of foreign actors into the local game totally changed the stakes, the teams, and the rules. At the same time, certain concepts and value sets gained pivotal roles. One of these was the idea of a "constitution." To the new social forces that had come into being in the Middle East, the vocabulary of the West and the Western media meant that their desire for a voice in government and for access to decision-making could be articulated as the desire for a parliamentary system. Conversely, to some rulers, a constitution became another instrument for balancing their polity; in times of dire crisis, one could announce that one was reviving the constitution, that one's opponents were being released from prison and censorship loosened, etc. George Antonius has described vividly the employment of the constitution by Abdul Hamid, first granting it to his populations in 1978 "in a panic caused by the sudden outbreak of a military revolution."[7] The Pahlavis, too, tried to operate with constitutional promises and revocations, with the founding and abolishing of political parties and the incarceration or release of political prisoners, and succeeded for some time.

These few examples should already suggest that the effects we are discussing were going on at two levels. On one level, the political, social, and military interaction with the West cut a rent into the fabric of Mideast society. This does not mean that disorder and despair were the only available responses and that things had been going splendidly before; on the contrary, some political actors manipulated the situation adeptly, making the best of it for themselves, their group, or their country, and many existing disaffections and inequities won a new lease on life.

These responses varied, but they can be simplified into four ideal-typical categories. These categories emerged as responses to the dependent position of the Islamic world in the international power balance; that is to say, they are the Islamic variant of the basic task faced by all political groups who find themselves operating in a political environment dominated by external actors. The degree to which outside powers figured in this, both as a reference point and as actual or potential "participants," is reflective of a political process distorted by a high degree of foreign control.

Responses to Domination

Those who are at a power disadvantage—economically, militarily, politically, and culturally—have a limited number of choices. They can conclude that defeat is evidence of the functional inferiority of their culture, and try to become as much like the victor as possible while redefining their identities along new lines to survive the abandonment of the old ones. This is a hazardous undertaking, and from the viewpoint of political psychology not a very gratifying one, since it requires admitting the superiority of the other side. What is more, the assimilationists will often fail in their efforts to become part of the dominant order, which may want to dominate rather than integrate them, or to integrate them permanently in a structurally inferior position. A second response is to feel morally superior to those who are materially stronger. The superiority of the enemy can even be viewed as stemming from moral inferiority (he has fewer scruples and can therefore fight more viciously, defeating those who have stronger ethics). Or, one can argue that present conditions are temporary, that one is really the equal or superior of the currently dominant culture, but that owing to an unfortunate combination of circumstances one has been put momentarily at a disadvantage. One is now faced with the task of identifying and eliminating these unfortunate circumstances, after which one's rightful position in the world will be restored.

All these responses have been chosen by groups and movements within Islamic society in modern times, although their relative importance varies with time and place.

Secularist Westernizers

Some, particularly those whose business or studies have brought them into frequent contact with the West, have tried to assimilate themselves as far as possible to dominant Western culture (in either its "socialist" or its capitalist manifestations). In order to improve social conditions, build modern nation-states, and become competitive in the international world, members of this group believed, their countries have to become westernized. This was taken to require the adoption of modern Western institutions in education and politics, in social and economic relations; it usually meant going so far as to adopt the outward signs of the West in dress and manners. All this involved abandoning elements of one's own culture, in some cases including the previous alphabet, and trying to displace and eliminate old elites. These westernizers are secularists and regard religion as an obstacle to modernity. Their societies are backward, they believe, because certain important events in world history were missed and vital growth did not take place. Two things were to blame for this: religion/tradition, and imperialism. Secularists have used the goal of westernization to undermine their rivals, especially those associated with religion. In Iran, too, they have been a significant political force since the early part of this century. The westernizers have included secular nationalists, liberals, various Marxist groups, and social democrats. At times they have been a radical opposition movement and at times they have dominated the official policy of the state, such as in Ataturk's case, and with less success in the cases of Afghanistan's King Amanullah (1919–1929) and Reza Khan. In Iran, groups such as the Tudeh Party, Peykar, and various factions of the Fedayeen-e-Khalq also belong to this broad category of secular westernizers.

Islamic Modernists

This second broad group argues that Islam is a positive force and a crucial part of the identity of their countries and people. Initially, they feel, Islam was the equal or superior of other cultures, and there is nothing in it that would block science, progress, or social reform. They support this argument by reference to Islamic scholarship, medicine, and

philosophy in the past and to the social reforms introduced by Muhammad. Over time, however, Islam has become too rigid and too perverted
by individuals exploiting it for their own purposes. It has to be brought
back to its essentials, adapted to the requirements of the modern age, taken
out of the hands of the currently ruling elites. Radical modernists, too,
have been highly critical of traditional religious leaders, arguing that Islam did not recognize any "priests" and that religious leaders had no special claim to authority. Ali Shari'ati writes: "Islam has abolished all forms
of official mediation between God and man, and the Qur'an mentions
the third manifestation of Cain—the official clergy—with harsh words,
even going so far as to curse them. . . . We have scholars of religion;
they do not constitute official authorities. . . . Islam has no clergy; the
word clergy (ruhaniyun) is recent, a borrowing from Christianity."[8] Secular and religious rulers diverted Islam from its true path: Islam "was re-
shaped under the Arab Caliphate," until it "became a rationale for the
acts of the most savage conquerors . . . [and] cast an aura of religiosity
over the feudal order of the Saljuqs and Mongols and bound the Muslim
people in the chains of predestination."[9] Shari'ati and his followers have
stated with varying degrees of directness that Islamic principles demanded the nationalization of the means of production and the creation
of a classless society. The most important group representing this viewpoint for Iran are the Mujahedeen-e-Khalq. The modernists are by no
means uniform in their goals or their choice of preferred means; they
manifest different degrees of radicalism and span the range from what we
might consider Islamic Marxism to social and parliamentary democracy.
The middle class has been the source of support for the modernists.
Moderate modernists have had more support in the traditional middle
class than in the modern one. Radical modernists have their base of power
in the modern middle class. Islamic modernism has been an important
political force in Iran since the late 1940s.

Traditionalists

These groups are conservative in the literal meaning of the term. Unlike the modernists, with whom they share an admiration for the Islamic
past, the traditionalists feel that accommodation, reform, and flexibility

are steps that will insidiously weaken the remaining power of Islamic culture and play into the hands of the enemy. One has to go back to the
original precepts and follow them to the letter, applying them as literally
as possible. At the same time, they accept the practical patterns of rule
that have emerged in their respective countries. They insist on the application of Islamic law in matters such as marriage and divorce and fight
against erosions of their role in education, and some of them want a voice
in legislation (often in the form of a veto over un-Islamic laws and decisions), but in general they accept the role and authority of secular institutions and governments. In the Iranian context this means that they would
accept the division between kingship and religion, and would oppose the
monarchy only on specific issues, not on principle. Where conflict arose,
they would try to pressure the state authority by using the by no means
negligible machinery available to them: exhorting their followers, using
the influence of relatives and associates who hold secular positions, en-
dorsing opposition groups, etc. They may at times be engaged in vehe-
ment oppositional politics, but their purpose will be to restore a perceived status quo ante that will allow them once again to withdraw from
active day-to-day politics into their sphere. In Iran Shariatmadari represents such a traditionalist position. He wants government to be Islamic
and to provide a supervisory authority over legislation to religious experts, but he does not oppose the idea of a secular government. In Michael Fischer's words,

> Shariat Madari . . . championed the interpretation that wilayat-e-faqih,
> could be accomplished very nicely under a fully-democratic form of
> government, without multiplying boards of clerical overseers in all areas
> of government[10]

and certainly without taking the place of the government. In fact, traditionalists generally regard secular government as not only tolerable but
necessary. The moral power of religious authorities is dependent on their
not corrupting themselves with the bargaining and compromise necessary in daily politics. Bazargan, for example, has stressed that religion and
politics must remain separate; Islamic associations must not engage in day-
to-day politicking.[11]

Traditionalists, being conservative, do not tend to be expansionist in
their politics. If anything, they incline toward isolationism, wishing to

block off the potentially hazardous effects of foreign, especially Western, influence. On this point, the Pakistani fundamentalist Maulana Maududi shares the traditionalist view:

> Cultural aping of others has very disastrous consequences upon a nation; it destroys its inner vitality, blurs its vision, befogs its critical faculties, breeds inferiority complexes, and gradually but assuredly saps all the springs of culture and sounds its death-knell. That is why the Holy Prophet has positively and forcefully forbidden the Muslims to assume the culture and mode of life of the non-Muslims.[12]

Such a statement is clearly a defensive one characteristic of the conservative position, since it implies that one's own culture will not emerge as the dominant one, but that one's followers will, if offered the chance, adopt the habits of the other culture. The traditionalists have been around longer than any other group. In the twentieth century, their support has largely come from the traditional middle class, although on some occasions they have managed to mobilize the lower classes.

Fundamentalists

Fundamentalists regard the religious authority as the primary one and the state, at best, as its instrument. They are radical, expansionist, and totalistic in their approach to foreign and domestic affairs. Unlike the traditionalists, they do not want a designated part in government, they want to *be* the government and to shape society in all its aspects. They refer to tradition as evidence that such conditions are envisioned by original Islam, but their claim rests on an idealized distant past rather than on the actual traditions of their society. To traditionalists, an Islamic polity is one in which Islamic precepts are followed in the life of the community. To fundamentalists, it is above all necessary that the government be Islamic, and the leadership religious.[13]

It cannot be stressed enough that all these categories are ideal-typical, and that they describe a dynamic situation. Each approach attempts to deal with problems and is subject to change as circumstances change and situations evolve. Groups can form tactical alliances, individuals can move from one category to another at different times or over different issues.

Most important, there are major divisions within each of the categories.

The most striking example of the tactical alliances these groupings have undertaken is the coalition between all four of them that overthrew the Shah. There are also historical examples, such as the modernist-traditionalist coalition during Iran's constitutional movement at the start of the century. Another important coalition was the recent tactical one between Tudeh and the fundamentalists. There are also many examples of individuals or groups who have changed their position, some quite drastically. Nikki Keddie argues that al-Afghani began as a secularist before becoming, perhaps in response to his assessment of the "pro-Islamic mood" dominating the Muslim world, an Islamic modernist.[14]

This brings us back to the "Islamic factor." How has it come to play such a consistent role in the current political expression of this region?

Islam in Politics

In explaining the centrality of religion in Iran's political course, three sets of hypotheses have emerged in the literature:

1. Islam is the most readily available means of articulating political sentiments.

According to this explanation Islam provided a network of organization and communication; it allowed the expression of political demands and sentiments in familiar words and concepts; since religion was one of the fundaments of the legitimacy claims of the state, it made possible a direct challenge to authority.[15] Islam was a vehicle for articulating dissent, then, because it possessed certain cultural, political, and tactical characteristics that made it effective. Fischer has referred to the Shi'ite "Karbala paradigm" as a "device for heightening political consciousness of the moral failings of the government" and for providing "multiple levels of channelling feelings of solidarity and conflict, of which the overt political metaphor of oppression by tyrannical kings is only the most obvious."[16]

2. The "Islamic revolution" was really an interelite conflict, with one side identified by its secular vocabulary and the other side, the traditional sector (with its own set of material interests), represented by the ulama and identified by its religious vocabulary.

Proponents of this view point to the highly pragmatic, sometimes clearly opportunistic political behavior of the ulama as reflected in their relationship with central authority, the monarchy, and other sectors of the elite, and in their alignment politics.[17] Of all the authors who follow this approach, Said Amir Arjomand proposes the most plainly pragmatic interpretation of ulama behavior and illustrates it by a review of the shifting alliances and tactics they engaged in since the Pahlavi reign. He even goes so far as to call the "Islamic revolution" a "clerical coup d'etat."[18]

3. Islam is different from other religions in its relationship to politics and/or Shi'ite Islam is different from Sunni Islam in its affinity for oppositional social thought.

This argument has gained the widest currency in the popular media. Islam, it asserts, does not lend itself to the division between politics and religion, since it seeks to regulate the life of the community along the guidelines set down. Shi'ite Islam, a variation of the argument continues, has been a traditional vehicle of protest against political oppression from the moment it was used to counter the domination of the Arabs and to forge a distinctly Persian politico-religious identity.

Each of these lines of argument has merit. However, they all assign to Islam an excessively central position, which tends to make the argument specious (politics in Islamic countries are Islamic because Islam is political) and to stress too much the uniqueness of Islam in explaining events in this part of the world. Christianity contains notions about property, government, and rebellion that can be interpreted to have highly political implications, and *are* so interpreted by Latin American guerrillas. Singling out Islam here carries with it the danger of sinking too deeply into the Great Dichotomy argument. Above all, however, it regards Islam too much as a uniform entity, thereby tending to obscure the domestic politics, i.e., the internal conflicts of interest and ideology between and among the actors and groups in the countries involved. The question of why political activity found an Islamic articulation may well be the wrong question altogether. Alternatively, we would like to look at events in Iran from the viewpoint of the three hypotheses we proposed at the beginning of this chapter.

Iran as a polity is composed of groups, actors, and classes engaged in those activities, consensual and conflictual, that comprise politics. The ulama was always one of the groups involved in this, as were the mer-

chants, the landowners, the bureaucrats, etc. The interests of foreign actors in Iran were always a factor in the political process.

Chronologically, the traditionalists were the first of the groups. They
represented a segment of the elite that stood in varying relations to the
authority of the state and to the other portions of the elite. To say that
the religious experts consistently challenged the legitimacy of the state and
the rulers would not be accurate; it would be more correct to say that
the ulama actively participated in politics at all times, sometimes in con-
cord with the government, sometimes joining in pressure against or even
deposition of a ruler.[19] In times of conflict, the government tried to challenge the legitimacy of the ulama just as the ulama assaulted the legitimacy of the ruler.[20]

Their position was not comparable to that of the Catholic church, since
there was no equivalent to the idea of papal infallibility. However, they
had moral authority, resources, networks, and an established way of participating in the political realm. They also had their opponents, those whose
ambitions were blocked by values and positions held by that elite of which
the ulama was a part.

. The secularists and the modernists represented those forces in the society that wanted basic changes. For a variety of reasons (because support
was forthcoming or hoped for from that quarter; because it provided the
concepts and terminology with which to express their ambitions; because
it was a model that proved one's aspirations could be realized) some elements of the society adopted postures that attuned them to the West. At
different times and in different countries this took different forms. Ultimately, Western-educated and westernized groupings emerged as nationalists and in many places led the anticolonialist uprisings. Their success
against the foreigners gave them popularity "in spite of, not because of"[21]
their secularism. In some countries, such as Turkey, a combination of
success, cultural predisposition (i.e., availability of identities that could
be more readily separated from religion), and timing allowed the secularists to establish themselves. In Iran, social changes were initially introduced within the traditional framework of government, that is, by a
monarch. The secularists remained weak, and tended either to become
modernists in the hope of broadening their base or to give way to the
modernists. The traditionalists initially behaved as they had in the past,
pressuring the monarch when they felt their interests threatened.

Khomeini himself appears to have been essentially a traditionalist during the 1940s and 1950s, and not to have become a genuine fundamentalist until the 1970s. In the beginning he had opposed changes in traditional life styles, particularly those he regarded as most threatening to Islamic values: the unveiling of women, coeducational schools, the introduction of Western dress, legal reforms affecting the family, and the sale of alcohol. He called for clergy participation in government, but not for the rule of the ulama. Yann Richard argues that Khomeini was already calling for religious government in the 1940s,[22] but we are unable to find any evidence for this. In his 1941 publication *Kashf-al-Asrar* (Discovering the Secrets),[23] Khomeini makes statements clearly to the contrary. "We do not say that government must be in the hands of the faqih," he writes, "rather we say that government must be run in accordance with God's law, for the welfare of the country and the people demands this, and it is not feasible except with the supervision of the religious leaders. In fact, this principle has been approved and ratified in the Constitution, and in no way conflicts with public order, the stability of the government, or the interests of the country." And he even goes on to assure that if ulama supervision over legislation, proposed in the Iranian constitution, were implemented, "everyone in the country, with no exception, from the religious leaders to the tradesmen, soldiers and hawkers in the street, would cooperate with the government. . . ."[24] Shahrough Akhavi has even described *Kashf-al-Asrar* as "a mild defense of the monarchical system,"[25] and it is true that Khomeini here supports the principle of secular rule as essential to keep order, arguing that "a bad government is better than no government."

This is precisely the traditionalist position. What brought about the change in Khomeini's stance? We believe it can be explained, with reference to our hypotheses, as a radicalization of tradition resulting from the combustible joining of new social forces with foreign interference (material and ideological) and the stress of multiplied domestic and international conflicts. All led some sections of the traditionalists, including Khomeini, to the conclusion that the traditional balance was too threatened to be salvageable by the customary means, and that to fight only for restoration of their traditional position in the old Iranian pattern this time would mean eventual defeat. The dynamics of the situation would in time sweep them away unless they took over control and radically transformed the system.

There is some support for this interpretation. Several of the leading

Islamic thinkers in Iran had voiced alarm over changes that they perceived not just as one more of the many power shifts that had characterized state-religion relations in Iran for so long, but as the portents of a
real and qualitative change heralding their own eventual elimination. In
his lecture "The Boundary Between Religion and Social Affairs" in 1962,
Bazargan clearly took this position. Politics and religion, he argued, had
to be maintained separately but in a balance, connected to each other both
by linkages and by a kind of institutionalized rivalry. However, politics
was threatening to dominate religion completely, and this might well be
the first step in the eventual annihilation of religion as a factor. Things
had reached the point of a "life and death matter." Therefore, religious
leaders and forces had to rally, for the sake of their own survival and to
save the society from the consequences of sole domination by political
power-holders.[26] In a 1964 speech from Qum, Khomeini shows a clear
awareness of the assault being launched on his sector by secular institutions. "According to a history textbook printed this year and taught to
our schoolchildren even now, and containing all kinds of lies and inac-
curate statements, 'It has now become clear that it is to the benefit of the
nation for the influence of the religious leaders to be rooted out.' "[27]

Shariatmadari, a traditionalist out of firm conviction that the religious
authority must occupy its own sphere and that it will be diminished in
its function and weight if it becomes too engaged in daily political and
administrative affairs, was highly conscious of this collision-course situation. In 1970 he had failed to respond to a call for a one-day strike issued
by students in Qum and Tehran; afterwards he was criticized for having
thereby demonstrated that he was "anti-nationalist and anti-religious."[28]
Shariatmadari consistently tried to avoid crisis and radicalization, to restore the correct order—including the role and influence of the ulama—
by other means. He seems to have perceived the successive radicalization
as a danger and to have felt the pressure on traditionalists to become fundamentalists. Opposing the declaration of martial law in November 1978,
he stated: "we have not made a decision on armed struggle, but if they
[the government] close off all other channels, we will have to take that
path."[29]

It is difficult to see, in the dynamics of radicalization the state and the
ulama became locked in, which side should be designated the initiator.
Was it the offensive taken by the state against the religious elite, the
crackdowns on oppositional clerics in the 1970s, and the effort, through

attempts to recruit religious students and through the establishment of a "religion corps," to encroach on the terrain of religion that marked the scene for confrontation? Or were these measures only taken by the Shah in recognition of an already threatening radicalization of a clergy determined to fight for its position?

Be that as it may, by the time he wrote *Islamic Government,*[30] Khomeini had changed from a traditionalist to a fundamentalist position. He now asserted governmental power had to be exercised directly by religious leaders. However, in that book he is still not explicit on how, exactly, the state is to be constructed. Political parties are neither excluded nor suggested; they are not mentioned at all. Whether there is to be a council of ulama or the selection of one of them as ruler is left open.

Statements made by Khomeini in Neauphle-le-Château were tactical rather than programmatic. The coalition with the modernists was still intact, and Iranians belonging to a variety of secular leftist groupings, including orthodox Marxists, spent a great deal of time with Khomeini and his supporters, attended his evening consultations, and came away with the feeling that there would be room for them, too, in the Iran he was fighting for.[31] Partly, this lack of clarity was deliberate, aimed at an audience. Ibrahim Yazdi instructed Khomeini's entourage to stress three things when speaking to the media: the rights of minorities, the rights of women, and the holding of democratic elections.[32] Khomeini, apparently, was fairly docile. Bani-Sadr reports that he and Yazdi drew up a list of eighteen points containing what Khomeini should say to interviewers and visitors, and that he cooperated. They had believed that their influence over him would continue after the success of the revolution, since they were expert at the pragmatic affairs of economics and statesmanship and he was not.[33] The ulama in their role as an elite acted on the basis of two broad motivations: first their world view and their social values; second their interests and position. Their goal was to maintain both.[34] To the traditionalists, maintaining order and avoiding anarchy were prerequisites upon which the competition over power and resources was premised. Arjomand and Shaul Bakhash[35] give evidence for the reluctance on the part of religious leaders to resort to the risky step of unleashing the masses; those highest in the hierarchy were at greatest risk from a collapse of social order, since their position as part of the elite necessarily must make them fear the consequences of a populist assault on authority. They were therefore the most reluctant. Khomeini, already in exile with no position to lose and with a status predicated precisely on his antimaterialistic stance, was the ideal kind of "marginal" figure[36] for carrying forward the radicalization.

The point that traditionalists were active in Iranian politics *as* political actors, and thus capable of the kinds of behavior politics requires, is worth making because it puts in context the argument that Islam is potentially revolutionary in part because it has no organized church. Obviously, it does not have a church organization in the Christian sense, but there are many senses in which the clergy acted as a coherent group and even a class.[37] Morris Janowitz has already pointed to the distortions in political analysis that result from underestimating the political efficacy of traditional actors.[38] The clerics were a religious group; they were also an interest group. This is evidenced most clearly by the skill they demonstrated in their interaction with other political interest groups.

Once the traditional interplay between clerics and monarchy had moved from its pattern of mutual accommodation to a period of chill and clergy losses, the ulama began looking around for new allies. It found them in the modernists, who, though they shared in principle some of the values of the modernizing monarchy, were dissatisfied with the pace, the means, and the direction the Shah had taken. Both sides undertook efforts to broaden their base, and the effort brought them, tactically, closer to each other. From the sociological standpoint, they were not alien to each other but came from essentially the same class and family background.[39]

As the fundamentalists entered into a dialogue with individuals such as Bazargan and Shari'ati and through them acquired access to the modernist and secularist intelligentsia, the modernists in turn were amenable to cooperation which offered access to the mass of the population to a degree the secularists alone could not hope to achieve.[40]

To get a better picture of the "platforms" that came together in this coalition, it is instructive to juxtapose the writings of their two most prominent ideologues: Ali Shari'ati for the Islamic modernists and Khomeini for the fundamentalists.

Shari'ati and Khomeini: Authors of the Coalition

According to available biographies, Ali Shari'ati came from a family of rural religious scholars; his father wrote and taught, and Shari'ati himself began by studying to become a teacher and by lecturing at the Center for the Propagation of Islamic Truth in Mashhad, of which his father was a founder. Subsequently, Shari'ati spent five years at the University of Paris, an experience that left an indelible mark on his later writing, imbuing it with an aura of classroom discussion on existentialism and leftist student debates over Marxism vs. anticolonialism in the Third World. Shari'ati acknowledged the influence of Fanon, and there are stylistic similarities. Shari'ati's book *Man, Marxism, and Islam,* republished in 1980 under the title *Marxism and Other Western Fallacies,*[41] reads remarkably like a term paper, conscientiously reviewing and discarding all the major Western schools of thought in a systematic if sketchy fashion. Other pieces, notably the "Philosophy of History: Cain and Abel," reflect clearly the impact of the French structuralists and are reminiscent of Lacan. These observations are not at all intended to disparage Shari'ati by making him the object of literary criticism, but to venture the supposition that the eclecticism of the modernists is a product of their biographies and a feature of their thinking, not just a tactical ploy.[42]

Shari'ati is in many ways the personification of populist, modernist, possibly even socialist Islam. His death in 1977 (alternately attributed to cancer and to assassination) deprives us of the knowledge of how he would have responded to fundamentalist rule, what position he would have taken and what course he would have advocated. At the same time it makes his writings available for much more flexible use and interpretation on the part of those who consider themselves his followers.

Shari'ati's writings reflect contradictory approaches to the question of leadership and social order. The anticolonialist and progressive social justice line remains constant, but then it can be found in Khomeini's writings, too. Shari'ati is a reformer, but who is to conduct these reforms, how exactly they are to be implemented, and what their nature will be remain open. This is not necessarily a criticism, since Shari'ati died before the phase of "implementation" had arrived and while the negative imperatives of opposition dominated the need for operationalization.

We can identify three points of consensus in the writings of Shari'ati and Khomeini:

1. The argument that Shi'a Islam has traditionally been the vehicle for political change;

2. An elitist approach to leadership and government, and a populist

notion of legitimacy combined with a totalist approach to authority (i.e., the idea of change through mass mobilization, and of an absolute imperative for this change stemming from divine authority and historical necessity);

3. A strong "nationalist" identity culminating in a Third-Worldist self-definition.

Ideologically, the mix of anti-imperialist nationalism and militant Islam is common to both, as is the vague picture of a subsequent political order with strong leadership, firm ethical values, and cultural autonomy. We will begin by identifying some of the random elements in common, and then attempt a more coherent picture. The writings of both the fundamentalists and the modernists reflect a strong antimaterialist stance.[43] Talmon's concept of the division into a pragmatic and a totalistic political view is useful in this connection: Islamic oppositional thought takes a clear stand against material measures of power, linking possession with corruption and material indifference with righteousness.

Shari'ati: "Shi'ites turn their backs on the opulent mosques and magnificent palaces of the caliphs of Islam and turn to the lonely mud-house of Fatima."[44]

And Khomeini: " 'Ali lived a life of utter simplicity while managing a vast state in which Iran, Egypt, Hejaz and Yemen were mere provinces under his rule. I do not believe that any of our poor people can live the kind of life that the imam lived . . . despite the control they had . . . and the power and authority in their hands, the prophets did not have the greed to be preoccupied with the good things of life, to acquire ephemeral things. . . . The prophet's life was one of utter simplicity. He himself did not possess any money . . ."[45]

This does not imply a rejection of private property, the owners and adherents of which were the main base of fundamentalist support. Khomeini repeatedly mentions that under a correct Islamic government, the possessions and property of individual Muslims would be safer than under current conditions and cites the damage to trade and the economy as important failures of the wrongful rule of the Shah. Rather, the realm of political leadership is considered to bear ethical demands that place it outside the mundane concerns of privilege. Power manifests itself not through its worldly attributes but through a moral absence of concern for personal advantage: the austerely moral state as opposed to the "theater state,"[46] displays of self-restriction rather than displays of lavish power and possession.

A derivative of this lies in the reversal of the usual political logic, which could be paraphrased as: because X is in power, X is rightfully in power. The legitimacy advantage inherently belonging to the ruler is claimed by the opposition, who can argue that precisely because they have no visible power or possessions, they are morally stronger. In Islamic opposition, this stance frequently has an antimonarchic dimension.

Shari'ati: "The history of Islam follows a strange path; a path in which hoodlums and ruffians from the Arab, Persian, Turk, Tartar and Mongol dynasties all enjoy the right of the leadership of the Moslem community and the caliphate of the Prophet of Islam, to the exclusion of the family of the Prophet and the rightful Imams of Islam" (*Red Shi'ism*, p. 10). In *Islamic Government*, Khomeini makes it abundantly clear that no political authority rests with the monarchy. Decisions made or judgments rendered by monarchical authority are invalid and wrong, even if the principle they state is an objectively correct one, because they stem from the wrong source: the "sultan" can at best be a "person working for the jurisprudents" (i.e., the ulama).

To both thinkers, the political values of Islamic opposition rest on a combination of populism and elitism. The method of documentation of current consciousness in the Islamic community is the spontaneous articulation of mass sentiment; the method of change is the channeling of mass sentiment by the oppositional leaders; the method of governance is obedience toward these leaders by the mass. The views of both Shari'ati and Khomeini might qualify for the label "totalitarian democracy" in regard to their authoritarian concept of a "vanguard" of the enlightened that is entitled to impose justice and the correct order in the name of the population, which is seen as incapable of self-government. This is clearest in the writings of Khomeini: "The rule of the jurisprudent is a subjective matter dictated by the Shari'a, as the Shari'a considers us a trustee over minors. The task of a trustee over an entire people is not different from that of the trustee over minors, except quantitatively" (*Islamic Government*, p. 38).

Khomeini does not state what form the governance of the Faqih would take ideally; he leaves it deliberately open whether the religious experts would rule "separately [that is, whether one of them would be the ruler] or collectively," whether government would be "confined to one person" or "shared equally" (p. 39). What is clear, however, is that the ulama are to be the government because neither the people nor the secular government are capable of recognizing and pursuing the right path.

Shari'ati, while more populist in style, is equally elitist. Rather than deriving the authority of the elite purely from religious tradition, he refers also to Third World revolution. Rather than a rule by the traditional ulama, Shari'ati favors a kind of "dictatorship of the intelligentsia," and makes the following case for it:

> This is the principle which today all of the intellectuals of the Third World, Latin America, Africa, Asia and especially the countries which have most recently become independent are basing their societies upon. . . . That is, they have a revolution. Through the help of their intellectuals and thinkers, they get rid of the colonizers and they free their society. Later, they see that if they act according to the votes of the people and rely upon them, these people are people who sell their vote for a nickel. They get together a hundred votes by offering them hot soup. . . . Therefore, if we want to elect a leader by public vote, the person who is elected will only serve the enemy.[47]

The solution Shari'ati ascribes to successful Third World precursors is "not to give leadership into the hands of the people who know nothing about leading." Instead, "they keep the revolutionary group who began the revolution. For a time, a stage exists which is called 'revolutionary' or 'democracy engaged in social action' which is ruled by the revolutionary group and the generation after the revolutionary group chosen by the revolutionary leader. They rule the people even without the vote of the people." This is to continue, Shari'ati proposes, until the population has developed into an educated and independent citizenry. The principle of rule by an elite group is, Shari'ati insists repeatedly, "an Islamic principle." If Islamic society had developed properly, if the descendents of Ali had ruled instead of the succession of tyrannical rulers, illegitimate caliphates, and opportunists, then "we would [by now] have elections."[48] Like Khomeini, Shari'ati designates the educated as the proper leaders of the population. The emphasis on learning is so strong that Khomeini quotes prominently a hadith that "the ink of the learned people is better than the blood of the martyrs" (p. 117). The difference between them is that for Shari'ati and the modernists, the "learned" are the revolutionary intelligentsia of the Third World, while for the fundamentalists they are the ulama.

What has been referred to as the anticlericalism of Shari'ati is to be found less in his criticism of the opportunist collaboration of the ulama with the powerful—a criticism shared by Khomeini—than in his belief in a new kind of political leadership. Both Shari'ati and Khomeini denounce the "crime of silence" as a major historic flaw of the ulama. Khomeini speaks of the "sin of silence" committed by the ulama and ridicules the contemplative approach to religion. Shari'ati laments the times when "piety remained silent against tyranny." However, Khomeini and Shari'ati place the emphasis cautiously but clearly on different actors. Khomeini approaches the intelligentsia as potential allies and exhorts his followers to enter into a coalition with them. His assurance that "Islam will be welcomed ardently by college people" because "college people are most hostile to repression, agentry, treason, the plundering of wealth and resources and unjust gains and will find in Islam—whose teachings in the sphere of government, the judiciary, economy and social affairs you will convey to them—traits that will attract them to it" (p. 97) should be read—particularly in view of his later comments about these "college people"—as tactical instructions. He orders his supporters: "unite for the purpose of planning for Islamic government with whomever demands freedom and independence . . . " (p. 105).

For Shari'ati, the intelligentsia are not potential coalition partners; they are the direct audience and his envisioned leadership, intellectuals with an independent Islamic identity engaged in anti-imperialist struggle on behalf of the politically immature masses. His tactics are weighted in the opposite direction: Islamic imagery borrowed to lend familiarity to new political goals for that portion of his audience that has not read Fanon or Sartre.

Writing a history for the Islamic opposition movement, Shari'ati cites the struggle against Mongol domination as a successful Shi'ite revolution, and his choice of terminology is revealing when he describes it as "a revolutionary movement based on Alavite Shi'ism, against foreign domination, internal deceit, the power of the feudal lords and large capitalists . . . led by peasants 700 years ago" (*Red Shi'ism*, p. 23). Underlying the varied arguments used by Islamic opposition thinkers, two strands of thought stand out and link up with oppositional movements in general. One is the emphasis on the mass base of the movement; the other is the focus placed on what is opposed rather than what is sought after. In the situation of struggle against a dominant ruler, neither of these is surprising. They are worth mentioning because they are such fundamental parts of the oppositional consciousness, a frame of thinking we will return to shortly.

In a prerevolutionary situation, the material advantages initially appear to be all on the side of the dominant group. Control over the repressive apparatus and the instruments of power, access to resources and money, and the sheer weight of being in the position of ruler all operate to the advantage of the power-holders. Against this, there is the weight of discontent, which is more a quantitative than a qualitative force, more a sentiment than a policy. Khomeini sensed this and described it in *Islamic Government;* the people generally, he wrote, were more a potential than an actual Islamic following. They were generally "ignorant of most of its laws," but they could be won over. They were susceptible to the appeal of Islam, he suggests, less because they knew what Islam stood for and approved it than because they were so urgently in search of leadership. "When I make a speech," he explains, "I feel a change in the people and I feel the impact on them because they are displeased with the condition under which they live. Fear of the tyrants is filling their hearts and they are in direct need of people who speak courageously and firmly" (p. 100).

He is touching here upon a point that is perhaps crucial in a comparative review of the modernist-fundamentalist coalition: the fact that the modernists were less consistent, more accommodationist, than the fundamentalists. Shari'ati tries to build a uniform chain of argumentation; Khomeini does not mind if his arguments contradict each other, so long as they all arrive at the same conclusion. Khomeini argues for the rule of the ulama on three sometimes redundant, sometimes clearly contradictory grounds: first, on the ground that the ulama are necessarily and always the government, either as assistants to the Imam who cannot be everywhere in person, or as his trustees in his absence; second on the ground that while secular government may or may not be acceptable in principle, in fact this government has displayed its ineptness and ineffectiveness, so that religious rule is pragmatically superior. A Shariah judge can decide in two or three days what it will take the civil court twenty years to rule on (*Islamic Government,* p. 10). The Shah was also inept at charting economic policy and has paved the way for the "decline of the Muslim markets" (p. 91). Third, the times are exceptional, an acute crisis is at hand, and a kind of Islamic martial law is required to save the day. Here, he allows that direct intervention may be a departure from traditional practice, but that it is justified by the crisis: "Will Islam be preserved if we kiss the Koran, put it on our heads and recite its phrases with a beautiful voice night and day?" Whereas in some places he distinguishes Islam from other religions, he also argues that modernization sounds the death knell for religion generally and that Islam must be warned by the fate of Christianity: "Their debate on the trinity, the hypostases and on the father and the son preoccupied them and left them with nothing else" (p. 110).

The modernists are on the defensive vis-à-vis Islamic fundamentalism; most of them have lived "un-Islamic" lives abroad and been attracted by a variety of thoughts and schools. They are also divided against each other, as becomes obvious when they help the fundamentalists rise to sole power by turning against each other.[49]

The eclectic style was to remain a feature of their approach after the overthrow of the Shah. This is well illustrated by a publication of Bani-Sadr's speeches under the title *Work and the Worker in Islam*.[50] The title page looks like the cover of the GDR's latest Five Year Plan, with muscular workers smashing a chain with their spades; but a pencil outline of Khomeini's face, twice the size of the burly workers, hovers in the background, and the introduction stresses that Bani-Sadr's father was the Ayatollah Sayyid Nasrollah Bani-Sadr. The content of the lectures is mixed, ranging from a defense of temporary marriage and polygamy on modernist grounds (temporary marriage has the purpose of allowing young students to live together before marrying permanently in order to see if they are compatible, and polygamy provides sexual gratification for all women in situations of a statistical shortage of men) to economic theory to a critique of Marxism and Iranian Marxists. By embarking on their coalition with the fundamentalists, the modernists acquiesced in establishing a set of rules by which they would not win because they were not the best players. They acquiesced because that seemed to offer the greatest chance for success, and possibly because they too did not realize the extent to which tradition had been radicalized. From the viewpoint of revolution and modernization theory, the weakness of the modernists that forced them into this coalition poses some interesting questions. In proposing some possible answers, we would like again to refer back to our hypotheses, and make the following observations:

The interaction between the monarchy and the new sectors of the society was affected decisively, to the Shah's advantage, by the support he received from outside powers, mainly the United States. One can make a case for the argument that, left to their own devices, political actors in Iran would have had more leeway for action against the monarchy, which would either have accommodated some of them more or been forced into a confrontation earlier. It is also possible that the National Front would have taken a different development without U. S. opposition to Mossadeq.

The relationship among the actors in Iran was affected decisively by the Third World status of Iran. The necessity for nationalism, especially in its cultural dimension, which resulted from this status made impossible a modernist rejection of those aspects of tradition which, in classical European history, could more easily be labeled reactionary and opposed. If the Shah had not been so dependent on the U. S., he might have been more of a nationalist figure; if he had not had the U. S. to fall back on, he might have been obliged to cultivate the modern elements as his backers; if secularization had not been associated with the foreign West and the repressive monarch, religion might not have become such a symbolic indicator of opposition.

CHAPTER THREE

Iran—What Happened?

In the wake of the turmoil, little agreement exists on the part of scholars, politicians, or journalists as to what this social phenomenon is that has overturned the Shah and ushered in an extended period of upheaval and violence. Is it a revolution? Is it typical of Islam, of the Third World, of belated modernization, of Shi'ism, of Persia? Who is responsible—the U. S., Khomeini, the abuses of the Shah? Or is it all just a brief interlude, the rule of an Islamic Savonarola, soon to be replaced by more predictable actors? The analysis of striking contemporary events carries with it the temptation to compare, to generalize, and to define. Events as dramatic as those in Iran lend themselves particularly well to what Gerschenkron has called "easy extrapolations."[1]

In agreement with Gerschenkron's view that the constructive purpose of comparative analysis lies in broadening the frame of reference against which events can be interpreted, in this chapter we seek to organize the questions raised by the events in Iran into a more systematic pattern. The question "what happened?" in literature dealing with this general topic produces answers that fall into two categories. First, there is "what happened" in a structural sense, an attempt to identify patterns in the preconditions, the course, and the political dynamics of the event. Second, there is the analysis of quality and content, of the essential significance that distinguishes one kind of change from another. In looking briefly at the concept of revolution, we will begin with the second aspect.

Revolution as Content

"The world is turning like a potter's wheel. Servant women are rebellious. The rabble goes freely in and out of the courthouses. Everything is in disorder."[2] Thus, contemporary commentators in Pharaonic Egypt criticized a period of social uprisings that threatened the established order and protested existing social injustices. Many prominent analysts of revolution take the position, however, that this phenomenon is the prerogative of the modern age. "The history of reform and revolution is relatively short," Michael Walzer asserts, arguing that the "active, ideologically committed radical" is a creation of our times.[3]

"Revolution," Huntington agrees, "is characteristic of modernization." Great civilizations of the past, such as the Egyptian, the Babylonian, Persia, the Incas, Greece, Rome, China, India, and the Arab World, had "revolts, insurrections, and dynastic changes, but not social revolutions."[4] Hannah Arendt, to whom he refers for support, writes: "Although history has always known those who, like Catiline, were . . . eager for new things, the revolutionary spirit of the last centuries, that is the eagerness to liberate and to build a new house where freedom can dwell, is unprecedented and unequalled in history."[5] This ready dismissal of premodern political events serves to define our age as the age of revolution, and the West as its spearhead. The argument is circular: because we are modern, we have real social revolutions; because we have had real social revolutions, we are modern. It is a definition less by argument than by fiat. As such, it is an element in historiography[6] rather than an insight about history. It is connected, in this view, with other key concepts, especially that of secularization. For example, Hannah Arendt, who may fairly be taken as representative of scholarly revolution theory of the non-Marxist school, has listed secularization as being invariably linked with revolution:

> Secularization, the separation of religion from politics and the rise of the secular regime with a dignity of its own, is certainly a crucial factor in the phenomenon of revolution. Indeed, it may ultimately turn out that what we call revolution is precisely that transitory phase which brings about the birth of a new secular realm.[7]

Elsewhere, revolution is defined by Arendt as a situation where

change occurs in the sense of a new beginning, where violence is used
to constitute an altogether different form of government, to bring about
the formation of a new body politic, where the liberation from oppression aims at least at the constitution of freedom.[8]

If revolution is defined as an abrupt and intense upheaval of the social
order which aims at, and partially succeeds in, establishing a new and more
just, freer order in its place, then the imperative for a secular content becomes much less obvious, the exclusion of prior mass movements for social justice less understandable. Why was the popular movement of ancient Egyptians against the tyranny of the established priesthood, the ruling
elite, and the inequities of the economic and social structure not revolutionary? Why was the movement led by the Prophet Muhammad against
the existing elite on behalf of certain moral values and in cooperation with
certain upward-striving social and economic elements not revolutionary,
though it clearly led to far-reaching social, legal, and political transformations of Arab society? And: would a leftist Catholic mass movement
in Latin America that overthrew a dictatorship in the name of egalitarian
Christian-Communist values be, as a nonsecular movement, automati-
cally nonrevolutionary?[9] Hannah Arendt leans clearly to the affirmative.
"The rebellious spirit," she writes, "which seems so manifest in certain
strictly religious movements in the modern age, always ended in some
Great Awakening or revivalism which, no matter how much it might 're-
vive' those who were seized by it, remained politically without consequences and historically futile."[10] How much evidence supports her con-
clusions, of course, depends on how one understands the term "strictly
religious."

The restriction of the term revolution to the modern age seems arbitrary. Therefore, it remains for us to discern the persuasive criteria distinguishing a revolution. Consensus exists that the change effected by a revolution must be sharp, that it must be achieved by mass involvement,
that it must bring about a new order and allow expression and leadership
to new forces within the society whose emergence had been blocked by
the old order, and that the change must be effected in the name of greater
social justice and political freedom.

Two problems remain with this definition. One of them has already
been touched upon above: the requirement that revolution must be instrumental in bringing about lasting and genuine changes that transform

an old order into a qualitatively new one. This means that judgment cannot really be passed on whether a genuine revolution has taken place except retroactively. This is connected with the second problem, one raised by Charles Tilly[11] in his critique of predominant theory on Third World revolution: that our study of revolutions is based on revolutions that succeeded. He illustrates his point by beginning with a description of an uprising against the monarchy in Sicily in 1848. Declaring it as their aim to "establish reforms and institutions proper to the progress of this century," a coalition of various socioeconomic interest groups led insurrections all over Sicily, setting up revolutionary committees and initiating a set of reforms. After only a few months, their coalitions collapsed and the monarchy was able to reestablish control. Arguing that its "incompleteness, ineffectuality and reversal" raise questions that studies of the more spectacular and successful revolutions avoid, Tilly asks whether "events such as those in Sicily constitute a number of separate revolutions, a single revolution, part of a larger revolution, or no revolution at all."[12] We will return to his argument later, because the answer he proposes involves leaving the content of revolutions behind and focusing on the form. For now, we will add two clauses to our loose definition of revolutionary content: that to be a revolution, an uprising must succeed not only in overthrowing the existing ruler but in establishing a viable and *new* social and political system, and that a decision on whether these criteria have been met or not can only be made after a significant amount of time has elapsed.

A contemporaneous political scientist, looking at the French revolution as its turbulent phases of radicalization, counterrevolution, expansion, and finally consolidation were unfolding, could not have seen it in the way we do now: as an erratic but continuous change, and part of an era of revolutionary changes in Europe that combined to create today's modern industrial West.

Besides awaiting the outcome, we have the option of studying revolution as a process: the circumstances under which it comes about, the actors involved, the phases of its unfolding, etc. This brings us to the question of form, rather than content, in defining revolution.

Revolution as a Process

Tilly's goal in the above-mentioned piece is to eliminate, one by one, the current notions about revolution until it emerges as a specific kind of power struggle. In a revolutionary situation, there are two sets of actors: the government, and the contender(s) for the power currently held by the government. The contenders can be subdivided into actors and groups who are recognized by the system and those who are not (in his terminology, "polities" and "challengers"). Proceeding from this set of actors, Tilly defines revolution broadly: "Revolution occurs when a government becomes the object of effective, competing, mutually exclusive claims from two or more separate contenders," and ends when one contender gains control. A revolution, for Tilly, takes place when three essential conditions are met: the appearance of contenders advancing claims to power; the support of their claims by a significant part of the population; and the unwillingness or inability of the existing government to suppress the opposition.

Obviously such an approach is premised on abandoning the distinctions that separate a revolution from some other forms of abrupt political change, and the author defends this by arguing that some coups, some wars, and even some incidents of banditry can spark the consequences generally associated with a revolution. Clearly under Tilly's conditions, the Iranian upheaval was a revolution.[13] Brinton's *The Anatomy of Revolution*[14] provides a much more precise model of the structural aspect of revolutionary change. We will now examine whether Iran meets Brinton's conditions as well.

What conditions bring about a revolutionary situation in the first place? The prerevolutionary situation, Brinton writes, is characterized by a few universal factors. First, there are growing and serious economic "or at least financial" problems. The economy is out of gear, or particular groups are severely and systematically disadvantaged, or there is a crisis of payment. "It is the government that is in financial difficulties, not the societies themselves," Brinton adds. The potential productivity is not the problem, and living conditions do not have to be extremely bad. Sometimes there will be major disparities between different sectors of the population, or between the population's expectations and reality. Economic decline as such is not the spark igniting the revolution. However, there will be some groups with serious economic grievances, and the government itself will experience a financial crisis. Perhaps more important, some groups in the society will feel that their chances are blocked by the policies of the government.

Looking at Iran, we find this description suprisingly apt. Revenues were high and had improved significantly compared with the pre-1970 situation. However, economic resources were not matched by financial stability. Owing to the vast arms expenditures, the allocation policies, and the uneven development, Iran's government consistently overspent. That the economy was on a worrisome course was perceived by international economic experts. A 1971 report of the International Labor Organization warned about serious structural imbalances in sector allocation, insufficient development in agriculture, and spending policies. The Report of the U. S. Congressional Research Service in July 1978 warned against the economic problems being produced by waste, unmanaged inflation, and unbalanced growth.[15] Others noted the overextensions of the budget causing Iran, despite high oil revenues, to borrow heavily on the Euromarkets, the overspending on military acquisitions, and the maldistribution, including growing urban-rural disparities, and warned that "positive forecasts made concerning the country's improving prosperity by the end of the century will obviously be academic exercises" unless these trends were halted.[16] Instead they increased. Government spending rose by 208 percent between 1974 and 1975, imports were up by almost 100 percent, amounting to 1.2 billion dollars a month,[17] and by 1978 military expenditures were $10 billion in excess of the budget plan.[18] This system of allocations caused important sectors of the society to feel themselves underprivileged.[19] Traditional sectors of the economy felt themselves in danger of displacement. The ulama resented decreases in traditional allocations as the Shah reduced their subsidies.[20]

A second major characteristic of the prerevolutionary situation, Brinton writes, is the inability of the central government to get a grip on the country's administration. The existence of old administrative units and resistance in the countryside to extensions of central authority, especially in such perennially unpopular areas as taxation, frustrate the efforts of the central power to rationalize its apparatus and perfect its control; at the same time, central authority is effective enough to menace the traditional sector and rouse it to resistance.

The case of Iran shows general conformity to these conditions. While his efforts to control the country's administration and to extend the reach of the center had made significant progress, the Shah's determination to maintain effective personal control led him at the same time to systematically weaken the apparatus of modern institutions in order to decrease the danger of opposition and the emergence of alternative leadership. In this, he followed a general Pahlavi policy established by his father; Reza Khan was described by Arthur Millspaugh as "following the advice of the Greek dictator" in "lopping off all heads that rose above the rest" (as in a grainfield).[21] His son's policies rested on a good measure of distrust, a system of surveillance, and the elimination of individuals who seemed too popular or effective. Amin Saikal offers an extensive description of the Shah's elaborate system of playing different individuals and departments of the bureaucracy, the military, and the police against each other in an effort to "rule by separating and by repression," with regular purges.[22] Robert Graham gives evidence for the systematic halfheartedness of the Shah in allowing the changes and institutions he was introducing to become genuinely effective. He wanted to industrialize but at the same time he feared the political consequences of a growing body of industrial workers; his political power system, including the prime minister's office, the majlis, the political party, the provincial government, and the press were matched by a set of "covert" counterinstitutions designed to make sure that democratization did not go so far as to threaten the Shah's personal rule; these "twin institutions" included the SAVAK, the Imperial Inspectorate, the military tribunals, censorship, corruption, and the strategic placement of loyal individuals and relatives.[23]

The armed forces, which were a central institution in the Shah's system of rule and, as we have seen, absorbed such an enormous proportion of the country's budget—about 40 percent in the late seventies[24]—are an instructive example of the Shah's efforts to maintain personal control and the consequence, the failure of these institutions to become effective. To circumvent the danger of coups, the Shah systematically disrupted the chain of command and hence the functioning of the military as a cohesive unit. Again, it was his father who had initiated this system of precautions. Reza Khan is described in contemporary texts as removing from office "any army commander who shows himself too successful in the field. . . ."[25] To maintain rivalry, avoid plots and coalitions against the throne, and secure his position as exclusive and indispensable center of command, the Shah built a number of precautions into the structure of the armed forces. They included a system comprising 12 different organizations for internal and external defense, all set sufficiently at odds or at least in competition with each other that there would be mutual distrust, surveillance, and reporting on each other. Commanders of the individual branches were not allowed to meet with each other, only with the Shah. Headquarters closed every day at five to decrease the likelihood of a coup. At times, the Shah would deliberately override such considerations as seniority and move loyal junior officers up in the ranks. Air Force General Rabbii was one person thus promoted, and part of his qualification may have been that as a Kurd, he would be less able to conspire with high-ranking officers of the dominant ethnic affiliation.

The purpose of all these measures was to make the army a personal institution, controlled by and loyal to the person of the Shah. Modern institutions, on the other hand, are generally defined by their nonpersonal, functional structure. This made for a fundamental ambiguity in the Shah's effort to introduce modern institutions.

James Bill and Carl Leiden characterize the result of all this as a condition of "organizational tension"[26] that maintained the Shah in the pivotal position of control. However, while a defense system with built-in traps to catch and eliminate those who are too efficient and to avoid independent coordination may make the military less effective in preparing a coup, it also makes them less effective in defending the country and, ironically, the regime itself.

As the crisis started coming to a head, military officers[27] were puzzled by the Shah's seeming indecision; since he had always exercised the autocratic last word in the military command, they first assumed that he had access to privileged information and/or was pursuing a deliberate strategy. After awaiting orders for a while, they began to be alarmed by the Shah's continued lack of action and by the peculiar behavior he displayed in his meetings with them, including fits of weeping and seeming disorientation. However, past experience did not encourage direct speaking or criticism; therefore, rather than talking to the Shah themselves, some officers met with American diplomats and tried to urge them to push the Shah to decisive action. Some, concluding that the Shah was subjectively incapacitated and unable to lead, contemplated carrying out a coup. The system of distrust and divisiveness that governed the military was such, however, that nothing came of these plans. Instead the officers in responsible positions, anticipating the outcome, sent their families out of the country. The lack of cohesiveness fostered by the Shah's system of distrust had brought about a mentality of "sauve-qui-peut," and the military, powerful by the objective standards of equipment, financing, and manpower, was overcome by confusion, declaring its neutrality in February 1979.

Even those institutions less affected by the Shah's personal ambivalence had not succeeded in establishing themselves throughout the country. Integration of nonurban areas was haphazard, and old networks and administrative units had not been effectively displaced.[28]

In the final stages of a revolution, according to Brinton, a country experiences what we may summarize as a legitimacy crisis. There is a great deal of free-floating discontent without a particular affiliation. The educated classes and portions of the elite are alienated increasingly from the government and from their class. Alienation manifests itself in great outpourings of polemical literature, in endless political discussions, and in receptivity to ideas of radical change, often with markedly utopian content. Members of the ruling elite are willing to "betray their class"; perhaps more important, they are unwilling or unfit to defend it. This includes a fatal self-doubt at the highest levels of the current government that will manifest itself, once the revolution has begun, either in indecisiveness or in irrational excesses, or in a combination of both—responses that will fuel the unrest. In Iran, the legitimacy crisis took the shape of an alienation of both traditional and new sectors of the population. Political restrictions had created an international diaspora of alienated Iranian intellectuals in many Western capitals, and a wide range of dissidents remained in Iran, too. At the same time, the Shah's policy of keeping his supporting institutions divided created a fatal irresoluteness once the crisis came to a head. There was the massive reaction of Jaleh Square (estimates of the number of demonstrators killed vary from several hundred to several thousand), followed by indecisiveness and a lack of effective response either by the Shah or by the military.[29]

We can only speculate on what might have happened if the Shah, following a route considered and then rejected by his father, had "modernized" himself into a constitutional monarch, supported the emergence of effective institutions, or alternatively, failed at suppressing the emergence of more radical modernists.[30] The success of the Shah, in which the U. S. was instrumental,[31] appears in retrospect to have crippled the development of precisely those modern institutions that might, under other circumstances, have carried the day.

The unfolding of the crisis, too, followed Brinton's pattern. There was an extended period of crisis punctuated by violent episodes and culminating in a massive countrywide explosion; a period of euphoria and exultation when it appeared that the overthrow of the old order had really succeeded; a phase of more moderate government culminating in a takeover by the extremists; a period of great repression and purges of opponents and critics. Assuming this is correct, then the present phase of the "Terror" should give way finally to "Thermidor": a period of "convalescence" and stabilizing normalization. As we stated earlier, a revolution deserves this title not only because it displays certain regularized characteristics of form in the way it transforms the power structure; it must also bring about a qualitative and lasting change that releases new social forces. It is too early to thus classify Iran.

Before returning to the question whether the "Islamic revolution" in Iran is likely ultimately to be classed as a revolution, we should look at the other things it could possibly have been. Four plausible and overlapping explanations offer themselves: that Iran experienced a peasant rebellion; that Iran is engaged in a millennialist revolt; that Iran has chosen the path of totalitarian democracy; and that current developments represent an idiosyncratic Iranian course of modernization, in keeping with its historic tradition of oscillations between centralistic order and centrifugal power diffusion.

Peasant Rebellion

While, as we have briefly reviewed above, there are a number of parallels between Iranian events and what is commonly held to make a revolution, there are also many features of Iran's experience that match descriptions of peasant uprisings, and it may be useful to look at Iranian developments in that light for a moment.

The classic peasant rising (jacquerie) occurs when social and economic transformations have changed the base of the society without integrating the mass of the population. Old authority lines are replaced by new ones, and the state undertakes efforts at centralization. Old elites and new elites coexist, with the old elites and the old economic patterns successively finding themselves crowded to the margins, not dominated so much as simply superseded. The mass of the population, living in poverty, dislocated from the old patterns of life, aware of great disparaties and ominous changes but unable to comprehend them or visualize a desirable new order, presents a fertile base for mass movements led either by charismatic individuals or by elites of the old authority.

The dissent of this population articulates itself, of necessity, in the vocabulary and the concepts familiar to it, and these are most often religious or pseudo-religious. Usually, the goals pursued are not really traditional. They build on traditional thought and justify themselves by reference to a past order, but they go far beyond any real prior condition or traditional goal. They accomplish a qualitative leap between—in the vocabulary of the sociology of religion—"Heilstranszendenz" and "Heilsimmanenz,"[32] by seeking to bring salvation from its place in the next world or some chiliastic future into the present moment.

These movements have usually been classed as fundamentally reactionary, because their impulse is to halt the forward thrust of their society, but this is not so much their nature as their consequence: the basic tragedy of the peasant uprising is that its population is powerless, without a grasp of the social trends taking place and without the resources to really affect them. They can express an accurate perception of injustice, but the power will remain elsewhere. It is in this sense that experts define the peasant rebellion as a doomed political form.[33] In this context the judgment of Ibn Khaldun deserves to be recalled, and his assessment of the chances of such a movement is damning:

> The common people . . . who make claims with respect to the Mahdi and who are not guided by any intelligence or helped by any knowledge in this connection, assume that the Mahdi may appear in a variety of circumstances and places. . . . They mostly assume that the appearance will take place in some remote province out of the reach of the ruling dynasties and outside their authority. . . . Many weak-minded people

go to these places in order to support a deceptive cause that the human soul in its delusion and stupidity leads them to believe capable of succeeding. Many of them have been killed. . . .[34]

Just from this brief paragraph, important differences between Iran's recent movement and the classic peasant uprising emerge: for one thing, because of the social and demographic dislocations resulting from modernization, the tumult was no longer confined to "remote provinces"; instead, the membership of formerly "rural" movements was to a large extent to be found in urban surroundings in the Iran of the 1970s; for another, the "intelligence" in the shape of the oppositional intelligentsia was available to them as it had not been in the classic instances of peasant uprisings.

Nevertheless, lack of information about the interests at issue and the division of real power, vulnerability to the leadership claims of charismatic figures, a rejection of the authority of the center and a belief that this authority is corrupt and illegitimate, and finally, a great deal of bloodshed—these characteristics, cited by Ibn Khaldun, describe millennial movements and peasant rebellions in many parts of the world. To conclude that they are not the agents of genuine social change does not amount to a political dismissal, because it says little about their role. As creators of social turbulence they may well play a central part in preparing the ground for revolutionary situations to follow.

This is a question raised by Eric Wolfe in his important study *Peasant Wars of the Twentieth Century*.[35] Wolfe describes peasant uprisings as "parochial reactions to major social dislocations set in motion by overwhelming societal change."[36] Though the movement itself is doomed to a costly failure, Wolfe writes, "when the battle is over, the structure will not be the same."[37]

The problem with peasant uprisings, in this view, lies in the inability of the peasantry to be an independent agent of change; it can only be the vehicle, providing the chaos and uproar that allow other political actors to rise to dominance. However, one can hardly think of a revolution in which the mob of declassée masses did not fulfill such a function. Even were we to agree that events in Iran bore a striking resemblance to peasant wars, this would not mean that they could not develop into a genuine revolution. Such a resemblance would also fail to take into account a similarity with still another political phenomenon, that of the millennialist rebellion.

Millennialist Movements

Even in the classic peasant rebellions of Western Europe, the religious component was strong. The following description, taken out of its context in time, sounds surprisingly applicable to any number of historical unrests:

> The population grows more rapidly than the productive capacity. The rural masses lose their base of existence and flee to the cities, where they form a restless urban proletariat. A beginning industry expands. The onset of modernity rouses hopes and expectations in the population that are not met. The stabilizing social ties of the old order are in disarray, the individual feels isolated, threatened. The ambitions of the intelligentsia are blocked—without adequate opportunities for upward mobility and expression, they become dissatisfied. Messianic movements arise, in the course of which some of those leaders who seek to employ the popular enthusiasms for their own ends lose control of their following. The real power of the chiliastic movement comes from the classes that vegetate along the margins of the society and have no secure and recognized place.

This description, taken from Norman Cohn's *The Pursuit of the Millennium*,[38] refers to the European Middle Ages from the eleventh century onwards, but the parallels to today's Third World are apparent.

Religious movements are characterized by their large following, often recruited from the peasantry or the urban subproletariat (it would, perhaps, be more accurate to speak of a rural and an urban peasantry).[39] Like the peasant rebellion, and unlike the revolution, the millennialist movement is characterized by its inevitable failure. At best, it creates the momentum and the disorder necessary for other actors, with a more coherent ideology and more resources, to pursue their political aims. Eric Wolfe describes these marginalized peasants as a group lacking political consciousness or understanding of the transformations under way in their society, but one could just as well describe them as possessing an all too acute awareness that these changes, however they may ultimately turn out, will not include them and will not preserve their way of life. Barrington Moore cites the existence of an "unresolved peasant problem" as one of the pivotal factors in bringing about dictatorship, but it is a Communist dictatorship he has in mind.[40] Finally, peasant wars and millennialist movements are most commonly led by heretics; they are not led by the established religious authority, as was the case in Iran. The Iranian example, viewed in this light, is full of ambiguities.

In one of the few works of the 1960s that credited political revivalism as having the potential to be a serious political factor in the Middle East, Manfred Halpern dealt with the phenomenon of what he described as "neo-Islamic totalitarianism" and as an "essentially fascist" strain in Middle Eastern political life. "As a movement resisting the changes of a multiple revolution in telescoped time, this Middle Eastern version of fascism is also stamped . . . by a kinship with certain religio-political movements which spread in Western Europe at the beginning of its modern age."[41]

In addition to parallels with the "militant social chiliasms of 15th century Europe," Halpern also sees significant similarities to modern European fascism, with the difference of a stronger traditionalist note in the Islamic version. We will return to the question of fascism later in this chapter.

In the meantime, the chiliastic component of Shi'ite Islam being proffered as an explanation for events in Iran, a review of the work on religious movements is clearly in order. There are two versions of this theory: one that deals with mass religious movements generally, and another that believes they have a particular quality in Third World societies undergoing modernization.

A millennialist or chiliastic movement is a movement that aims at bringing about an immediate and profound social transformation that is expected to replace the present corrupt order with a utopian one, through the intervention of divine or divinely commissioned leadership. These movements have in common with each other, and in common with revolutions, their stress on justice and on immediacy: the world must be turned around completely, and the time for it is right now. They have in common with peasant rebellion usually (though not necessarily) their actual or potential mass base. Their world view is totalitarian; politics encompasses everything, the enemy is Evil, and compromise is unthinkable. The momentum of such movements can be sustained only as long as the

movement is in the role of the opposition, before particularistic interests
of the participants emerge, before the business of compromise and pragmatism sets in, and as long as the high degree of violence still appears to
be part of the struggle, and has not yet been identified as Terror.

There are many resemblances between millennialist religious movements and revolutionary ideology, since revolutionary ideology commonly contains millennialist components. In addition to a postulated
mythical past (whether in the form of the rule of the Imam or of original
communism) and a projected utopian future that set the parameters for
both movements' concept of political time,[42] the direct employment of
religious imagery and concepts by revolutionary ideology is often striking.[43]

What are the conditions favoring the emergence of a charis-
matic/chiliastic movement? T. K. Oommen cites four:[44]

—repressed discontent;
—the failure of previous measures to affect disparities;
—the onset of a crisis;
—support of a traditional authority group such as the priesthood
for the oppositional movement.

Not surprisingly, these conditions resemble closely those Crane Brinton
lists for revolutionary situations and Eugen Lembert cites as descriptive
of the expansive phase of ideology.[45] It is unsurprising because these are
the conditions one might expect to be necessary; a movement of great
magnitude involves a great deal of risk for the participants, and also sig-
nifies a departure from the more static-passive behavior of normalcy. One
requires a great deal of motivation to overcome the barriers against opposing authority, and it is clear that such motivation will have to be man-
ifold: will require a system of thinking that permits such action, and will
require grievances severe enough to justify the risk, and a feeling that
success is at least possible. Purely by deductive reasoning, then, we could
arrive at a set of preconditions: signs of weakness on the part of those in
power (so that one could hope to overthrow them); serious social dislocations; the participation of persons who had some link to authority and
could thereby ease the gravity of sedition; and a framework of thought
that justified rebellion. When does this take place within a reli-
gious/chiliastic framework? Authors agree on one precondition: a severe

sense of social disorientation, an acute need for order. Shils speaks of the "perception of chaos" and the flight to symbols of order, often with a sacred and traditional character. Clifford Geertz speaks of bursts of "ideological activity" resulting from a loss of orientation.[46] Erik Erikson refers to periods in history that are marked by "identity vacua," in which a feeling of alienation spreads and the profound conflicts of the society attract its members to a leader who personifies their disturbed consciousness.[47] Georges Balandier, speaking of Africa, views both nationalism and messianism as "reactions to the process of group dissolution."[48]

What about this is specific to the situation of the Third World? Reference to spiritual values as a means of cementing the social order is not the invention of any particular culture. In *Sacrum Imperium*,[49] Alois Dempf traces the development of the institution of kingship as it evolved from charismatic, martial, and administrative power. Authority being unsolidified and identity often unclear in the Third World at the present time, one line of argument goes, the ground there is particularly fertile for such foundational and transitional means to authority as charisma and religion. This is Wallerstein's point[50] when he sees the charismatic individual as a means of transferring loyalty from traditional structures to the bureaucratic ones. In regard to the Third World, messianic movements could be one of two things: they could be a directionless response to uncomprehended changes (antimodernist in thrust) or they could be instruments of modernization, bridging the gap from old to new in the person of the modernizing hero.

The charismatic leader, typified in the eyes of the authors of this school by such figures as Kwame Nkrumah, functioned as the "symbolic referent" for societies that had lost their frameworks of orientation.

The Shah made every effort to be such a figure. He attempted to practice what Geertz calls "exemplary politics," building showcase projects to symbolize his power through lavish displays of dynastic splendor. He tried to link himself to religion in order to make his displacement of traditional religious authority more palatable to the population, and presented himself as the recipient of religious messages and visions.[51] But charismatic sentiments did not crystallize around him, or did not, at any rate, remain associated with him.[52]

What emerged instead is a movement that bears some of the characteristics of a millennialist movement. It is chiliastic, orienting itself by the expected return of the Twelfth Imam. It is totalitarian, encompassing all areas of life, seeking to regulate behavior, impulses, and interactions of the private as well as the public sort and dividing the world into good and evil. Enemies are referred to in existential terms, such as the most common appellation for the U. S., "world devourers." The movement distinctly aspires to transcend worldly affairs, which are dismissed as trivial. "I cannot believe that the purpose of all these sacrifices was to have less expensive melons," Khomeini has said.[53] The similarities of Iran's experience to a millennialist peasant uprising are evident, and again our final definition will have to be postponed; just as a revolution is contingent on its success, a millennial movement is characterized by its failure, as it gives way to the rise to dominance of elements within its membership or to the reassertion of part of the former ruling government.

Totalitarian Democracy

Another concept that should be introduced into an assessment of Iran's current developments derives it relevance from the all-encompassing approach of the present government to the life of the community and its refusal to allow for any realm of life where control should not be exercised. This exercise of government control over all spheres is a feature of totalitarian rule, but in order to assess whether this is a transitory phenomenon inherent in the crisis situation or whether it is likely to be a qualitative feature of Iran's political situation, reference to a wider context is useful.

The central features of totalistic social thought involve the following ideas:

— that the world is divided into good and evil, virtue and sin, right and wrong;
— that individual freedom is not a relevant value, but that the correct life of the collectivity is the main goal;
— that human society is perfectible and that this perfection must be implemented immediately;
— that there exists a body of truths, or a law, in which the mandate for human behavior is given, and which must be applied;
— that whoever does not participate in this effort and share these values is wrong, and evil, and is to be treated as an enemy.

How do these conditions apply to political systems? One answer is attempted by Jacob Talmon in his books *The Origins of Totalitarian Democracy* and *Political Messianism—The Romantic Phase*.[54] Talmon's premise is that the revolutionary spirit of eighteenth-century Europe produced two distinct political models, which he refers to as liberal democracy and totalitarian or messianic democracy. The difference between them centers on their different view of politics, the liberal political image being that of pragmatism, problem-solving, and a division of spheres between the political realm and other areas of social and individual life. In this view, politics is a limited endeavor managing certain functions of the community and validated by its successful solution of the problems that arise. To the totalitarian-democratic model, on the other hand, politics encompasses all the life of the community. Its validation lies in the pursuit of certain abstract and nonnegotiable principles and not in any empirical functionalist criteria. It considers that there is an elite group charged with realizing the moral aims of social order, which are absolute and universal, a "vanguard acting as a trustee" and "fully justified in using force and repression because this elite alone knows the true path to follow and therefore exemplifies the will of the collectivity."[55] It is evident that the image of politics proposed by the Shah[56] fell into the first category, while that of the fundamentalists conforms to the second.

To the Shah, his legitimacy derived in part from the fact that his policies "worked." Iran was progressing, growing according to various empirical indicators; he held power in the country and in the region. Certainly he made an effort to draw on other types of claims, too—the dynastic heritage, religious visions[57] that he claimed to have received, etc.—but on the whole, he drew on the "empirical" validation for his political legitimacy. To Khomeini and the fundamentalist school, a government can be "wrong" no matter how prosperous the nation and no matter how enlightened its policies. If it is not Islamic then it is illegitimate. (However, in fact Khomeini attacked the Shah on both levels, alleging that he was both morally wrong *and* pragmatically ineffective, and countering the expected argument that clerics were not qualified to rule by replying that they could not possibly bungle things worse than the Shah had.)[58]

Talmon has illustrated his study of totalitarian democracy with reference to eighteenth- and nineteenth-century Europe, but he notes that the duality of the two concepts of politics is a constant strain in the history of Christianity from its inception. An articulation of totalitarian values can be found, for example, in Augustine's concept of the *City of God*.[59]

Persian history contains many instances of conflict between these two views, which reflected sometimes a sincere conflict of world views and sometimes a tactical effort to undermine the legitimacy of the other side. Persian monarchical tradition rested very much on the pragmatic principle. A king was not necessarily someone who was the son of a king or even the issue of a special family. A king was, on the contrary, someone who could lead the country. Dynasties were repeatedly founded by "commoners," by military men who freed the country from a foreign threat and thereafter installed themselves on the throne.

Traditionally opposed to this at frequent intervals was the Muslim clergy, representing an absolutist and purist position regarding the political realm. Marginal to the business of making compromises or pursuing goals with systemic violence, they could afford to insist on nonnegotiable principles. This balance between two views of politics, sometimes only a superficial mask for the highly pragmatic identity of interests between monarchy and ulama, may have been a unique feature of the Iranian polity. The relation between church hierarchy and state hierarchy in medieval Christian Europe, while showing some parallels, is at the same time different because the Christian religious elite was far more institutionalized. And Hodgson argues that the decision *not* to be coopted into the power structure distinguished the Shiʻi ulama.[60]

The Iranian system maintained a balance between two different kinds of power—a more constant one, held by secular authorities and subject to the shifts of daily politics, and a more latent one, capable of constant but fluctuating influence and periodic mobilizations of the population when deemed necessary. The legitimacy of the secular government was always in question as far as the religious authority was concerned, but secular authority was able to respond in kind by challenging the legitimacy of the religious elite.[61] Besides, the opposition in principle generally went along with a de facto policy of accommodation on the part of religious leaders.[62]

Compared with the past framework of this system, recent events represent a qualitative departure in two ways, both of which conform to totalitarian radicalism. First, the idea of rule by the religious experts was transformed from a passive, abstract ideal into an immediate arrangement. Second, the leader personifies the unity of the people and the movement.[63] For this radicalization of a long-established pattern of ulama behavior, one plausible explanation emerging from fundamentalist writings seems to be that the religious leadership felt its position to be existentially threatened by the changes begun by the Shah, so that a continuation of the former pattern was no longer an option if they wanted to survive.

The Islamic Republic in Iran displays the characteristics of a totalitarian system, and conforms to Talmon's description in a number of important ways. Its world view is premised on the division of the world into the just and the unjust; it believes that a good society can and must be brought about by application of the principles handed down in the Islamic religion; it considers violence and repression justified in the pursuit of this goal; it sees the collectivity, not the individual, as the significant frame of reference; it considers individual freedom to be an irrelevant concept, defining justice instead as the result of living according to moral injunctions under a just Islamic government. Besides this general conformity, there is congruence in details, such as the attitude to property and economics. Talmon describes a mix of egalitarian-welfare values— such as the notion of a ceiling on property, the subsidizing of basic supplies, and a guaranteed minimum life standard in shelter, food, and work opportunities—that coexist with acceptance of private property and profit within certain limits.[64] The reference to Talmon's work is particularly important because there is a strong tendency on the part of analysts to exaggerate the uniqueness of Islam in this connection.[65]

Perhaps the most important quality of this political condition is the state of crisis mentality it requires to keep its momentum and justify its system of rule. The violence exercised against opponents needs justification, as does the continued existence of social and economic problems and inequities. "In order to make its message prevail, a total revolution needs implacable opposition, treacherous plotting by a national enemy, counter-revolutionary uprising, in brief a state of emergency," Talmon writes.[66] Iran's political culture is characterized by ongoing oppositional and terrorist activity, the continuation of war with Iraq and agitation in other states of the region, heavy stress on the plotting of foreign enemies, especially the American CIA, and the maintenance of high tension. It also contains the idea of austerity that Talmon describes as an important component of totalitarian democracy.[67] Khomeini continuously transmits the message that these are times of absolute crisis during which sacrifices must be made and sufferings undertaken.[68] There are usually limits to how long a society can believe in a state of emergency. Eventually, something else has to follow. The most important alternatives to date are described by Barrington Moore, and we turn now to his model of social change.

Routes to Modernity

Barrington Moore's study on the *Social Origins of Dictatorship and Democracy* remains one of the most valuable sources in charting political constellations during periods of great social transformation. His analysis of the English, the French, the U. S., the Chinese, the Japanese, and the Indian cases of modernization consistently stresses that class alignments, in situations of upheaval, will generally be far from clear; that economic developments are not the prime cause but only set the framework in which political events will unfold; that some historical configurations are not repetitive but consecutive (and that, therefore, developments in one wave of social transformation will not be reproduced later). He notes that "certain institutional arrangements such as feudalism, absolute monarchy, and capitalism rise, have their day, and pass away."[69] To some extent, then, the evolution of political systems is nonrepetitive. They stand to one another in a sequential relationship. The developments that took place in Europe were unique in two senses: unique because historic constellations are not repeated, and unique because they evolved without a prior model. Finally, Barrington Moore articulates what political scientists as a group find it so hard to acknowledge: that elements of chance are inevitably high, and that conformity in the starting point is no guarantee of an identity of outcome.

With that in mind, it is interesting to review the Iranian case against the backdrop of Moore's observations. Barrington Moore identifies four basic paths to modernity: the path of bourgeois revolution; the capitalist route culminating in fascism, termed by Moore the route of "revolution from above"; the peasant rebellion leading to Communist dictatorship; and a vaguely indicated fourth pattern of countries such as India where mixed indicators are present without clearly inclining to one of the prior routes. For each case, Moore sketches the factors he considers most important in the determination of which pattern a society is most likely to follow. Some of his most important observations, however, are made in the form of unsystematized comments in the last section of his book. For the purposes of our discussion, we would single out three of Moore's observations about revolutionary change, and some of his concluding cautions.

Which path a society will follow depends on a variety of factors. The democratic route is most likely if the following circumstances exist:

1. The society's tradition includes some notion of the right to resist unjust authority and to participate in some form in the political process, and there is a group of people sufficiently removed from the coercive control of the ruler(s) to exercise these rights.

2. Countervailing forces constrain to some degree the power of the crown.

3. The commercialization of agriculture, creation of a viable urban economy and, in line with that, the settlement of the "peasant question" through absorption of the peasantry into other sectors of the economy have made significant strides.

Where these three conditions are present, the chances for developing a measure of democracy are in the view of Moore the greatest.

Looking at the case of Iran in this light, the problems with translating the groups and actors involved from one cultural context to another are immediately apparent. While we can compare the relative strength of the monarchy and its alliance with other powerful groups within the society, we cannot compare the French monarch and the aristocracy with a Reza Shah; there are too many new factors involved. There are two superpowers, one of them encroaching from geographically contiguous areas, the other having been an immediate political, economic, military, and cultural presence for decades, both offering resources and influences no industrializing European nation ever had to deal with. A European king, faced with restless populations, could call on royalist sentiment, could compromise, could present the image of enlightened authority, but he was neither able nor obliged to address extra-continental audiences to a comparable extent. In Iran, as we have seen, the authority of the monarch was taken by Western observers to be nearly complete. Retrospectively regarded, it is clear that in fact the Pahlavi monarchy conformed more to Moore's picture of a monarchy that has failed to achieve a clear coalition with other centers of power, above all in bringing about a settlement of the crucial peasant question. This was overlooked because the religious leaders, the middle-level manufacturing and trading elites, and the landlords were not perceived as a possible political force. If we regard these groups—who were in Iran bound to each other not only through shared traditional values but also through ties of family—as a type of aristocracy, the new urban elites as a type of bourgeoisie, and the rural masses as an unabsorbed peasantry, then Moore's model would predict few chances for democratic modernization and would lean much more to his third possibility—peasant rebellion, authoritarian rule, and greatly delayed economic transformations.

There are problems with this. For one thing, one could make a good case for seeing Iran as a modified example of the second instance, modernization from above. One could argue that the Shah had initiated fundamental changes in his society's economic, cultural, social, and political system. While we have previously enumerated some of the areas in which his efforts had failed, it would also be possible to cite evidence for his successes.

We could argue that what had happened in Iran was the following: the Shah had initiated modernization from above. This had awakened some resistance from the traditional sector, but it had also strengthened the forces that sought modernity.[70] These forces developed their own dynamic, and their demands eventually overtook the aims of the Shah, whose desire to modernize was coupled with his determination to retain personal power and to control the process of change. Partly through his ability to draw on foreign support, the Shah was able to meet the threat from the more radical modernizers. This forced them into an alliance with his other opponents, the traditional sector. After his removal, the traditional elements emerged victorious from the struggle with their coalition partners, the modernizers. Had the modernizers won, Iran would have experienced a continuation and radicalization of the modernization begun under the Shah.

Since the traditional sector won, Iran at present can be classified as a "counterrevolutionary" situation. Those forces that opposed modernization came to the top (as they did in parts of France during the French revolution). Iran would thus be a case of modernization from above that did not fall to an alliance between those forces that in the European instance led to pro–industrial right wing extremism (and fascist rule). Instead it brought about a coalition between progressive intellectuals, disaffected parts of the elite, the peasantry, and the traditional elite, taking the form of a millennialist peasant rebellion participated in by the progressive radicals who hoped it would turn into a revolution.

The outcome of the revolution-from-above, in Moore's model, is fascism; of peasant rebellion, a Communist dictatorship. Neither possibility can be ruled out for Iran. It is conceivable that a right-wing radical dictatorship will consolidate, combining "repression at home and expansionism abroad"; it is also possible that the radical left, possibly with some support from the Soviet Union, will take advantage of the administrative collapse or an intensification of internal unrest to take power. However, it is also possible that the modernizing elements may yet succeed to power.

Authors who study the past in the hopes of finding there a label that can suitably be attached to Iran are bound to be thwarted. There will always be an essential point that does not fit. Fascism in its classic instances in Western Europe, for example, resulted from a seeming convergence of interests of the petit bourgeoisie, the lower middle class, and the declassée elements; it did not involve a coalition with leftists, the intelligentsia, and substantial elements of the old elite. One can say of the Iranian fundamentalists, as Polanyi[71] does of the European fascists, that they "put a political religion into the service of a degenerative process" and are characterized by their intolerance once in power, by their "sham nationalism during the revolution, and their imperialistic non-nationalism" afterwards (i.e., by their expansionism). There are similarities here, but there are important differences, and the similiarities may derive from the totalistic (or even totalitarian) quality they share. The fascists rose to power on the crest of very different economic constellations; they tended to value industrial productivity highly and did not share the explicitly antimaterialistic stance of the Iranian fundamentalists.[72]

As for the peasant rebellion leading to communist dictatorship, in Moore's model, this too may be applied in various ways, owing to two important differences. First, does the dictatorship have to be communistic, or can there be variants? In the chapter dealing with the consolidation efforts of the fundamentalists (chapter 5), resemblances to totalitarianism will be noted. Second, what role will outside actors, particularly the superpowers, play in the ongoing ideological and material conflicts within Iran? Can any movement, including a fundamentalist one or a revolution, play itself out in the Third World without the distorting interventions of outside forces?

In order to pursue this question further, and examine more closely the situation to which the Iranians were responding in their uprising, the next chapter will turn to the question of how this oppositional movement was constituted and why it chose the method of articulation that eventually emerged as the dominant one.

CHAPTER FOUR

Prejudice as a Cultural Weapon: Orientalism vs. Occidentalism

In common linguistic usage, prejudice is often taken to mean a kind of defect of reason, a prior judgment based on excessive or incorrect generalization and hostile to the admission of new evidence. However, as soon as the study of prejudice is conducted with reference to a specific instance, such as racism, sexism, anti-Semitism etc., it becomes obvious that prejudice is not just a kind of arbitrary ignorance but that it performs important social and political functions, and that there are elements within the society that benefit, or believe themselves to benefit, from its maintenance. Where it has been studied in this light, its role as an instrument of domination has stood in the forefront. Analysts have explained how it keeps groups apart who might otherwise discover an identity of interests and join to rebel against the dominant elite; how it helps keep the subordinate down; how it provides short-circuited explanations for social problems and thereby redirects social protest, which might otherwise be aimed at the government, at a weak group within the polity; how it prevents the members of a society from questioning certain crucial aspects of the value system and the coercive structure.[1]

However, it would be wrong to see it primarily as a kind of large-scale case of mistaken judgment, and would be wrong to regard prejudice only as a power instrument. Instead, it may be useful to approach prejudice as the social and political employment of certain patterns of simplified, overgeneralized, nonrational thinking. It can operate, as such, on different levels: to maintain the cohesiveness of the group, to maintain a certain order, to defend a power relationship or to challenge it.

In its most elementary form, prejudice is a means of dealing with the sheer existence of other groups. Berger and Luckmann explain in their book *The Social Construction of Reality*[2] that a social order is always a fragile thing, since it represents a decision for one way of dealing with a problem at the expense of another. As long as that decision can be presented to the members of the society as the best, the correct and necessary one, conformity is easier to achieve. However, the existence of another society, which operates on very different principles and yet still manages to survive (and perhaps even to prosper), challenges the inevitability of the decision for one order over another. When the other society is more successful than one's own, the problem accelerates; when it conquers one's own, a real crisis sets in.

The German political theorist Carl Schmitt[3] has defined the "fundamental political decision" as being the "distinction between friend and enemy." August Nitschke, building on this definition, extends it to the hypothesis that "political groups can be understood most clearly when we ask: how do they look at their enemies?"[4] It may be more productive to revise this sentence, replacing the term "enemy" simply with the term "the Other," and to ask how groups view the Other—the Other who may appear as opponent and stranger, but also as a trade partner, a model, a rival, or an exotic curiosity. Above all, it will be useful to analyze how societies manage to maintain the Other, over long stretches of time and in spite of sustained interaction, as the Foreigner—one who can be transformed from a tactical ally into an enemy, from a trade partner into a belligerent foe, as circumstances change. World history testifies eloquently to the ease and frequency with which such shifts are effected, and prejudice is one of the means that societies employ for this exercise. The "fundamental political decision" appears to be less the distinction between friend and enemy than the consciousness of difference: a consciousness that can be hostile and discriminatory, objective and pragmatic, or indifferent, or enviously imitative, depending on the nature of the interaction. Above all, it can change over time.

Prejudice and Culture

The interaction between cultures is a subject that has gone out of fashion in political science. This is not a coincidence, but stems largely from the fact that this kind of analysis acquired a (well-earned) bad reputation for its past proclivity to ethnocentrism, geopolitics, and neo-Darwinism. This has meant the loss of an important dimension in conflict study and political analysis, because it is at the level of cultural interaction that the operation of prejudice as a sociopolitical tool can best be observed. As a tool, it is both a defensive and an offensive device; it operates both at the domestic level and at the level of foreign affairs; and like any weapon, it can lead to consequences not intended by the user. It is a means of dealing with the environment and particularly with Others, and just as most polities or serious political movements will have an arsenal of weapons for the event of an armed conflict, they will have a reservoir of prejudice, capable of being employed for the various interactions the group will be engaging in, from trade to warfare. As in the case of trade and weapons, different groups and societies will have different kinds and amounts of resources available to them, and varying degrees of skill at employing them, in the area of prejudice and cultural conflict.

At the cultural level, it is helpful to conceptualize this kind of interaction as a kind of dialogue, an exchange. When the groups are unequal, when one of them is dominant and the other subordinate, the dominant group will attempt to convey a message like: you have been conquered by us because you are inferior, our dominance is inevitable, you had best adjust to it. Or the message may be: we are not really conquerors, we have come to help you and liberate you from your backwardness. To its own population, the dominant group may have to offer some justifications for the actions it has taken: we are not really savage oppressors subjugating these Others—ours is a cultural mission to educate, elevate, and convert them.[5]

To this, the subordinate group must respond. It must explain to its own population what happened, and why one is not really defeated and existentially inferior. "We have been defeated because the other side is unscrupulous and immoral and fought unfairly, for which they will be punished as soon as our inevitable triumph is effected," the message might run. Various kinds of arguments will be drawn upon to substantiate the claims on all sides, with the dominant side having the advantage of both empirical evidence of its greater success and control over most of the channels of communication and socialization, by means of which it can often virtually monopolize the cultural dialogue. Those who oppose existing power relations have the more difficult task.[6] If defeat was recent, they will be in a state of shock and disarray; if the pattern of domination has existed for a long time, it will begin to appear more and more inevitable. If one is trying not just to reverse a defeat but to transform an entire structure of power relations, then the task of surmounting the obstacles and convincing enough people of the possibility of change is truly enormous. In the words of Adorno, "Theory can hope to move the excessive burden of historic fact only if that fact can be made to be seen as what it is, illusion become reality, and the historic moment as no more than a metaphysical coincidence."[7] To this effort, the ruling order will respond by making itself appear as eternal, true, and inevitable as it possibly can.[8] This effort will take place on all levels of social interaction. Habits of daily life, when questioned by another culture, become bound up with associations of morality and national consciousness; they are part of the social code, and when more than one nation or culture is involved, they become political. Norbert Elias tells of the eleventh-century Greek princess who, upon her marriage to a Venetian doge, tried to introduce the fork into her new environment. This developed into a major issue, with church leaders denouncing such decadence, the population at large resisting the foreign innovation, and the lady's untimely death being cited by religious leaders as the just punishment for her eccentricity.[9] In our age, numerous examples of this kind of cultural confrontation can be cited. One of the most central is obviously the conflict between an advancing Western civilization and a Third World seeking ways of survival, adjustment, and resistance. Iran is touched by three aspects of this conflict: between industrial West and Third World, between Islamic civilization and Christian civilization, and between Persian/Iranian and Foreign.

The West Looks at the East—Orientalism

The interaction between Christianity and Islam has a long history, and a varied one. Many centuries of exchange and animosity have built up a great collection of sentiments, knowledge, grievances, assumptions, and fears, and by no means can the power balance generally be said to have favored one side, the West, over the other. Theologically, culturally, scientifically there has been mutual borrowing as well as competition, and both have at times been in the ascendant. At times mutual toleration in monotheistic brotherhood was the ideal; at others the forced conversion or conquest of the other seemed more worthy of pursuit. For both sides, religion was at different times a component of variable significance, sometimes more and sometimes less important as a motivating force in political behavior. Curiosity, ascriptions of barbarism, and a lingering fascination with the life styles and habits of the other culture, along with the feeling that those life styles and habits are deviant, ungodly, and immoral, have characterized the popular as well as the official sentiments of both parties, while managing to coexist with envy and admiration.

The scholastic work that has been done on these issues recently has tended to reflect the current power balance even while criticizing it. Edward Said's important study *Orientalism*[10] made the contribution of introducing a new category into the study of prejudice; at the same time, however, it implied (by omission) that the Orient was a passive victim of this relationship, rather than an active participant who merely happens, at present, to be in a disadvantaged position. Studies such as Hamid Naficy's analysis of popular images of East and West in Iranian film examine Eastern ambivalence vis-à-vis the West without taking the opposite phenomenon into account.[11] Prejudice is a simplifying code, but it is not simple; dominance requires apologetics and contains guilt, hostility includes fascination, and the instrumentarium for managing prejudice will be diffuse, complicated,[12] and many-stranded. Whether the authors are Turks describing the Viennese they are besieging, ancient Egyptians portraying their tributaries, tenth-century Muslims encountering the Franks, British colonial administrators diagnosing their subjects, or men in a patriarchal society describing the feminine character, the attitudes of dominant toward subordinate always tend to display a high degree of uniformity; they will also contain a steady degree of ambivalence.[13] We will illustrate this briefly by drawing on two levels of articulation: the East in popular European literature during the previous century, and Iran in policymakers' perceptions at the start of the U. S.-Iran interaction.

Persia as Entertainment

The blend of fascinated curiosity and denigration that often characterizes prejudice can be clearly identified in popular literature during the nineteenth and early twentieth centuries. During this time, travelogue-style descriptions of Persian culture enjoyed great popularity in Western Europe. The authors were most commonly doctors, colonial administrators, or their wives who had visited Persia and upon their return published books with titles like *Persia As It Is, Unveiled Iran, Under Persian Skies, Through Persia in Disguise, Persian Lions—Persian Lambs, A Doctor's Holiday in Iran,* or *To Persia for Flowers.*[14] Ranging from relatively informed to almost completely fantasized, the books centered on a few standard themes: the exotic backwardness of Persian culture, the childlike character of its inhabitants, the position of the women, a number of pronouncements on the national character of the Persians, and a prognosis for the future which almost always foresaw some slow but incremental success in raising the Persians to the level of the West both as individuals and as a nation. The accounts are certainly as revealing of contemporary Europe as they try to be of their subject. The harem, for example, appears to have exercised unending fascination for British audiences; the theme was standard, and nearly always accompanied by amusing descriptions of a wealthy sultan's efforts to purchase the author (where the author was female) or the author's narrow escape from death after accidentally wandering into a harem (where the author was male). Often the "travelogue" was only a pretext for titillating, semipornographic passages. Harem women are described as wearing "nothing but a few diamonds" and there are lurid descriptions of unfaithful wives drowned in the "Well of Death."[15] Various humid Western fantasies[16] found their way into the pages of this literature under the guise of anthropological reporting. Besides allowing the author to evade censure for his erotic outpourings by elevating the status of his product to that of scientific inquiry, the subject of Persian women and Eastern sexuality held a number of other attractions. In many texts, the authors managed at the same time to describe Eastern women as the archetypes of sexual desirability, to do a rapid volte-face and insinuate that they are generally ugly, depraved, fat, and shrewish, to deplore the bondage they are held in and view it as evidence for the backwardness of Eastern culture, to strike a blow at Eastern men by questioning their masculinity, and finally to land an attack on their own domestic radicals by approving of Eastern society where women still know their place.

This pattern has remained consistent into our own century. In 1955, James Cleugh published a book entitled *Ladies of the Harem* which con-

tains all the above notions. He regrets the downtrodden position of Eastern women, contrasts their character favorably with that of British women
(who are too domineering and castrating), ridicules Eastern men, and
concludes with the triumphant observation that "Eastern women, even
the young, are more often hideous than not."[17] C. J. Wills had described Persian women as "fat," "sharp-tongued," and occupied inces-
santly with making confectionery and going for drives in large glass coaches
in order to make the assignations for which they would subsequently be
executed in the "Well of Death." He then turned around to make a set
of unflattering observations about the women of his own nation.[18] The
style remains the same in current literature. In his successful book *The
Fall of the Peacock Throne,* William Forbis writes that "a voluminous black
chador worn to expose only the eyes and the nose is unquestionably a
fast turn-off for seducers—particularly if, as I noticed more than once,
the nose has a large wart on it."[19] This underhanded, adolescent slap at
Iranian physiology does not prevent him, seven pages later, from rhap-
sodizing on the "Iranian configuration of molten dark eyes and lush eye-
brows" that "makes for seductive looking women."[20]

The East also served as a hypothetical audience, a mirror in which was
reflected, by virtue of the contrast, one's own level of greatness. The tone
of these reports was usually condescending and benign; they assumed that
eventually the Orientals, in their humorously inept fashion, would arrive
at some form of modernity, and in the meantime their social conditions
were good subjects for anecdote and folklore. Roland Barthes has identified this variant of the fascination with the "exotic" as an important in-
gredient in the colonial mentality.[21] Its bonus of apologetics for social
injustice is clear in this excerpt from Angela Rodkin's book *Unveiled Iran.*
On the subject of the child labor she witnessed, she has this to say:

> The final spinning is in the hands of children. Small boys ranging from
> 8–12 years stood in rows on each side of 2 machines, putting in fresh
> bobbins and mending broken threads with the extraordinary deftness
> which Iranian children develop so young. They were a cheerful looking
> lot, though their overseer seemed to keep them closely at it. They spend
> 11 hours a day at the factory, working for about 8 hours altogether.[22]

Later she quotes as clever the observation of one of her travel companions, inspired by the small children who carried their luggage: "Why bother

about mules when one has the inhabitants of Deh Kord to help one?" Importuned by villagers who turned to them for help in hopes of medicine and superior knowledge, Rodkin and her companions devised the game of inventing false remedies and amusing themselves with the credulity of the "natives"; following British advice, one mother forced her sick child to swallow a raw fish. Poverty, illness, and underdevelopment are humorous to Rodkin, and presumably to her readers, because the objects of the jokes are too exotic to be fully human, and because she presumes these conditions to be transitory. "Persia," she writes, "is on its way to becoming modern Iran."

The Persians as Allies

The image of the subjugated in the minds of the dominant is usually composed of a fairly standard set of assumptions, and the Western consensus regarding the nature of the Persians reflected this set very well. The Persians were regarded as childlike and dishonest, vain and oversensitive, irrational, unorganized, and dependent on strong, authoritarian leadership. They required a firm hand, desired an autocrat, and had to be treated with distrust. It is clear that such assumptions will be both an asset and a liability for the dominant group; an asset because they will facilitate domination and excuse any abuses, and a liability because one's picture of what the subjugated are like and what they might be up to will be badly distorted. Political estimations regarding their subject population had a lot in common with the travelogues. In his book *Persia and the Persian Question*,[23] for example, Lord Curzon approached his subject like a narrative. Chapter 8 contains the following highlights: "The personal element in Persian government—Nasr-ed-Din Shah—His appearance—Health and habits—Intellectual attainments—Tastes and caprices—Sense of humour—Fancy for animals—The Shah as ruler—Atmosphere of flattery—Cruelty or humanity—His European journeys—" etc.

Similarly, Balfour's book *Recent Happenings in Persia,* an incisive study of British policy and interests in Persia and the social conditions in that country, is punctuated by derogatory anecdotes illustrating Persian cowardice and backwardness, the uselessness of democratic institutions for such a population (most Persians, he surmises, don't know if the Constitution is "something to eat or something to wear," and in any case they would lose interest "once they found it was neither one of these desiderata").[24]

The attitude of exasperated colonial condescension was one of the British legacies to their American successors in Iran. In the years between 1948 and 1951, the U. S. was developing a policy toward Iran. U. S. diplomats and policymakers were not certain what to make of the Shah, they were not clear about the aims of the Soviet Union, and they had not decided on their own priorities for that region or the part Iran could play in them. Some of these uncertainties were articulated and resolved by reference to the stereotyped picture of the East, a process that reflects itself quite clearly in the communications between U. S. diplomats in Iran and the State Department. One goal of U. S. policy in the early years was to urge the Shah to resist Soviet threats and advances without, however, embroiling the U. S. in any potentially hazardous confrontation. The Persian government, on the other hand, wanted assurances of U. S. support in the event of Soviet aggression. U. S. diplomats were instructed to give no firm promises; if something absolutely had to be conceded, one was at all costs to avoid putting it into writing. After one such session, Ambassador Wiley telegraphed the State Department that he had delivered a virtuoso performance in evasiveness, putting on "the biggest act since Sarah Bernhardt."[25] At the same time, it is the Persians who are constantly described as inscrutable and manipulative. Wiley, busy formulating deceptive statements on U. S. policy and exchanging privileged information with the staff of other Western embassies, found time to compose homilies on the Persian character. "In our dealings with the Medes and Persians," he reflected, "we must always recall that we have to do with a people for whom the intrigues of the day suffice."

The Shah, meanwhile, was seen as a kind of child; sometimes it was best to appease him with a few concessions,[26] at other times the U. S. ambassador diagnosed the need for some "gentle harpoon therapy."[27] Not for an instant does the notion arise that one is dealing with the sovereign of an independent country. Instead there are discussions on whether one should "pull the plug on Mansur" (a prime minister unpopular with the U. S. administration),[28] and outrage runs high when the Shah is discovered to be negotiating with the British; Ambassador Wiley sees this as a manifestation of the "traditional Persian conviction that unique policy is that of playing off one great power against another."[29]

Prejudicial images of the Persian national character facilitated the pursuit of the one goal the U. S. ultimately decided it valued most highly in the Third World: stability. The contradiction between the democratic intentions with which policymakers justified U. S. presence and the dictatorial measures they often encouraged the Shah to take was bridged by theories about the "Persian character." Thus Ambassador Wiley, during a period when the U. S. was pressuring the Shah to be a "strong ruler," observed: "There is in Iran an underlying psycho-political factor of great significance; the Iranian people from top to bottom much prefer to be governed by a strong hand, even if wrong, than by a weak one, even if right."[30] Departures from democracy were perfectly all right: the Persians *needed* authoritarianism, their makeup demanded it.[31]

The correspondence between diplomats and State Department officials points to a paradoxical conclusion: U. S. policy did not jell until the Shah and the Iranians had been fitted properly into their negative stereotype of "Asia." At first, the documents reflect great uncertainty about the Shah, and there is much speculation about his personality and character; is he a liberal, humanitarian, open-minded, and perhaps even slightly *too* advanced monarch for his population? Or is he, conversely, weak, immature, and dishonest? It is not until a decision was reached on this point that the discussions stop, and the decision was to file him under "Oriental despot" and stop worrying. "The Secretary asked if this was not a case of corrupt and incompetent government which no matter how much equipment or money we put into it would be doomed to fail. Mr. Hare said that this was somewhat the case," one report from March 1, 1950 puts it. A State Department paper concluded that the Shah's "indecision was monumental and his moral courage debatable," that his decisions were made on the basis of "devious Oriental reasoning."[32] With him thus labeled and diagnosed, the way was open for the Shah to become America's "Oriental ally." This image contained a whole set of political assumptions that were to structure U. S. relations with Iran: that repression must be something the population took for granted and even required, from their psychopolitical structure; that the workings of the political process could only be erratic; and that to deal with all this, extraordinary methods might well be called for.[33] The Shah himself was certainly aware of these thought-maneuvers by which the U. S. justified departures from democratic values when it seemed expedient to do so. His sarcastic reply to U. S. criticism of his government's corruption during one of the troubled times in the relationship reflects this: "What is corruption in Persia," he asked rhetorically in a radio-broadcast reply to U. S. charges, "in comparison with corruption elsewhere, particularly in those countries which already receive substantial free American aid?"[34] Even in the last hours of the Shah's rule, the stereotypes were not revised. In 1977, the U. S. ambassador saw in him a "wounded sovereign sulking on his orange-scented terrace, in his black pajamas, above the bright-blue Caspian Sea."[35] By 1979, asked by the U. S. ambassador whether he should inquire on his behalf if the U. S. might grant asylum, he is "leaning forward, almost like a small boy, and saying 'Oh, would you?' "[36] In a rare burst of self-criticism, a U. S. government report[37] subsequent to the ousting of the Shah raised the question of why U. S. policy had failed to recognize the warning signs that in retrospect one could see had existed. The report concluded that the warnings had not been seen because they involved problems one did not *want* to be aware of and would have required revisions one did not want to make.

Insights such as these are rare. More commonly, perception moved smoothly along a track that had the "splendor of Persepolis" fantasies at one end and the "savage Muslim hordes" at the other.[38] Not only that, the images were apparently transferable to the Shah's successors, as unlike him as they may be. Of Yazdi, the American chargé notes that "in true Persian fashion, he will probably be moderately assertive in public and more reasonable in private."[39] The question whether this was the character of Persians or the nature of diplomacy was not raised. In another passage, a meeting is described as "ending on a Persian note. As we were taking our leave, Ibrahim-Zadeh drew an American official aside. He said he had some friends. They needed visas. Could we do anything for them."[40] Any embassy will be able to give examples of such attempts; there is nothing peculiarly Persian about them.

The case of Iran illustrates that condescension, moral diffidence, and disdain characterize the attitude of dominant toward inferior, but do not tell the whole story: elements of fear and fascination are usually present as well. Explorers and travelers to the East may have been motivated mainly by the search for profit, but some went because they were profoundly alienated from their own culture[41] and projected their expectations onto the Orient in a lifelong odyssey that only ended, for some, when they were finally laid to rest in an Arab-style tomb erected in the British coun-

tryside.[42] A second and much more significant flaw in the façade of supremacy was the fear that was never very far beneath the surface of colonial smugness. If the East had really been regarded as so inherently
inferior, so obviously in need of guidance and change, then the "retour
d'Islam," the specter of an Islamic mass movement, would not have been
such a haunting notion to the administrators.[43]

As noted in chapter 1, development theory provided its own version
of the inscrutable East under the heading of a "non-Western political
process." The conviction that personal, autocratic leadership was something inherent in the psychosocial makeup of Third World societies helped
explain the coups, the charismatic leaders, and the seemingly nonrational
mass behavior; it also made it easier to tolerate dictators and accept the
human rights violations committed by one's allies. One might even venture to argue that policy and theory merged here to produce a predilec-
tion on the part of Western decision-makers to deal with and support
individuals on the premise that this kind of leadership, with all its dis-
advantages, was what the Third World wanted. Analysts such as Rupert
Emerson noted and criticized this attitude, pointing out that

> the emergence of Fascism, the virtual deification of Stalin, the return of
> De Gaulle to supreme power in France, the abundant Latin American
> experience, and even the wartime preeminence of Churchill and Roo-
> sevelt, among many other examples, make it absurd to regard this em-
> phasis on personal leadership as in any way a peculiarly Oriental or Af-
> rican aberration.[44]

It seems quite possible that the emphasis Western stereotype placed on
personal Third World leadership had a certain effect on diplomatic interaction, and combined with massive support for individual leaders served
to make true its prejudice. The famous comment ascribed to several
U. S. presidents in regard to such Third World dictators as Somoza or
the Shah himself that "he may be a son of a bitch, but at least he's *our*
son of a bitch" says as much about Western diplomacy as it does about
the political system of the polities under discussion. The "personalism"
in the relationship between the U. S. and individual rulers in pivotal Third
World countries is an aspect that would certainly be deserving of further
study.[45]

The East Looks at the West—Occidentalism

"Their understanding is dull and their tongues are heavy,"[46] tenth-century Arab commentators smugly noted in describing the Europeans they encountered. "You shall see none more filthy than they," al-Qazwini is disgusted to report in the thirteenth century, speaking of the Franks. "They are people of perfidy and mean character. . . ."[47] The cultural balance and the balance of power favored such pronouncements. Ibn Jakub, visiting Krakow in 966, found a shabby town supporting itself by maintaining a large slave trade.[48] Throughout much of Western Europe, the economy stagnated and coins, where they were in circulation at all, were of Muslim origin. From the ninth century on, a stream of refugees from Muslim-occupied parts of Europe sought the protection of feudal warlords, and a backward and beleaguered Western civilization struggled to rally itself with a Christian consciousness against an "infidel" superior in nearly everything—except the true faith, that useful political category where truth is in the eyes of the believer.

To pursue the definition of prejudice as a conflictual tool it is important to look at this side of culture conflict during times when the power balance was not to the disadvantage of the East. We will discover then that Islamic "chauvinists" have certainly participated in the cultural war, and from several perspectives. During the times when they were culturally and materially in a superior position, generalizations about the inferiority of Christians and Europeans assisted in cementing the power balance. And prejudice was not restricted to "Orient-Occident" relations; it was also employed as an instrument in Islam's regional and domestic politics.

Prejudice Within Islam

While cultural arrogance covers all aspects of the Other, aspersions on their political life stand in the foreground. The inferior Others are portrayed as incapable of contributing to culture and civilization; they command no power of lasting significance; they are incapable of governing themselves according to civilized precepts. These ascriptions, most familiar to us in a colonial context, are in fact widely employed throughout history; by no means are they the invention of one particular culture. This is perhaps best illustrated when one looks at the example of intra-Islamic controversy.

Hostilities between Arabs and Persians operate by precisely the same methods of discrimination as East-West stereotypings do, and contemporary Shi'ite consciousness continues to reflect an awareness of this.

The conversions to Islam that followed the Arab conquest of Persia did not equalize the status of Arabs and non-Arabs. Partly this appears to have stemmed from the material consideration that one did not wish to lose revenues formerly derived from taxing non-Muslims, and partly it was the product of Arab consciousness during this period of power and expansion. The Persian "nationalist" Shu'ubiyya movement arose in large part as a response to the experience of racial and economic discrimination in the ninth through the eleventh century. The ensuing dispute between this movement and the dominant Arabs was a classic instance of cultural war, with mutual claims of civilizational superiority and accusations of the other side's corruption, political incapacity, and inevitable historical decline. One instructive text is the one by Ibn Abd Rabbih,[49] whose approach documents the universality of certain recurrent arguments in politico-cultural disputes. One great strength of the Arabs is obviously Islam, whose ideological, military, and material success goes hand in hand with that of the Arab rulers. Rabbih's task is to disrupt this linkage between "Arab" and "Muslim." All Muslims are equal in moral terms and before the law, he argues, and the Arabs are racists in refusing to acknowledge this.[50] "We rebut the argument you use in boasting against us," he writes. But this is not enough. Not only is the supremacy of the Arabs based on illegitimate claims, it is also doomed to failure. Rabbih goes on the offensive to challenge the political supremacy of the Arabs:

> Do you consider pride of ancestry to lie in kingship and prophethood? If you answer that it is in kingship, then the non-Arabs say to you: Ours are the kings of all the earth, the Pharaohs, the Nimrods, the Amalekites, the Chosroes, and the Caesars. . . . If on the other hand you claim that pride of ancestry rests only on prophethood, then all the prophets and apostles from Adam onward are ours, save only four—Hud, Salih, Ismail and Muhammad. Ours are the two chosen ones, Adam and Noah, who are the original stocks from which all mankind derives. We are thus the roots and you are the branches—indeed, you are but one of our twigs.

One powerful argument for Arab superiority remains: the pragmatic argument for their obvious existing power. Rabbih attempts to defuse this advantage by arguing that their military might is not matched by political achievements: "non-Arab nations in every part of the world have kings who unite them, cities which gather them . . . the Arabs, on the other hand, never had a king who could unite their main part and draw in their outlying parts . . . they achieved nothing at all in the arts and crafts and made no mark in philosophy. . . ."[51]

Recently, supremacist sentiments have been ascribed primarily to the West in its dealings with the Muslims, and Shi'a Islam has been seen as a kind of oppositional voice vis-à-vis the Sunnis. These interpretations can be true at one moment in history without being true at another. Circumstances permitting, the Arabs can be arrogant supremacists vis-à-vis the West, and Persian Shi'ites can be repressive and violent toward their Sunni population. In the sixteenth century, for example, Ismail "erected a zealously Shi'i state . . . Sunni tariqas were dispossessed, losing their Khaniqahs and endowments, and Sunni ulama were executed or exiled."[52]

In their dealings with the culturally backward Christians of the Middle Ages, the Muslims conformed perfectly to the pattern of cultural prejudice.[53] For nearly every stereotype and every stylistic detail of contemporary "Orientalism," history offers an inverse equivalent. European habits and customs were described as quaint and amusing in travelogues. The appearance, morals, and social condition of the other side's women received a lot of attention, and the harem fantasies of Westerners had their counterpart in Eastern speculation about the promiscuous young ladies of Nice or the reports that Viennese ladies went without underwear. Just as the author of European accounts usually infiltrated the harem at risk to life and limb, Muslim authors amazed their readers with accounts of perilous love affairs they had had with court ladies and even Viking queens.[54] The authors also undertook to compare the relative position of women in the West and in their own societies, generally producing the same kind of contradictory and subjectively distorted summary as their Western colleagues would later supply. Some noted that the legal position of Western women, for example in regard to the ownership of property, compared unfavorably with that of women in Islam. Others dwelled long and luxuriously on the decadence and depravity of Western sexual mores and on the failure to place the proper restraints on the freedom of movement of women, who in consequence were to be found strolling about on the streets, looking out of windows, and conversing with men.[55]

Prejudice and Defense

Beginning in the seventeenth century, and continuing up to the present time, Islamic civilization suffered a series of setbacks that destroyed its political and military structure, subjugated its economics, and made it a subordinate part of an international system dominated by Western civilization. Such an experience deals a profound blow to any social order, which must explain the reasons for such a defeat and try to find ways of countering it. To a culture that is in the ascendant, or that lives in relative autonomy, the question of identity is not acute.[56] Identity becomes self-conscious in times of crisis. Different groups within the society will choose different routes of defense.[57] One group will conclude that the victorious side must obviously have the better weapons, not just militarily but also in regard to science, technology, economy, and social organization. The thing to do is to acquire these instruments so that one will be able to defend oneself on terms of equality. The difficulty lies in distinguishing the instruments from the rest of the cultural fabric; the idea is to adapt but not to disappear, to become as good as the superior Other without losing one's own distinct identity.

In Islam, this approach is taken by the secularists, and their response to Western dominance is to try and acquire what they think makes the West successful. In the process of so doing, they are obliged to abandon much of their culture's tradition, and the abandoned parts have to be declared nonessential; they will usually even be declared responsible for the lagging of the East behind the West. Also, a substitute for what is abandoned has to be found, and it is often sought in nationalism.[58] The argument by which these secularists would counter the apparent fact of Western superiority is the following: first, the Islamic world has to bring itself up to date in weaponry, science, productivity, education, and life styles. It has to form itself into the successful shape of modernity to be competitive once more in the international system.[59] The risks implicit in this approach are self-evident. The admission of the superiority of the

Western social and political process leaves unanswered the question of how this superiority came about, a defect it seeks to overcome by concentrating on the argument that the superiority is transitory and that one's own culture will soon be even better at modernity than the West is. The view of the West that this group had was necessarily schizophrenic, combining admiration with resentment and a desire to be acknowledged as equal by the West with an awareness that the West should not be one's judge.[60] Another problem was the difficulty of persuading the population to follow in the leap from tradition and religion to nation and race as the fundaments of identity. Nationalist leaders, Charles Cremeans concludes in his study,[61] tended to be "far more secular and Westernized than their population," and to possess popular support *in spite of,* certainly not because of, their secularism. Secularist nationalism depended very much on the personality of the leader and on the linkage to nationalist issues with universal appeal, such as wars of liberation and anticolonialism.[62]

Some of the problems facing the secularists in their political work were avoided by the modernists (and analysts like Khadduri argue that some secularists became modernists for precisely this reason).[63] For Islamic modernists, the identity question is answered much more affirmatively. Economic problems and the violence of imperialism, they argue, along with the inevitable attrition of time, had thrown Islamic culture into a period of stagnation. This was natural; it happens to all cultures, and in any event is now passing. Islam in its essence is just as dynamic, just as democratic, and just as creative as anything the Western world has to offer. In fact, whatever is useful in Western thought already existed in original Islam (socialism, land reform, technological ingenuity, women's emancipation, whatever the respective author wants to stress). The Islamic modernists of Egypt were the most productive, though there are many earlier and other representatives. The names most commonly associated with the initial period of this school are Sayyid Amir Ali, Muhammad Abduh, Muhammad Iqbal; in Iran, al-Afghani was perhaps the most influential.[64] Islam, this school argues, is a socially progressive code and it established a militarily victorious, scientifically and culturally productive, politically and legally advanced society.[65] At a certain point in its history, however, problems occurred. How these problems are defined will depend on the ideological bent of the author arguing the case. Radical Islamic modernists such as Qaddafi will forward a primarily militar-

istic explanation: Western force, unfairly and immorally employed, oppressed the Muslims.[66] A more leftist version, such as that of Ali Shari'ati
and Ahmed Rezali, will give the blame to the development of class society in the world, including the Islamic world: the clergy, who become a
class, pervert religion into an official institution and a power instrument
for the ruling classes.[67] In either case, the West is subject to rejection; by
the radicals, because it is an imperialist power, by the leftists, because it
is the embodiment of the materialistic values that threaten human development.[68] Islam emerges from the debate as the superior social framework and as the most effective revolutionary ideology. Those aspects of
Western life and thought that one wishes to adopt can be coopted under
the premise that they are not Western at all, just updated versions of things
originally present in Islam. Obviously, this posture is ideologically more
gratifying that the one secularists are obliged to adopt. However, modernists face difficulties of their own.

We have already mentioned that many authors express doubts about
the sincerity of the Islamic modernists; these doubts are frequently shared
by their domestic opponents, who occasionally regard Islamic modernism as a vehicle for smuggling Marxism, secular westernization, and other
foreign affiliations into the culture. Fazlur Rahman believes the modernists to be politically and ideologically the most vulnerable sector in current Islamic debate, "always on the defensive against the aggressive
revivalists"[69] and trapped by the dual necessity of arguing in such a way
that the secular West will be impressed without alienating the religious
domestic audience.[70] Another of their problems lies in the fact that, while
they are able to claim Islam as a positive part of their political identity in
theory, in fact they are often in the position of trying to put the brakes
on the fundamentalists. In many Islamic countries, modernists are engaged in a day-to-day struggle with fundamentalists over the interpretation and implementation of Islamic law.[71] To a tradition-minded population, the fundamentalists will appear as unconditional supporters of Islam,
while modernists at times will seem to be overintellectual quibblers and
"fellow travelers" of the secularists.[72] They will not be able to use Islam
anywhere near as effectively as the fundamentalists do, while the necessity of always stating their essential agreement and loyalty to Islam will
be a persistent handicap in conflicts with the fundamentalists. The fundamentalists can (and do) accuse the modernists of being impious. If they

want to counter with their own accusations against the ulama, the modernists usually have to employ a vocabulary that is not very familiar to their audience. Shari'ati's accusation that the ulama assisted in the destruction of the original classless society is a clear case of this. Traditionalists share with fundamentalists a common view of the West. Their distinction lies in the greater (real or purported) indifference to it.

"We can be just as modern as the Westerners," the secularists might say. "True Islam, cleansed of the distortions of history, is just as dynamic and progressive as the West," the modernists would argue. "Islam is superior in all ways and the superiority of the West is an illusion," fundamentalists insist. But the traditionalist position would come out more like: "Why compare ourselves with the West at all? If we could only get rid of their material and intellectual presence, our culture would be perfectly all right." Traditionalists tend to present the West, its beliefs, its criticism of Islam, and its accomplishments, as essentially irrelevant to Islamic civilization.[73] They will not tend to be political activists except for a clearly defined, short-term purpose. Traditionalists believe that Islam can resolve its own problems, that it is a viable and complete system that only needs to be protected from the dangerous influences of an alien and decadent way of life. This position, like the three preceding ones, suffers from a number of inconsistencies. Like some of the antiemancipationist women who travel far and wide in order to argue that women should stay at home, traditionalists cannot act in consistency with their principles without already thereby contradicting themselves.[74] The most dramatic case in point is probably Saudi Arabia, where a declared traditionalist regime relies heavily on the most sophisticated foreign techonology to maintain its desired social organization.[75]

Islamic fundamentalists, the fourth group, are the most vigorous employers of the prejudice weapon in their conflict behavior; while the other groups are more ambivalent, the fundamentalists' approach to the West and their mental framework correspond closely to Orientalism. They are expansionist; they may also be nationalist, but their nationalism will not admit to boundaries. They want to see their values, which they declare to be the only correct ones, established all over the Muslim world and beyond. Fundamentalists portray Islamic culture as being superior not only in the past or in some ideal future but in the present time as well. Islam is the only true moral order, and they are the only true representatives of

Islam. Fundamentalists such as the Egyptian Sayyid Qutb, whose work remains influential throughout the international fundamentalist community, firmly dismiss Islamic modernism: "Islamic society is not one in which people invent their own version of Islam and call it, for example, 'progressive Islam,' "[76] Qutb judges.

The challenge presented by Western supremacy is dealt with by presenting supremacist counterclaims. Sayyid Qutb ridicules the approach of Islamic modernists who

> when talking about Islam, present it to the people as if it were something which is being accused and they want to defend it against the accusation. Among their defenses, one goes like this: "It is said that modern systems have done such and such, while Islam did not do anything comparable. But listen! It did all this some fourteen hundred years before modern civilization!"
>
> Woe to such a defense! Shame on such a defense![77]

Why is this modernist line of argument so reprehensible? First of all, Qutb argues, because it is absurd to lower oneself to such comparisons. One does not need to justify oneself to the West or even to regard Western criteria as applicable. The world is divided into two systems; one of them is Islam and the other "jahili," or ignorance. To defend oneself against ignorance is ridiculous. Furthermore, it is wrong to defend the present condition of Muslims. They are in dire straits because they have abandoned Islam, not because they have failed to adopt Western ways. "The argument which Islam presents is this: Most certainly Islam is better beyond imagination. It has come to change Jahiliyya, not to continue it."[78] To look for analogies and similarities in achievement with the non-Islamic world, as the modernists do, is completely wrong; Islam is different, and in this difference lies its essence and its superiority. From a propagandistic viewpoint, the superiority of such an approach is self-evident; Qutb, who diagnoses the Islamic modernists as uncertain and "full of contradictions," claims to have been one of them in the past until he recognized that it was a mistake to accept Islam as being "something accused and standing at trial, anxious for its own defense."[79] Instead, it is far more efficacious to "take the position of attacking the Western jahiliyya, its shaky religious beliefs, its social and economic modes, and its immoralities."[80]

The borderline between defense and attack is a thin one. Sayid Mujtaba Rukni Musawi Lari's book *Western Civilization Through Muslim Eyes*[81] is a good illustration. This text, written by an Iranian from a family of prominent theologians, is of interest for another reason: because of its striking stylistic similarities to Orientalist literature. As with Orientalism, the book describes itself as a scholarly and objective study of the other culture, and the author's credentials are similar to those of the authors we reviewed in the corresponding Western section: one visit to the civilization in question and an eclectic collection of "data." The stated goal of the book is to present "a balanced study" of "both the superiorities and the deficiencies of the West in its concepts on all life's affairs."[82] The table of contents somewhat qualifies this introduction; only one-third of the book is actually about the West, while the remaining two-thirds elaborate the superiority of Islam. The chapter headings also provide a clue:

On the West:	*On Islam:*
Anti-Islamic propaganda	Islam and political theory
Morals in the West	Islam and legislation
Sex in the West	Islam and nationhood
Social dropouts	Islam and economics (1)
Alcohol	Islam and economics (2)
Shortages and uncharitableness	Islam and intellectual advance
Savagery in a civilised age	Medical science
Reasons for Christianity's advance	Hospitals
Landslide in family life	Chemistry
Love of animals	Industry
Childhood traumas	Mathematics

Lari's argumentation follows the classic lines. He begins by arguing that those areas where the West appears to be superior are more than irrelevant as criteria, they are in fact evidence for Western inferiority. The excellence of science and technology only shows how low, correspondingly, the moral and spiritual values have sunk. "Science," he writes, "plunges human conduct into deeper dark and murk," a development from which the Islamic world, by remaining outside it, has been spared. Prejudice is an instrument of conflict, not a tool of logic; it is therefore possible for Lari to argue, a few pages later, that it is in fact the East and not the West that has produced all really significant science and technology and that the West has merely taken over and expanded upon these essential

Islamic discoveries. The sections on morality are impressive in their eclecticism. Freud, Dale Carnegie, and the *Encyclopaedia Britannica* are the main
witnesses to the depravity of the West; there are quotations from authors
such as Montaigne or Tolstoy taken utterly out of context to read as tes-
timonials to Islamic superiority. There is evidence ranging from tapped
telephone lines in New York that reveal the promiscuity of American
housewives to a purported speech by Khrushchev declaring the "grip of
sexual passion that has fastened on our youth" to be the "single most
important threat facing the Soviet Union," to statistics on the number of
children bitten by dogs in various Western capitals.[83]

Lari concludes on the classic fundamentalist note: the conviction that
although at present, Muslims suffer from an "inferiority complex" in the
face of the West's "industrial prowess" and long to adopt its "manners
and morals, laws and legislation," eventually Islam will emerge from the
culture conflict as the superior side, and "man by man, Europeans will
come to adopt the Islamic faith."[84]

The ideal-typical fundamentalist image of the world is strictly dualistic.
There is truth and there is falsehood, Islam and jahiliyya, Islam and the
materialism of the West in its capitalist and socialist versions. At the same
time, and to differing extents, fundamentalists, like all beleaguered parties in the cultural war, are obliged to operate within the framework set
by the opponent.[85] Khomeini went to great pains to win over the Western media while in France. This fell under the heading of tactics, but it
nevertheless obliged him to formulate his goals in language plausible to
his opponents, thereby embroiling him in just the kind of inconsistency
fundamentalists deplore in their modernist rivals. His coalition with the
modernists, though he emerged from it as the victor, caused another break
in the purity of fundamentalism. That it left its mark may be seen in his
speeches, which are permeated, often incongruously, by leftist and de-
pendencia school phrases bearing the unmistakable signature of Bani-Sadr.
The infiltration of the term "hegemony" into fundamentalist vocabulary
is one example.[86]

Prejudice and Sexual Politics

The relationship between the sexes, the status of women, and the organization of the family are issues that receive a great deal of attention

by all the participants in cultural controversy. We have seen that sexual images and ascriptions were a frequent element in the popular Orientalist literature, past and present. To the fundamentalists of today, the issue is suitable to demonstrate the decadence of the West and to establish the distinctness of one's own position. Qutb declares, "The family system and the relationship between the sexes determine the whole character of a society and whether it is backward or civilized, jahili or Islamic."[87]

In the Western and the Islamic modernist critique of existing Muslim society, Muslim laws of marriage and divorce and the place of the woman in society in general were pivotal issues. Salama Musa writes of the Egyptian nationalist movement at the start of the century that "there were two subjects we used to discuss more than anything else . . . they were the English occupation, and Qasim Amin's movement for the liberation of women."[88] This phenomenon deserves our attention for two reasons: first, because of what it tells us about the dynamics of the political psychology involved, and second because this assignment of the role of symbolic indicator to women has such grave consequences both for their social status, which becomes a proxy battleground on which the struggle between ideological groups is fought, and for their own political behavior.

The literature offers striking evidence for the inclination of all parties involved to sexualize the debate, and to draw on sexual imagery for their most intense arguments.

Khomeini denounces the immorality of Western civilization so much that Western and immoral tend to become synonymous. "Westernization," in his vivid language, meant "parading around the streets with a European hat on your head watching the naked girls" (i.e., the women in Western dress).[89] Today, too, Western-dressed Iranian women are denounced as "cabaret dancers" by Khomeini, while coeducational elementary schools are classified as "houses of prostitution."[90]

Islamic modernists and secularists use this imagery in a variety of ways; to attack rigid and corrupt tradition, or to associate both the Shah's Iran and the clergy's oppressive wielding of Islam with the most drastic sexual allegations. In *The Crowned Cannibals,* for example, leftist author Reza Baraheni accuses traditional society of producing a pattern of sociosexual perversion on the fundament of repressed but nearly universal male homosexuality and a sadistic hatred of women's sexuality.[91] Sexual imagery is also highly suitable for denouncing imperialism, as in the following rendition of Western civilization by Bahman Nirumand:

> The image presented to the Iranians for self-identification reflected, in importunate, superficial and seductive colors, imported European-American features. . . . Not only does this physiognomy appear behind bluish glass panes on the back seats of big American sedans, not only does it smirk from toothpaste billboard ads, not only does it flick across the screen as . . . a fashion model, or appear as a strip-tease star through the early morning hours in dim, feudal enclaves of the plutocracy; it lies over the land like a poisonous mist and enters like a deadly tumor into the consciousness of the astounded Iranian. . . .[92]

Nirumand is a leftist political economist. He studied in Europe, refers to Marcuse as his mentor, and was formed by the European student movement. Though aimed westward, this paragraph is also a vivid expression of the ambivalence felt by some secularists and modernists.

The positions taken on the "woman question" by the four ideal-typical groups are predictable and consistent. Secularists will consider the position of women and the attitude toward sexuality that prevail in the West to be superior and worthy of adoption.

Modernists will argue that while the status of women in the areas of work, education, legal position, and political participation is superior in the West today, Islam was originally an emancipatory movement that improved the situation of women in the Arab world dramatically. Purdah, child marriage, and women's disenfranchisement are classified as non-Islamic and stemming instead from local customs, while marriage laws and other Islamic rulings are taken to require reinterpretation according to the principles of Islam. In addition, focus will be put on the negative aspects of women's situation in the West. The Mujahedeen platform argues that women must be freed both from the "dark, reactionary oppression" of the fundamentalists and from the "capitalist conception of women as a commodity."[93]

Traditionalists will reject the comparison with the West, while fundamentalists will argue that the Islamic system is the only one that does justice to nature and morality.[94]

All the groups subscribe in one form or another to Marx' and Engels' dictum that the status of women is the most reliable indicator of the level society has achieved. Qutb refers to the relationship between the sexes as the "only measure which does not err in gauging true human progress."[95] With the symbolic directness of the chador, the woman question generally thus becomes a symbol for one's position in the ideological struggle. There appear to be three major reasons for this:

1. Sexuality and the family involve basic elements of individual identity and social organization. Attacks on the morality of the other side's women, or allegations regarding their abuse, have a high emotional content.

2. The status of women is a relatively low-risk issue. This has advantages both for the fundamentalists and for their opposition. The fundamentalists are able to signal the dawn of a new age by means of some relatively simple changes, such as rules of "Islamic" dress for women. Also, steps taken in this area will be less likely to endanger the process of consolidation, since the resistance of some women to the new measures can be managed much more easily than if one alienated more potentially troublesome opponents. In the same way, it is a cheap means of offering benefits in the form of a raise in status and a vicarious share in authority to traditional men vis-à-vis women. For the modernists, verbally progressive stances on this issue will identify them as liberal without really obliging them to implement their stand.

3. This area of social organization is one that is genuinely fundamental and therefore worth controlling, comprising as it does the pattern of primary socialization, linked to the structure of work, distribution, and communication.

The behavior of the fundamentalists after the removal of the Shah illustrates these points. Immediately upon his return to Iran, Khomeini began issuing a series of decrees in regard to women and to his conception of Islamic morality, an easy way to signal the dawn of a new social order. At the start of March 1979, he directed the Minister of Justice to eliminate from the Family Protection Act any passages contradicting Islamic principles. The act, which had introduced such relatively moderate reforms as requiring husbands to get the approval of their first wife before taking a second one and making it slightly less difficult for women to initiate divorce procedures, represented an effective but low-risk starting point for the fundamentalist takeover of the judicial and legislative system.

PREJUDICE AS A CULTURAL WEAPON   99

Modernist women resisted with demonstrations, strikes, conferences, and even an attempt to assassinate the head of television and radio, a man known for his antifeminist stance. The fundamentalist response to this opposition corresponded to their conflict behavior vis-à-vis other elements of the modernists: they avoided a direct confrontation, concentrating on splitting and discrediting their opponents and on steadily consolidating their position. Khomeini initially "reinterpreted" some of the restrictive proclamations (concerning dress, for example), but at the same time he proceeded with legislative and judicial cancellations of previous reforms and tolerated the widespread harassment of nonconforming modernist women on the part of male vigilantes among his following. Since 1979, a rigorous fundamentalist version of Islamic law has even included such practices as setting the compensation to be paid in the case of murder of a female victim at half the compensation required for a murdered male. Though the politically active modernist women were forewarned and aware at each point, their response to the fundamentalist undermining of their rights was ineffectual and disorganized.

The schizophrenia which is the main political weakness of Islamic modernists is well illustrated by the political behavior of these modernist women, who are often expected to participate in assigning low priority to their own social rights for some pragmatic consideration. They are also required to share in the apologetics and defensiveness with which modernists explain some of the traditional treatment accorded to women, partly in order to disclaim Western superiority, partly in order to avoid the accusation that they are separatists cooperating with bourgeois Western feminism, partly in order to avoid alienating traditional women or providing fuel for fundamentalist claims that modernist women are immoral, and partly because of the ambivalent attitudes held by their male counterparts. Qasim Amin himself, whose tracts against veiling caused much controversy in turn-of-the-century Egypt, did not permit his wife to abandon the veil or to socialize with his male guests at home.[96] More important than these individual examples is the way in which modernist male authors use the question of women's rights in a clearly derivative and symbolic way. Almost never will one of the them argue that education, freedom of movement, political participation, and equal legal status are inherent rights of women; almost always these rights are justified by arguing that such changes will be for the best of society. For example, a woman should receive an education not because her rights are equal to those of men but because she will educate her children (some authors do not hesitate to say: her sons) better. She should be allowed to participate in politics not because it is her right but because so many women have died in the struggle and thus "earned" the right for their gender. (This is the line taken by the Mujahedeen.) Other modernists use women to signal changes in their own affiliation. Algeria's Ben Bella, for example, signified his move to a greater stress on Islam and his tactical coalition with the fundamentalists by requiring his wife, a former Communist, to wear the chador in their Paris exile.[97]

For the ambivalence and tactical confusion of politically active women, the case of the Egyptian feminist modernist Nawal as-Saadawi is instructive. Her book *The Hidden Face of Eve* details graphically the physical, legal, and emotional abuse experienced by women in a traditional context; however, she is careful to assign the blame for these practices to pre- or non-Islamic cultural practices and to class society. When the Iranian revolution took place, she initially endorsed it; she subsequently regretted this as she struggled to explain to disparate audiences what she thought had happened and what Arab women were to learn from it. When she was jailed by Sadat as an Islamic radical, feminist groups in Europe and the U. S. agitated for her release. Her response to the experience and her subsequent performance before mixed European and Arab audiences have been expressive illustrations of modernist confusion.[98]

Gender has always been a peculiarly indicative variable in relation to political consciousness and political behavior. Although there are important similarities between the status and the political behavior of women and that of other marginalized populations, sex is in many ways unique as a factor determining political identity; of all populations, it is the most difficult for women to act in a coherent political fashion, because they are least a "group" in their social condition. Their bonds with nonmembers are stronger, their scope for activity is narrower, their loyalties necessarily more schizophrenic and their identity more ambiguous than is the case for any other subordinate group. In Iran—and more broadly, in the Islamic world—the political dilemma of women can serve as a metaphor of the general political dilemma: of the subordination of crucial social questions to issues determined in large part by outside powers, and of the fracturing of critical dynamics by this subordination. Women provide a

particularly clear illustration because it is a characteristic of their condition never to be the primary issue, always to be subject to more powerful
interests and more forcefully embattled issues.

The four conflicts sketched in chapter 2 (North/South, East/West, tra-
ditional/modern, and ideological) cross-cut the political behavior of women
in Iran in an immediately demonstrable fashion. The lines between tradition and modernity divide women on issues such as education, participation, family structure, and civil rights. The lines between North and
South, East and West, and left and right determine what place women's
issues will be granted in the hierarchy of importance on any given dispute; and the divisions will run along different lines depending on the
issue, the timing, and the main actors. As with the ethnic groups, wom-
en's rights will never be the primary issue for any of the other active groups
involved; they will be a tactical instrument or a lower case element of the
platform at best, and a manipulable variable at worst, with the issue of
ethnic minorities and women used to signal new allegiances. A crackdown on minorities or an abrupt disenfranchisement of women, for example, will often be a symbolic way of announcing a new general line of
policy. Unlike the rights of ethnic groups, however, women's rights will
rarely be the primary issue even for those affected; except for a small minority, women themselves will generally rank women's rights as a subordinate political issue. This fact intensifies the fractures imposed by the
four constraining conflicts.

For example, in the demonstrations prior to the expulsion of the Shah,
women of all ideological affiliations chose the chador, a symbol of tradition, to demonstrate their rejection of the transformations personified by
the Shah. "Modern" women found, later, that their rallying to tradition
on this issue had more consequences than they may have expected; that
not only the chador but the social position of women generally was going
to be the symbol of the new course Iran was to be placed on. When
members of the international women's movement rallied in support of
their Iranian wing, yet another fracture line intervened to prevent any
political gains that might have accrued from this solidarity: support from
the outside, particularly from the West, activated the North/South line of
conflict and obliged Iranian women, in the name of nationalism, to reject
"foreign intervention" of any sort. When restoration of traditional dress
was followed by restorations of traditional work and education sys-

tems—that is, when secular education and qualified jobs began to be denied to women—the movement rallied again, only to shatter against yet
another line of division, the ideological one. Revolutionary pragmatics in
Iran, as elsewhere, are designed by male ideologues in whose view wom-
en's rights are an issue best held in reserve until some later postrevolu-
tionary date. In the name of the common struggle ("common" being defined as unilateral imposition of the male view) women are exhorted to
place pragmatism before particularism and to realize that other issues must
be given priority.

The Many Uses of Prejudice

In volatile political situations, prejudice has numerous functions. It can
be employed in domestic power struggles to discredit opponents by linking them or their values to a discredited association. It can serve as a mo-
bilizing agent. It can defuse opposition and discontent by providing a
short-circuited explanation and redirect aggression toward a scapegoat.
In international and intercultural relations, it is deployed both by the
dominant and by the challengers. When the conflict subsides, prejudice
will show its second face, easing the reestablishment of "normal" relations without qualitatively affecting the fundamental premise of Otherness.

CHAPTER FIVE

The Islamic Republicans in Power

By the summer of 1981, out of the coalition comprising fundamentalists, traditionalists, modernists, and even some secularists, the fundamentalists had managed to emerge as the dominant force after either eliminating or substantially weakening their rivals. They have attempted to consolidate their domestic power through a phased process of ideological and functional activities.

The Coalition Phase

The upheaval in Iran was effected through a mass movement that cut across the lines of class and ideology. Nonfundamentalists, especially modernists, believed that Khomeini and his fundamentalist supporters would share power with them in the kind of arrangement where the fundamentalists were custodians of moral authority while modernist experts and professional politicians ran the affairs of state. At the very least, it was expected that nonfundamentalists would be allowed to operate freely. Ibrahim Yazdi, who was Khomeini's adviser in Paris, and a modernist himself, told Henry Precht of the U. S. State Department that after the overthrow of the Shah, various ideological groups would "enjoy full freedom of speech and the press, including the right to attack Islam."[1]

This view appears to have arisen from two factors. The first was the experience during the initial phases of the coalition, when Khomeini appeared to be cooperative and amenable to the ideas of his modernist allies and at times gave the impression that he would return to the holy city of Qum and not get involved in politics. Second, the modernist view of government presumed a distinction between ethical functions on the one hand and the pragmatic functions of politics on the other—tasks such as administration and diplomacy, for which the clerics in their view were so obviously unsuited that the point appeared to require little discussion. The role that personalities like Khomeini and the network of religious structures could play in crowd mobilization was seen as a short-term phenomenon.

The fundamentalists did not come to dominance immediately, and developments after the ousting of the Shah tended to support modernist expectations. At the lower levels, political authority was exercised in random combinations by all the participating groups, as thousands of committees (komitehs) appointed themselves to be in charge of various administrative tasks from stamping passports and directing traffic to confiscating land with an eye to its redistribution.[2]

Several interpretations of the break between fundamentalists and modernists have been proffered, and even the participants themselves do not seem to be clear on the exact nature of the fundamentalist strategy. Did Khomeini initially intend to withdraw once the Shah was overthrown, and were the fundamentalists gradually encouraged by the weak, irresolute, and disunited behavior of the modernists to seek control themselves? Did the modernists realize from the start that the clerics intended to govern, and dismiss this threat because they did not take their fundamentalist allies seriously?

Evidence seems to point to the conclusion that Khomeini's view of government was consistent from the start: that he felt the actual power of government was a moral one and should belong to him and the fundamentalists, while the modernists could usefully provide the administrative skills necessary in implementing the fundamentalist program. To the modernists, given their concept of politics, running the day-to-day affairs of the state was not a matter of secondary importance but the crux of government. To Khomeini, experts were a kind of hired help with specialized skills, professionals like electricians or surgeons. Once it had become clear that these particular "tools" had ambitions of their own contrary to his goals, he moved to eliminate them. Some modernists like Bani-Sadr still believe that the requirements of the modern age do not allow the kind of approach that fundamentalists have chosen, that eventually they will be forced to rely once again on the experts, that normalization implies a return to rational government by professionals and therefore spells the displacement of the clerics.[3] Fundamentalists, on the other hand, continue to believe that experts are interchangeable, though loyal ones should be preferred over the others; nonfundamentalists should be depended on only when there are no alternatives.[4] But this was not clear to the modernists during the initial phase.

After the collapse of the Pahlavi Shah those who formed the provisional government at the center were westernized intellectuals from the middle class. Mehdi Bazargan, who came from a prominent Bazaari merchant family, had a long history of opposition to the Shah and was appointed prime minister. In the early 1950s he was one of the main figures in the Iran National Front, a coalition which supported Prime Minister Mohammad Mossadeq (1951–53). In June of 1951 he was named chairman of the National Iranian Oil Company, empowered to implement Mossadeq's oil nationalization program. Later he became Mossadeq's director general of the Tehran water system. After the 1953 coup, Bazargan was dismissed; in 1955, he was jailed for a short time. In 1957 he was one of the founders of the National Freedom Movement of Iran (NFMI). Later he, with several other NFMI leaders such as Ayatollah Taleghani, was convicted of treason by a military court and sentenced to 19 years of solitary confinement. After being pardoned by the Shah in 1967, he maintained a low profile until the 1978 uprisings. When he spoke at opposition rallies, he called for "a return of truly constitutional government," supported freedom of the press, total independence of the judiciary, and free elections.[5]

Bazargan's appointment as prime minister of the provisional government was taken by modernists in Iran and left-of-the-center supporters of the Shah's overthrow abroad as an indicator of Khomeini's desire to turn over power to modernist and nonclerical elements in society.[6] However, it became increasingly clear that substantial political power was being exercised by the Revolutionary Council dominated by the fundamentalists and the thousands of komitehs belonging to various political organizations. It also appears that Khomeini and other fundamentalists believed that the modernist-dominated government could buy time for the fundamentalists to become better organized. According to Ayatollah Mohammad Husseini Beheshti, the leading fundamentalist political figure after

Khomeini, the fundamentalists at this point were not organized enough to take over government. For one thing, they had not formed their political party prior to the Shah's overthrow. In an important document *Az Hizb Cheh Medanim* (What do we know about the Party?),[7] Beheshti reports that he himself and several others had given thought to the formation of a party and had been in touch with Khomeini on the matter in 1978, but because of rapid escalation of developments in Iran such a step had not been taken. It is possible that the fundamentalists believed the public declaration of the establishment of such a party might frighten their modernist and other allies. In any case, according to Beheshti, soon after his return to Iran Khomeini "insisted" that the party's existence should be declared as soon as possible. The Islamic Republican Party was declared one week after the declaration of the Islamic Republic.

Upon his return from Paris Khomeini appointed, besides a provisional government, a Revolutionary Council (Shura-yi Inqilab). The members of this council included four fundamentalists who had been Khomeini's students in Qum in the past (Ayatollah Beheshti, Ayatollah Mottaheri, Hojjat al-Islam Rafsanjani, and Hojjat al-Islam Mohammad Javad Bahonar) and included two radical modernists, Bani-Sadr and Qutbzadeh, who sided with the fundamentalists against the two more moderate modernists, Yazdi and Bazargan.[8] The revolutionary komitehs, the Pasdaran or Revolutionary Guards, and the revolutionary courts dispensed justice, distributed food, set prices for goods, policed the streets, and decided on many important local and national issues. The government was unable to control their action. For example, Bazargan was unhappy with the executions, the land seizures, and the lack of control over the official media. He sought to convince Khomeini that the economic situation in the country must improve or the government would fall. To improve the economy, he wanted greater governmental power, less interference by clerics and komitehs, and more workers' discipline, which was being undermined by komitehs. As early as February 18, 1979, he complained that the revolutionary komitehs were seeking to establish a parallel government.[9] The most important indication of this was the establishment of Pasdaran under the control of the revolutionary council and Khomeini. The initial structure of the guards is set out in figure 5.1, based on a U. S. Embassy classified report released by the students who occupied the embassy. The guards, dominated by fundamentalist clerics such as

Figure 5.1 Pasdaran Organization

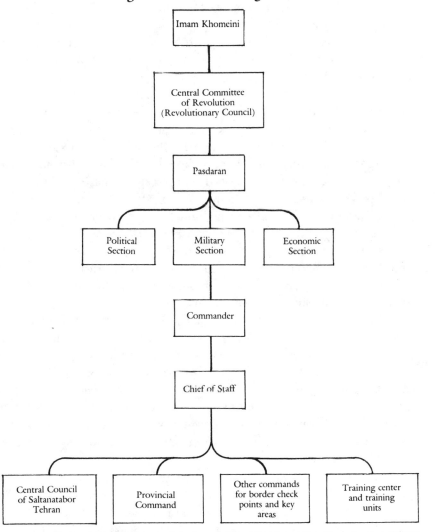

SOURCE: Muslim Student Followers of the Imam's Line, *Ifshi-i imperialisms* [Exposing Imperialism] (Tehran: Muslim Student Followers of the Imam, n.d.) 1:40.

Ayatollah Hassan Lahoti and Hojjat al-Islam Rafsanjani, were to act as the "eyes and ears of the Islamic Revolution" and as "a special task force of the Imam Khomeini to crush counter-revolutionary activities within the government or any political usurper against the Islamic Government."[10] They were also expected to prevent a coup by the military and indoctrinate others with Islamic values.

Over time, the conflict between the Bazargan government and the Revolutionary Council intensified. In July 1979, deputy premier Amir-Entezam complained in private meetings that the komitehs, Pasdaran, the revolutionary courts, and even Khomeini himself were working against his government.[11] Increasingly, Bazargan recognized that the fundamentalists did not intend to be satisfied with a ceremonial role but wanted actual power. Beheshti subsequently complained that the government and the Revolutionary Council had not functioned well because of lack of ideological cohesiveness.[12] The fundamentalist clerics dominated the Assembly of Experts responsible for the drafting of a new constitution for the country. Increasingly, the Revolutionary Council became involved in running the state. Rafsanjani, who headed the Pasdaran, became deputy minister of the interior, Hojjat al-Islam Khamenei became deputy defense minister, Ayatollah Mahdavi-Kani became another deputy interior minister. There were always some modernists who chose to continue their affiliation with the fundamentalists, because their aims were more radical than those of the other modernists. Two of these were Sadiq Qutbzadeh, who was the director of the National Iranian Radio and Television (NIRT), and Bani-Sadr, who became the country's finance minister in charge of banking. Another member of the Revolutionary Council who joined the government was Mustafa Chamran, a modernist, who became deputy minister of defense.[13]

Modernists were afraid that the clerics would get more than half the seats in the Islamic Assembly election. During the summer of 1979, Bazargan believed that Khomeini himself did not favor "Akhondism," a term that Bani-Sadr has anglicized as "mullocracy" or clerical domination of the political system,[14] but that some of the clerics around him, such as Ayatollah Beheshti and Hojjat al-Islam Rafsanjani, did. Again he tried to convince Khomeini that the domination of the political system by the clerics would be bad for the country and appealed to him not to endorse clerics in the assembly elections. However, he continued to believe that the need to regain the confidence of the middle class and bring about economic recovery would keep the working of the government in the hands of the modernists, even if clerics dominated the assembly.[15]

Bazargan's efforts were unsuccessful. As the tension between the middle-class-supported Bazargan-type modernists and the fundamentalist clerics increased, Khomeini came out in support of the clerics:

> Do not oppose the religious scholar . . . the power afforded the nation by the religious scholars is a God-given power; do not lose it. . . . You who imagine that something can be achieved in Iran by some means other than Islam, you who suppose that something other than Islam overthrew the Shah's regime, you who believe that non-Islamic elements played a role—study the matter carefully.[16]

In his speeches beginning in June 1979, Khomeini began attacking the middle class, Bazargan's power base, crediting the success of the revolution to the lower classes and fundamentalist clerics.[17] Beheshti reports that Khomeini had asked him and IRP leaders several times during 1979 whether they could form the government, but they had responded they were not ready yet because a "party's government should be a completely independent government and should have a specified program and we have not reached that stage yet."[18] Beheshti also argues that Khomeini had instructed his party to make an all-out effort to get as many seats as possible in the Islamic Consultative Assembly (Majlis).[19]

As Bazargan slowly recognized that Khomeini would not curb the increasing interference by clerics in the running of the state, he tried to take his grievances to the public. In an August 31 speech, he spoke of his powerlessness and of the subservience of his government to the clerics.[20] Later, he described his government as a "knife without a blade," charging that all power rested with the Revolutionary Council and especially Khomeini. He said: "all our affairs are in his hand, at his command, including the power of dismissal, appointment, decision making, issuing orders, everything."[21] In October he told Oriana Fallaci that he feared a "dictatorship of the clergy."[22]

As Bazargan's complaints about the fundamentalists increased, they retaliated with attacks of their own. In September, Ayatollah Beheshti, then vice-chairman of the Council of Experts, member of the Revolutionary Council, and the leader of the fundamentalist Islamic Republican Party

(IRP), accused the Bazargan government of not implementing the decisions of the Revolutionary Council (such as the council's decision for the formation of local councils at province, city, district, and village level) and of hostility to the clerics. He accused the government of forgetting that the revolution was led by the clergy. Several other ayatollahs, including Ayatollah Ahmad Azari-Qomi, Tehran's revolutionary prosecutor, criticized Bazargan for his "anti-clerical statements" and for "weakening revolutionary unity." Ayatollah Rouhani demanded that antirevolutionary elements be purged from the government. Others criticized the government for ineffectiveness.[23] Thus, the fundamentalists took a strong position, while the modernists did not close ranks. Bani-Sadr joined the fundamentalist attack against the government. The Bazargan government was ultimately removed from office after the American embassy had been taken over in November 1979.

A look at this first period of post-monarchy Iran raises two questions: If the fundamentalists intended to hold power themselves all along, why did they put modernists in office at all, only to sabotage their efforts, undermine their government, and eventually remove them? And why did the modernists, after holding high positions, offer such an ineffective resistance to the fundamentalist effort to displace them?

Beginning with the question of why modernists were instated in office at all, three possible explanations offer themselves. First is the possibility that the fundamentalist leaders, or at least some of them, sincerely intended to establish a kind of coalition government with shared power. As we noted in previous chapters, the direct leadership of the political system was the goal that separated the fundamentalists from the traditionalists. Khomeini's *Islamic Government* had been a forceful statement of this position. However, during the actual struggle against the Shah there were reports that Khomeini was not really insisting on direct clergy rule. One source quoted him as stating in September 1978 that "our intention is not that religious leaders should themselves administer the state, but that they should guide the people in determining what the demands of Islam are."[24] Another source reported him as stating that the clerics would "not participate in official government."[25] While in Paris Khomeini appeared to moderate his position on clergy rule. This may have been due to his desire to make a positive impression on Western media and on the Iranian middle class. It may also have been the work of modernists, and especially of Yazdi, who wanted the international media to portray a moderate image of Khomeini, and who may, besides, have been engaging in some wishful thinking regarding future interactions and Khomeini's amenability to the modernists' influence. On the basis of our own conversations with Khomeini in Paris on December 31, 1978 and January 1, 1979, his Persian-language speeches, and the "Messages to the World" circulated while he was in Paris, we believe that he held fast to his concept of Islamic government in which "committed clerics" would play the dominant role. He referred to Plato's *Republic,* saying that in the Islamic Republic power would have to be exercised by those who knew Islamic law, the clerics.

When the Constitution was drafted, it gave clear legitimacy to the rule of the Faqih. According to the Constitution, "in the absence of the Imam . . . the leadership of the nation is on the shoulders of a just and pious faqih." Government institutions were to operate under his supervision, and he was to appoint the members of the defense council and supreme court, to supervise the armed forces, and to appoint and dismiss senior officers. He can declare war and peace. He appoints half of the twelve-member Council of Guardians, a body which reviews Majlis decisions and has the power to approve them or send them back to the Majlis for reconsideration. But even before the constitution was drafted—a job accomplished by a committee dominated by fundamentalists—Khomeini had supported the increasing role of the fundamentalists, including the concentration of power of the Revolutionary Council and the independence of revolutionary courts. Bazargan's many appeals to Khomeini to allow greater authority to his government, to bring Pasdaran, the NIRT, and the komitehs under government control, and to support secular candidates in the Majlis elections went unheard; instead, Khomeini encouraged Ayatollah Beheshti to speed up the organizing of the IRP. All the evidence seems to indicate that Khomeini intended a fundamentalist-dominated government from the beginning.

The second reason why he might have appointed modernists to office, if that is the case, is that he might have thought the modernists could be useful and would accept both his ultimate authority and the dominance of the clerics. If so, it did not take long for him to realize that such an arrangement did not hold much promise. Bazargan opposed the Constitution, fought against the increasing political role of the clerics, and sought

improved relations with the U. S., all steps that antagonized the fundamentalists. When the modernists began directly attacking the clerics with
such statements as Deputy Premier Amir-Entezam's comment that the IRP
program wanted to "turn time 1000 years back,"[26] when they came out
in clear opposition to "Akhondism" and "clerical dictatorship," the stage
was set for their elimination. So if Khomeini thought the modernists would
be malleable instruments, their actions changed his mind.

There is a third possible explanation. The appointment of the modernists may have been a tactical move, intended to avoid antagonizing the
modernist political groups, such as the various factions of the old National Front and their supporters among the modernized middle class,
the large industrialists, and the military, which Khomeini and his group
feared.[27] The Bazargan period bought time and weakened these potential
adversaries. The armed forces were purged, the position of the large industrialists weakened by nationalizations, the middle-class political
groupings discredited and weakened. At the same time, the IRP was established, the Revolutionary Guards founded and strengthened, and the
Constitution passed. When Bazargan ceased to be necessary and began,
instead, to become a source of trouble, he was dispensed with. This explanation, while it cannot be definitely proven, seems consistent with the
coalition politics Khomeini was following all along. It would also explain
why Khomeini was so unresponsive to the pleas of Bazargan and later of
Bani-Sadr to allow more weight to the modernist forces.

This brings us to the next question: why were the modernists so weak
in resisting their own elimination from power? When it became clear that
a sharing of power was not possible, two courses were open to them:
they could accept the terms of the fundamentalists and try to remain on
in a limited function, or they could confront the fundamentalists. While
there was opposition and disagreement, a hard-line confrontation did not
take place while modernists still held power. There appears to be more
than one reason for this.

First, unlike the fundamentalists, the modernists failed to establish a
political organization of their own. Second, they were divided among
themselves as well as being against the fundamentalists. Instead of unit-
ing in support of Bazargan when he ran into trouble with Khomeini, some
modernists who were members of the Revolutionary Council joined in

the attack on him, although they were ideologically closer to him than to the fundamentalists. Bani-Sadr attacked the Bazargan government in a speech on September 15 for not accepting "constructive criticism," for opposing the nationalization of banks (one of Bani-Sadr's favorite projects), and for bungling the Kurdish problem.[28] Qutbzadeh, who was in charge of the country's TV and radio during much of this period, often supported policies that were in conflict with those of the government. In addition, there were serious divisions within Bazargan's government on important economic issues. For example, Abbas Amir-Entezam and Ali Moinfar clashed over monetary policy. The modernists who held more radical socioeconomic goals than Bazargan apparently thought they could sustain their own alliance with the fundamentalists and push forward the radicalization of social change. Hence they failed to consolidate the modernist forces, assisted in their own partitioning, and were eliminated in successive waves. The fate met by Bazargan was repeated by Bani-Sadr. After his election to the presidency in January 1980, modernist forces rallied around him, but the growth of a parallel fundamentalist power center continued. The IRP won the Majlis elections in May 1980. Like Bazargan before him, Bani-Sadr wanted to weaken the komitehs and the Pasdaran, to extend the center's authority and reduce clerical interference in the running of state affairs. Again, Bani-Sadr tried to persuade Khomeini to help him; but to no avail. Bani-Sadr later came to believe that his greatest mistake was in not confronting Khomeini in time.[29] What deterred him is connected, in part, with the third apparent reason for modernist weakness: their intimidation in the face of what they saw as the overwhelming continued popularity of Khomeini. Both Bazargan and Amir-Entezam believed that whomever Khomeini endorsed would be elected. Some of the problems experienced by the modernists that are related to their factionalist tendencies have continued now that they are in exile or underground. We will return to this question later.

The Islamic Republic as a Regime Type

By the summer of 1981, the protracted period during which various rival forces contended for control of the state apparatus had given way to fundamentalist supremacy. From the point of view of comparative politics, what type of a regime seems to be emerging, and does it fit into the available categories of political systems?

The problem of categorizing governments into various regime types is a complex one, and the terminology favored within the discipline has passed through several fashions. Past categories have included terms such as absolutism, despotism, plutocracy, tyranny, monocracy, oligarchy, autocracy, dictatorship, and numerous others.[30] Some of these still remain useful. Although categorizing regimes continues to be controversial, three categories have found a substantial degree of acceptance: totalitarianism, authoritarianism, and pluralistic democracies, with various subtypes. Using these categories, we find that while Iran's Islamic Republic shares some of the features characteristic of other regime types, it conforms most closely to the totalitarian regimes in their consolidation phase. It is important to keep in mind that none of these categories are absolute. Conditions of each may also be found in other types of systems; it is their simultaneous and concentrated presence that favors one categorization over another.

There is substantial theoretical and empirical work on totalitarianism.[31] The essential characteristics of this system include:

1. A totalist, elaborate, and exclusive ideology;
2. Single mass party rule, but not necessarily a monolithic center of power;
3. Active mobilization of citizens for collective tasks.[32]

Although there are differences among totalitarian systems, in general several additional conditions seem to accompany such regimes, especially in their consolidation phase. These are similar to the conditions enumerated by Alexander Gerschenkron in 1962 for the "stability of dictatorships":

1. Maintenance of a permanent condition of stress and strain
   a. by the existence or creation of enemies both internal and external, and
   b. by imposing upon the population gigantic tasks that exert strong pressure upon its standards of well-being or, at least, greatly retard improvements in those standards.
2. Incessant exercise of dictatorial power.

3. Creation of an image of the leader as an incarnation of supreme wisdom and indomitable will power.
4. Reference to an allegedly unchanged and unchangeable value
system by which the action of the state is justified.
5. Proscription of any deviating values and beliefs coupled with
threats and acts of repression, sustained and implemented by
appropriate organizational devices.[33]

A review of the steps taken by Khomeini and his followers to consolidate their regime shows a striking similarity to this list, even though they
have some special characteristics of their own. The approach of Iran's
current regime shows the following characteristics:

—a totalistic approach to society seeking to dominate all its important institutions and interactions and to transform society in all its
aspects
—fundamentalist IRP dominance over the political system, through
a system of one-party rule
—a system of terror and repression of deviant values and political
identities

An Elaborate and Totalistic Ideology

Clearly ideologies differ in complexity. Although it may not be so
complex as some others, Iranian fundamentalism, like many totalitarian
ideologies, nevertheless provides its believers with a sense of mission and
a holistic concept of persons and society, and it has its own distinctive
style and rhetoric.

Samuel Huntington has commented that "the most important political
distinction among countries concerns not their form of government but
their degree of government."[34] A major characteristic of fundamentalist
ideology is its totalistic approach to politics. The regime wants the politicization of all spheres of social and even private affairs, and its world
view in fact is predicated upon a denial of these categories. In *Islamic
Government,* Khomeini had asserted: "there is not a single topic in human life for which Islam has not provided instruction and established
norms."[35] The IRP program states that it aims at establishing a *tawhidi*
(unitary) society, "a society in which Islamic values, commands, and laws

govern all social relations."[36] Since the overthrow of the Shah the government has sought to imbue all forms of activity, including the economic, cultural, and educational, with Islamic or rather fundamentalist values, although, as we shall see in economic policy, there are important disagreements among fundamentalists. The desire for politicization of all spheres of life has been justified with reference to the necessity for "elimination of foreign influence," and it has also been useful as a weapon against internal rivals.

The IRP program, required reading in Iranian schools, argues: "For decades our society has been consuming imported culture and education. In order to strengthen their political and economic imperialism, the world-devourers have used cultural imperialism."[37] Therefore, it goes on, Western patterns of life have to be eliminated in all areas: food habits, clothing fashions, architecture and city planning, education and manners.[38] In order to gain "cultural independence," Khomeini declared a "cultural revolution" in the spring of 1980[39] and established the "Headquarters of Culture" to coordinate the effort.

This "cultural revolution" provided a lever against secular education especially at the university, where many secularists and modernists still had a large following. Khomeini himself led the attack against the universities, characterizing them as "imperialist universities," arguing that "those whom they educate and train are in fact cloaked with the West. . . . Our universities in their present state are of no use to our people. The universities must become Islamic."[40] Intellectuals were also criticized.[41]

Khomeini's campaign against the universities and intellectuals was aimed at weakening nonfundamentalist groups, many of whom were active on university campuses. As a result of Khomeini's program, opposition professors and students were attacked and their organizations ousted from the campuses. Hundreds were wounded and many were killed in clashes leading to university closures. This in turn gave authorities time for the "Islamization" of the college curriculum.

The government Islamization program has affected nearly every area. Coeducation was outlawed. Media, art and entertainment, clothing, and the family became subject to regulations. The IRP-dominated regime aimed at converting the media, artistic expression, and films into morality exercises promoting the government viewpoint.

The IRP characterized the media as a "university," for the education of the population. It has declared that "printing anti-Islamic ideas and beliefs is not permitted in Islamic society."[42] The same is true of meetings and discussions. Radio and TV programs were to reflect "the true message" of the "revolution," and "art is to be political . . . in conformity with genuine Islamic and revolutionary themes."[43] The regime has increasingly moved toward monopolization of means of mass communication, banning opposition papers. Patriotic and religious songs have become the principle musical expressions; dancing is forbidden. The fundamentalist regime also has imposed *hijab* (the Islamic code of dress) on women.

One-Party Rule of the IRP

Related to the importance of ideology is the central role of the party in totalitarian politics. The party is an important instrument for mass participation and mobilization for the purpose of achieving ideological goals and regime consolidation. The relationship between the party and the state apparatus in various phases of regime evolution differs from one totalitarian regime to another. While the popular image of totalitarian regimes is that of "an efficient machine transmitting decisions from the top to the bottom,"[44] in fact there is considerable policy divergence and ideological infighting at the top.

In Iran, as we have seen, the IRP emerged after the overthrow of the Shah in order to take over the state and to compete with already established groups. Like many other parties in similar systems, it expanded rapidly, becoming a mass party and developing a broadly based organization. A core conflict between the IRP and other groups has been over the fundamentalist desire to monopolize power. The IRP argues for the primacy of politics and domination of the political and social systems by "true believers." According to the IRP program:

> if in a society all its members are Muslim and they observe Islam in their personal lives while their social relations are not governed by pure Islamic laws, it is not an Islamic society. On the other hand, if in a society all its members are not Muslim. . . . or some of its members are weak Muslims and do not behave according to Islam in all their personal ob-

ligations, while the values and laws governing social relations are Islamic, that society is Islamic.[45]

A major characteristic of the IRP is the preeminent role of the clerics in the party. The party favors the direct role of the clerics in running state affairs and supports the concept of the Vilayat-e Faqih (The Governance of the [Islamic] Jurisprudent) as the just form of government. It regards the clerics to have been the effective leaders of the revolution, which they date as having begun on June 5, 1963 (the Khordad 15, 1342 uprising against the Shah) and having taken sixteen years to succeed. The fundamentalists have argued that "leadership must always belong to clerics"[46] and that other positions, too, should go to clerics if they are qualified. Except in cases of urgent need, those less qualified but more Islamic in their behavior and approach should be given priority over those more qualified[47]—a kind of fundamentalist affirmative action. The political role of the cleric in the new system is symbolized in the Vilayat-e Faqih. As figure 5.2 demonstrates, the office of the Faqih occupied by Khomeini is the central institution in the state structure.

Since the Shah's overthrow, the participation of the clerics in exercising direct political power has increased substantially. According to James Bill,[48] already in the first Majlis "213 deputies were seated. Of 200 identifiable deputies, 43 were Mullahs. This number increased to 55 after the election of July 24, 1981, which was called to choose a new president and to find replacements for those deputies who were assassinated in the bombing of June 28, 1981. Seventeen of the 27 newly-elected Majlis deputies were mullahs . . . the clerics held eight of the chairmanships and seven of the deputy chairmanships of the 23 parliamentary committees. Since the establishment of the Islamic Republic, clerics have also held the office of Prime Minister and occupied many cabinet and subcabinet posts. They have also gained considerable influence in the country's security apparatus. After Rajai's assassination, a cleric, Hojjat al-Islam Ali Khamenei, was elected as the country's president. Ali Akbar Hashemi-Rafsanjani, a cleric, is the Majlis speaker, and another cleric, Ayatollah Musavi Ardebili, is the country's chief justice, thereby putting clerics in charge of all three branches of government. Six members of the Council of Guardians are clerics, the other six are jurists nominated by the Supreme Court and approved by the Majlis.[49] According to the "Headquarters of Culture" a cleric will be assigned to each college and univer-

Figure 5.2   State Structures of the Islamic Republic of Iran

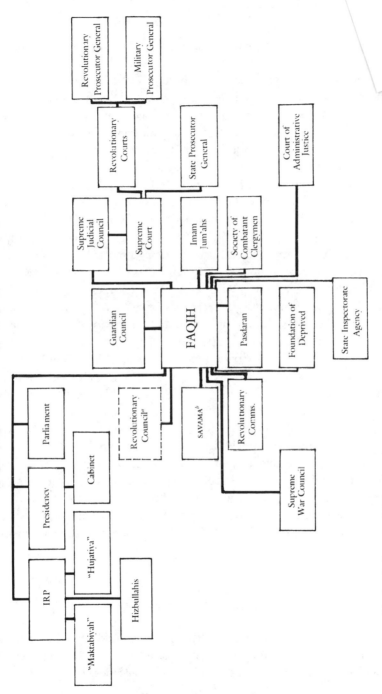

[a]Dissolved in September 1980.
[b]Secret police.
SOURCE: Shahrough Akhavi, "Clerical Politics in Iran since 1979," in *The Iranian Revolution and the Islamic Republic*, Conference Proceedings (Washington, D. C.: Middle East Institute, 1982), p. 19.

sity in order to exercise surveillance over the cultural activities in these institutions."[50]

The IRP provides people to hold political offices at all levels. Non–party members have held high offices (for example former President Ra-jai) but only as long as they enjoy the confidence of the party. The IRP has carried out several purges of the bureaucracy, "in order to cleanse government agencies of corruption," and staff them with party members, or those whom the party can trust. The party plays an important role in politicization of the masses. It has organized several thousand ideological classes, it has organized the Basij (a paramilitary force active both in do-mestic security and in the war against Iraq), and the Revolutionary Guards, and it continuously mobilizes support for the regime's policies, some of which, such as the war against Iraq, have required substantial sacrifices on the part of the population. Local IRP leaders and clerics representing the Imam have substantial power. Government leaders meet with them regularly, and they supervise the activities of the state apparatus. Islamic councils have been established in villages, counties, towns, and tribes to help in mass mobilization and supervision of government.

As in other totalitarian parties, there is considerable policy divergence within the IRP, especially on major economic policies. The party has been a gathering of disparate elements, lacking internal cohesion on a number of issues. Resolving differences consumes a good part of the energies of the elite. These conflicts undermine party effectiveness. However, at its first Congress organized in 1983, four years after its establishment, the party showed considerable discipline and responsiveness to its leaders. Party leader and President of the Republic Khamenei and Speaker of Majlis Rafsanjani along with others were elected to the Central Council of the party for two years.[51] The fundamentalists have successfully passed sev-eral bills, such as the retribution bill and penal code, in order to "Islamize society."[52]

The Role of the Leader

Several analysts have emphasized the role of an undisputed leader with a cult of personality as an essential characteristic of totalitarian systems.[53] A totalitarian system can exist without such a leader, but in general it appears that in the phase of consolidation such leadership is highly probable, in totalitarianism both of the right and of the left.

In Iran, obviously, this is true in regard to Khomeini. He has been the
regime's most important asset, giving it legitimacy and continuity in the
face of massive inconsistencies of policy and personnel. Other political
leaders have sought to associate themselves and their policies with him in
order to gain legitimacy, while religious leaders who are in disagreement
with his course appear at times to have consciously suppressed their disagreement in order to preserve his role as the integration point for a society already in uproar. Khomeini's supporters have built an image of him
as the absolute, wise, and indispensable leader of the nation. Songs are
written about the people's will to die for their leader. His name is chanted
in demonstrations and his portrait continues to be seen as a revolutionary
banner. He is not accountable to anyone for what he does. Like leaders
in other totalitarian regimes in their phase of consolidation, Khomeini as
the leader wields the ultimate power. Even though he allows the various
factions to express their views on subjects such as the war with Iraq, his
views when expressed are decisive and not seriously or directly challenged in the party. His will cannot be questioned. He has allowed the
cult of his own person to go forward. He possesses the aura of the founder of the republic and leader of the "revolution."[54]

However, in contrast with other totalitarian regimes, the relations between the leader and the party, although strong, are less formalized.
Though the party was formed with his support, Khomeini is not its Secretary General. There is no evidence that he attends party meetings, but
rather party leaders report to him and seek his views. The reason for the
absence of overt relationships between Khomeini and the IRP may have
to do with the definition of the role of the Faqih. According to the Iranian constitution, in the absence of the Hidden Imam, all rights and authority of the Imamate will be exercised by the Faqih. The process by
which the Faqih is selected is not directly a party decision. He is either
recognized as the Faqih by the people, as was assumed to be the case
with Khomeini, or a "popularly elected" assembly of experts chooses either
a single or a collective leadership. Thus at least formally the leader rules
on the authority of the Hidden Imam, not of the party. Therefore he
maintains public distance from the party, although he clearly supports its
role.

The Use of Terror

Massive and arbitrary use of terror is not an essential characteristic of totalitarian regimes. However, there is a high probability of occurrence of this in totalitarian regimes, especially in the consolidation phase. The degree has varied from country to country. It was exercised massively in Germany and the Soviet Union. In China, Mao reported in 1967 that in the first five years of Communist rule some 800,000 "enemies of the people" had been killed. Others give figures between 1 and 3 million. However, in Italy the Special Tribunal for the Defense of the State sentenced over the years 33 persons to death, of whom 22 were executed; an additional 5,619 people were tried, of whom 4,546 received jail sentences.[55]

In the case of Iran, there has been significant use of terror by the fundamentalist-dominated regime. Since the Islamic Republican leaders, including Khomeini, regard their government as "God's Government" and as one of "divine justice," measures taken against those who are "waging war against God" and who represent "corruption on earth" do not have to be moderate.[56] Those who oppose the system risk execution, and even some of those who support the system have not been safe. The state officially encourages an atmosphere of fear and denunciation, calling upon students to spy on their teachers and children to turn on their parents. Several thousand have been killed in street battles or executed by firing squads. In the case of executions, the accusations and the procedures for carrying out sentences have been highly arbitrary. The radical Islamic modernist organization Mujahedeen-e-Khalq has been the main target of regime violence, but other groups, including Marxists such as the Paykar or the Aqaliat faction of the Fedayeen-e-Khalq, and ethnic nationalists have also been under attack, along with some social and sexual deviants. In December 1982, Khomeini criticized the courts and komitehs for their excesses in arrests, executions, and invasion of privacy. Whether that reflects a genuine change in policy or greater confidence on the part of the regime in its security, or is merely a public relations exercise, remains to be seen.

The use of terror is motivated by a desire for "unanimity." In regard to the political system, the tendency to monopolize power is evident. Although the IRP platform and the Iranian Constitution allow the forming of political parties as a "natural right of people"[57] and state that "Islamic society is not a one-party system,"[58] the record clearly points in another direction. The IRP platform distinguishes between three kinds of political organizations: Islamic, non-Islamic, and anti-Islamic.[59] In the Islamic Republic, Islamic parties have complete freedom. Parties which are non-Islamic, that is, which "don't have an Islamic infrastructure but are not hostile to Islam," are also to be permitted. Those parties that are anti-Islamic and that "create disorder" are to be "dealt with decisively by the government." Non-Islamic parties are further defined as those that "have a dependent outlook" such as liberals, capitalists, or Marxists, or those that erroneously mix Islam with some -isms foreign to Islam.[60] Their behavior will determine whether they will also be defined as anti-Islamic, in which case they will be "dealt with accordingly." The main objects of this latter treatment so far have been the Mujahedeen.

The fundamentalist government has established several institutions for administering terror. One is the Revolutionary Guards. The guards are sanctioned as a permanent institution of the Islamic Republic by the Constitution. A separate Ministry of Pasdaran has been established. The guards have the task of organizing a large People's Militia, for which purpose the IRP program requires all men and women who can carry arms to get at least one week's military training.[61] The guards themselves grew from 30,000 in 1980 to more than 200,000 in late 1982 with tens of thousands of core members. Ideological conformity ("faith in Islam, and piety") is the first priority in applicants. The guards have their own heavy weapons, including tanks. They have been employed against both domestic and external adversaries. At the domestic level they have attacked opposition offices and demonstrators, and they have been deployed against the center's ethnic opponents. The guards have an intelligence branch which spies on the regime's domestic adversaries and participates in their arrest. This group was congratulated on the arrest of the Tudeh leaders. Externally, they have participated in the war against Iraq, where they organized the "human wave" attacks. The guards also train foreigners to "export the Iranian revolution." As was mentioned earlier, the expansion of the guards reflects the regime's distrust of the regular armed forces. The IRP also has another security arm, the Basij, which has also participated in attacking regime opponents and in the war against Iraq. Both the Basij and the guards are the party forces. Besides establishing new organizations, the regime has retained much of the Shah's security apparatus: the armed forces (at reduced size), police, and gendarmerie.[62]

Estimates of the number of people killed by the regime vary greatly. Amnesty International estimates that as of July 1982, about 4,400 executions had taken place. The Mujahedeen have cited 15,000 for the same period.[63] They also report some 40,000 political prisoners, a figure which is also higher than the Amnesty estimates.

Political violence is continuing, and the fundamentalist leadership itself has been the object of many violent attacks by its opponents. After Bani-Sadr's dismissal in June 1981, when a de facto state of war existed between the regime and the Mujahedeen, 74 members of the ruling elite were assassinated in a bombing incident. Those killed included IRP leader Ayatollah Beheshti, 4 cabinet members, 6 deputy ministers, and 27 members of parliament. The following list gives some idea of subsequent leadership losses:

President Mohammad Ali Rajai	killed August 1981
Premier Mohammad Javad Behonar	" "
Ali Qodusi (prosecutor general)	" "
Assadollah Madani (Khomeini's representative in Tabriz)	September 1981
Hasheminezhad (Kohmeini's representative in Mashhad)	" "
Dastghaib (Khomeini's representative in Shiraz)	December 1981
Ehsanbakhsh (Khomeini's representative in Rasht)	April 1982
Sadooqhi (Khomeini's representative in central Iran)	July 1982

The regime has withstood many challenges both from within and from without. Khomeini himself apparently believes that consolidation has occurred. He has declared: "We should no longer say that we are in a revolutionary situation."[64] However, there are reasons to be cautious about predicting total consolidation.

Although the regime's opposition has been seriously weakened, it is not to be discounted. The ability and willingness of the regime to continue using terror, and the preparedness of the population to tolerate it, will be factors in determining whether the regime remains in power. Whether the fundamentalists can fully consolidate in the long run, however, will depend on whether they can establish and maintain legitimacy. This in turn will depend, given the kinds of problems the government must manage, on whether they can incorporate professional elites, manage conflicts among the interest groups by means other than a sustained state of emergency, and neutralize the opposition while maintaining popular support. One basic condition for the regime's stability and survival will be its management of the economy.

Economic Policy

Economics, or rather living conditions, have not been assigned a high priority in the Islamic Republic, although this appears to be changing. Khomeini himself appears to be in accord with Lenin that "politics cannot but have primacy over economics." As far as economic philosophy is concerned, we can make the following observations:

1. The fundamentalists, especially the more radical ones, are in tacit or explicit agreement with many of the economic concepts of their harshest critics, the modernists, on a number of general principles including the goal of national self-reliance[65] and what could be termed a kind of limited dissociation; the encouragement of the agricultural sector and of return migration to rural areas from the cities; and concentration on basic needs.

2. To this is added a philosophy of austerity and a stressing of the crisis conditions.

At the level of ideology, both the fundamentalists and their opponents on the left and among the modernists exalt the interests of the collectivity over those of the individual.[66] (As we have seen, however, this is typical of many political movements in their phase of radicalization.) Both the radical fundamentalists and some of their opponents claim to desire a classless society. Both claim to represent the interests of the workers and the oppressed. It is possible that some fundamentalist economic concepts, if not in the ideas then at least in the vocabulary, are a legacy of their brief tryst with the radical modernists. While he was in grace, Bani-Sadr gave speeches with a fairly orthodox "Third World Marxist" content, apparently without encountering opposition from the fundamentalists. Even after his flight to Paris, when he had few good things to say about his former partners,[67] he still asserted that there had been no harsh disagreements over such issues as land reform. Disagreement had been over the issue of who was to hold power, and the only real conflict over economic questions had been in relation to the issue of foreign imports and consumer goods.

The IRP program, which reflects the views of those who are radicals on economic issues, is identical to many contemporary leftist programs. For example it is stated that "in Islam's revolution there will be no room for the domination of capital, such as is fundamental to capitalism."[68] Private property is recognized, but has conditions placed on it. These conditions are vaguely summarized as the "absence of exploitation," something that is to be achieved by workers working for themselves either by depending on their own capital or by borrowing it interest-free from the state.

Article 43 of the Iranian Constitution makes the state responsible for meeting the essential needs of the population in regard to food, housing, clothing, health care, education, and the "minimum necessary to establish a family." The Constitution also promises housing for everyone, and the IRP has argued that land for this housing should be provided free and the government should make interest-free loans available for construction. The Pahlavi Foundation has been succeeded by the Mustazafin Foundation.[69] Several other organizations intended to help the poor have been established, such as the Foundation for Housing and Imam's assistance committees. The state is also supposed to provide employment for all those who are capable of working. To foster self-reliance, this is supposed to take place by the provision of interest-free loans to small businesses. The parliament has passed laws nationalizing external trade, banks, and insurance companies, a goal important to the radical modernists. However, the Council of Guardians has opposed the nationalization measure even though the IRP program favors foreign trade nationalization, indicating disagreement among party members on the issue.[70]

Agriculture

In their programs and speeches, fundmentalist leaders place great stress on agriculture. In Paris, Khomeini had told us that the "Shah had destroyed the country's agriculture" and promised that the "agricultural health" of Iran would be restored.[71] The new regime declared a jihad against agricultural backwardness, too. An agency called Jihadi Sazandegi (Holy War for Construction) was established on orders of Khomeini in 1979. This organization among other things has focused on agricultural problems, building roads, digging wells, and providing tractors at subsidized rates. One main problem blocking agricultural growth is the uncertainty about land ownership. After the overthrow of the Shah there were many unauthorized land seizures. In some cases the takeovers were subsequently validated by the revolutionary komitehs, but in other cases the government ruled in favor of the landowners.[72] In September 1979, under the Bazargan government, a modest land reform program was passed. Fearing the breakdown of law and order in the countryside, the government discouraged unauthorized seizures. Khomeini himself intervened to prevent the spreading disorder.[73]

After the fall of the Bazargan government, in April 1980 the Revolutionary Council passed a sweeping land reform program. There was considerable opposition to this program within the IRP. Many religious leaders, such as Ayatollahs Qumi and Golpaygani, opposed the law on a doctrinal basis. The IRP platform itself does not take a position on land reform,[74] and some IRP leaders own considerable amounts of land themselves. Some of the clerics who had lost land under the Shah have since reclaimed their property and at times even augmented it substantially. The law was creating disorder in the rural areas; at times lands were taken and distributed without authorization. Some of the lands taken without authorization have been returned. The April law was suspended in November 1980. Subsequently the Majlis passed another land reform, but it was rejected by the Council of Guardians. So far the Majlis has not been able to reach a consensus on a new land reform law that would be acceptable to the Council of Guardians.

Data on what is happening to Iranian agriculture is sketchy. According to the Tehran government, agricultural production in terms of constant rials for the year after the overthrow of the Shah increased from 327.3 billion rials in 1356 (Iranian year, March 1977–March 1978) to 357.6 billion in 1358 (March 1979–March 1980). However, government data show a reduction in land cultivated for wheat and barley for 1359, perhaps reflecting greater concern about the uncertain government policy on land reform, and also because of the Iran-Iraq war and occupation of some Iranian territory by Iraq.[75]

Officials in rural areas have on occasion resisted the activities of the Jihadi Sazandegi, which they have regarded as intrusions into their sphere. The Jihadis, in turn, see themselves as independent and have no use for the existing bureaucratic structures. The Jihadis might get a ministry of their own. According to government data the Jihadis have provided considerable services for the Islamic Republic. They claim that during 1979 and 1980, they built 1,934 houses, 1,997 schools, 484 mosques, 1,464 public baths, 80 hospitals, dug over 2,000 wells of various kinds, distributed over 4 million books, and held more than 3,000 literacy classes.[76] Official data also point to change in government priorities from those of the Shah's period, a significant decrease in defense expenditures and major increases in investment in social programs.

Oil Exports and Industry

As in the agricultural sector, industrial policy too is based on the goals of self-sufficiency and on small-scale production. Initially capital-intensive industrial projects did not find favor, and many projects begun by the Shah were canceled or reduced in scale.[77] The IRP has proposed that the construction of industrial areas in rural parts of the country should be given priority over urban projects in order to encourage reverse migration. Implementing these ideas has proven difficult, and the economic situation of the country has been marked by severe problems. In 1981, almost one-third of the urban labor force was unemployed, inflation was between 30 and 100 percent, oil income was declining, many important goods were rationed, the GDP was falling, and the country's financial position was not good. The depressed level of industrial productivity is shown in the following index of output (Central Bank of Iran; 1974/75 = 100):

1977/78	150
1978/79	126.4
1979/80	121

According to the Iranian government, major domestic economic activities had declined substantially from 1356 (March 21, 1977–March 20, 1978) to 1358 (March 21, 1979–March 20, 1980). The services sector had declined in constant rials from 1,643.4 billion to 1,580.1, and industry and mining from 591.6 to 491.5, oil from 1362.7 to 764.2. Only agriculture showed some increase, from 327.3 billion rials to 357.6.[78] Therefore, major economic activities thus measured had declined by some 40 percent. The country's industry suffered from shortages of raw materials, spare parts, and technical skills.

As the above data illustrate, a major factor in the country's economic calculations is Iran's oil production and exports. In 1978 Iran produced more than 5 million barrels of oil a day and exported some 4.5 million barrels a day abroad. This brought Iran an income of $20.9 billion. The fundamentalists intended to reduce the country's oil exports, but not to such an extent. By 1980 Iran's exports had declined to an average of 1.1 million barrels a day, and it had been provisionally estimated that Iran would export an estimated 800,000 barrels a day in 1981.[79] However, in October 1981 it exported only 300,000 barrels. The war also negatively affected Iran's refinery capabilities. Before the war, it could refine 55 million tons/year. The Abadan refinery, which processed 25 million tons, was heavily damaged. Iran was forced to rely on its other refineries (Tabriz, Shiraz, Isfahan, Kermanshah, and Tehran). They have a capacity of 5,000 barrels per day, which met three-fourths of Iran's regular requirements. The government introduced rationing of gasoline and increased the price of gas. Other essential goods were also rationed (see table 5.1).

The decline in oil income increased budget deficits, despite reduced allocations. According to regime opponents initial government proposals for a $44 billion budget for the Iranian year 1981/82 were reduced to $37 billion. Even with the reduction, a $8.5 billion deficit was projected, and at least one source predicted a much higher deficit ($13 billion). The country's budget deficit for 1980–81 was $11.5 billion. To finance these deficits and to maintain at least some of the services promised by the fun-

Table 5.1   Goods Rationed in September 1981

Product	Monthly allocation	Price [a]
1. Energy		
Petrol/Gasoline	20 litres/consumer	30 rials/litre
Motor Oil	1 litre/consumer	45 "/litre
Kerosene	60 litres/household	2.5 "/litre
Gasoil	500 litre/household	10 "/litre
2. Foodstuff		
Frozen chicken	1200 grams/person	240 rials/kilo
Vegetable oil	450 grams/"	75 "/"
Sugar cubes	800 grams/"	29 "/"
Sugar	400 grams/"	29 "/"
Eggs	1 kilo/"	200 "/"
Milk	7.5 litres	35 "/litre
Rice	10 kilos/family	350 "/kilo
3. Others		
Soap	one 75 gram unit/person	20 rials/unit
Detergent	240 grams/person	350 "/kilo

[a] According to official rates: US $1 = 79.25 rials.
SOURCE: National Movement of the Iranian Resistance, *Iran 1981* (London, 1982), p. 2. This source estimates the "black market" rate for the dollar in Iran at 300 rials.

damentalists, the Iranian Central Bank has issued a lot of new money and tried energetically to sell more oil. A similar policy was followed by the Shah during his last two years of rule. In 1976, the total notes and coins in circulation amounted to approximately 600 billion rials, but by 1981, the amount had increased to almost 1,700 billion rials. This increase in the money supply helped fuel the country's inflation, which was between 30 and 100 percent in 1981/82.[80]

Another consequence of the decline in oil revenues and continuing high levels of imports ($8.4 billion in 1979, $12.5 billion in 1980, and $12.6 billion in 1981)[81] was a decrease in the country's foreign currency reserves. At the time of the Shah's departure, reserves stood at more than $15 billion. By the end of 1981, this figure had declined to less than $1 billion.

Besides the decreased income from oil, the war with Iraq resulted in major damage to the country's infrastructure and economic facilities. Thousands of hectares of land were not planted to capacity, because farm workers were called for military service. At the official level, the fundamentalists blamed the country's economic problems on domestic and external conspiracies. They maintained their emphasis on austerity. In fact, the economic problems have two main causes: the Iran-Iraq war and the persisting internal disarray. One analyst has estimated that the war expenses comprised 20 to 30 percent of government expenditure in 1981.[82]

However, in 1982 the country's economic situation began to improve, in large part because of greater success in oil exports. According to the Iranians, income from oil was $23 billion between March 20, 1982 and March 1983. This means that Iran must have averaged about 2.1 million barrels per day of export during this period.[83] This was achieved in large part owing to Iran's energetic marketing policy, which included giving significant price discounts. It successfully pushed OPEC to increase Iran's quota to 2.4 million barrels per day. Iran increased its refining capacity to 670,000 barrels a day. And as we shall see, it signed a number of trade agreements with countries, even those considered hostile, to meet the country's needs, from meat to sugar to industrial goods, indicating greater pragmatism. There are also signs of at least a degree of reversal from the originally declared policies against capital-intensive projects. For example, the regime has demonstrated interest in reviving projects such as a large petro-chemical complex and nuclear power plants, which had been started by the Shah.

In 1983 there were shorter lines for essential goods than in previous years, and economic recovery was emphasized. The country's reserves have gone up. The Iranian government has reported dramatic decreases in both unemployment and inflation.[84] The regime has been careful not to alienate the middle class with excessive radicalism in regard to private property and profit, although there are basic disagreements on these matters within the IRP. Even during the time of economic austerity, the regime apparently managed to meet the basic needs of the country's population in spite of the problems. It made special efforts to distribute goods to those sectors of the population it regarded as critical, the lower classes.[85] The government distributed food and other supplies at subsidized rates, through Islamic Cooperatives and mosques, hoping to maintain the religious institutions as central in the Islamic Republic.[86]

Several factors will affect Tehran's future economic performance. A major factor will be the economics of oil. Substantial reduction in Iran's oil production capability or its price for oil will have a negative effect.

Another factor influencing economic performance is the availability of technical and managerial skills. Since the overthrow of the Shah, thousands of skilled personnel and professionals have left the country. The closing of the universities and 122 centers of higher education, where some 400,000 students were registered in 1980, has also negatively affected the availability of skilled personnel and set the stage for even more serious shortages of expertise. The universities have been reopened, and the regime has made some effort to attract back some of the technical experts who had left the country. How many will return home is unclear. There are continuing reports of conflicts between technocrats and religious leaders who are at times put in charge of government agencies. Internal elite conflicts have prevented the emergence of cohesive programs and interfered with the government's ability to carry out those programs that do exist. Internal conflicts within the IRP have led to paralysis on major issues. Some of these problems are likely to persist. However, it appears that the regime, or at least the more conservative faction in it, believes that deemphasizing the significance of economic matters may be effective in the short term; but in the longer term, the "price of melons" acquires greater weight. An increase in economic problems might well increase regime vulnerability.

The Minorities: Nation-Building and Consolidation

Iran is a multiethnic polity. Although the relative number of various ethnic minorities in the population is a matter of controversy, a recent estimate of the German Orient Institute holds that the Iranian minorities (ethnic and religious) constitute as much as 53 percent of the population.[87]

As in other multiethnic polities, the subordinate areas have presented a major obstacle to the extension of central power in the past. Ethnic identity in Iran remains sharp and has become more politicized. Modernization literature has generally treated ethnicity as a problem to be resolved in the ordinary course of modernization. Fragmented loyalties were expected to give way to the larger ones, the nation-state, as the focus of identity. In fact, the reverse is happening, a fact that has become increasingly recognized.[88] The climate of nationalism, of social change, and of confrontation has encouraged not only trends toward national and even supranational movements, but also new trends toward particularism, such as ethnicity and sectarianism. Therefore, many countries, including Iran, face the threat of internal instability from politicization of ethnic groups. Some of the analyses based on this recognition have gone to the other extreme, predicting the disintegration of multiethnic states such as Iran under the pressures of ethnic nationalism.[89] Although ethnic nationalism will further complicate the many administrative and political dilemmas that states like Iran face, without massive outside intervention on the side of ethnic nationalists or total breakdown of the center, balkanization is unlikely.[90]

Like the Pahlavis, the fundamentalists oppose ethnic nationalism. According to the IRP, loyalty to Islam is "dominant" (or supreme) over all other loyalties. It wants to incorporate ethnic minorities into the state on the basis of Islamic solidarity. The emphasis on Islam has dramatically changed the relative position of religious minorities, especially the Bahais, who are not regarded as a recognized religious group. According to Khomeini, "the Baha'is are not a sect but a party; which was previously supported by Britain and now the United States. The Baha'is are also spies just like the Tudeh."[91] They have been defined as an evil group, making their persecution a morally acceptable deed.

On the ethnic minorities the official policy is that all Muslims belong to one nation and that ethnic nationalism weakens the unity of the Muslims and makes them vulnerable to external manipulation.[92] The Iranian Constitution includes some provisions for regional control of local affairs through local councils elected by the local populations. However, the fundamentalists have stated that they would respect ethnic languages and customs and that minorities shall be free to pursue their own literature and culture. The have also forbidden discrimination against ethnic minorities as anti-Islamic.

Since the overthrow of the Shah, relations between the central government and ethnic minorities have been problematic. After Khomeini's takeover, with the relative degradation of the center's power and the many conflicts within the ruling group, many ethnic nationalists detected an opportunity to push for a variety of local demands, especially increased autonomy. The Kurds were the most active and insistent. Their demands were pushed by the Kurdish Democratic Party (KDP) established in 1947 and currently headed by Abdol Rahman Qassemlou, who had returned to Iran after twenty years of exile. Similar demands were pushed by Sheikh Ezzedin Hussein, a local religious leader.[93] The KDP denied that it was secessionist. These demands had the support of centrist parties such as Fedayeen (Aqaliat) and Mujahedeen, who looked at the Kurds as one instrument for weakening the Khomeini regime. Monarchists have a similar approach toward the Kurds.

Another trend in Kurdistan has been to support Khomeini and seek a compromise between the KDP and the center. After the revolution several revolutionary committees sprang up in the area to rally support for the new government; even some elements within the KDP, who in June 1980 split from the party.[94] The Azeris in Kurdistan have also been pro-center and attacked those suspected of secessionist tendencies.[95]

A third approach was represented by a group called Komeleh. It opposed any compromise with Khomeini's regime, regarding it as hostile to progressive forces. It accused the KDP of being soft against Khomeini and of being sympathetic to the Soviet Union.

The interaction between the center and the Kurdish areas since the revolution has led to many violent encounters. The center's policies have vacillated between general use of punitive measures and occasional compromise. This policy has weakened groups such as the KDP and has pushed it to more extreme positions. KDP now opposes the Khomeini regime, and, along with Bani-Sadr and the Mujahedeen, has formed the National Council of Resistance against the Tehran government.

Shortly after the revolution, to indicate accommodation toward those Kurds seeking autonomy, Tehran for the first time in recent history appointed a Kurd, Ibrahim Yunesi,[96] as the governor-general of the area. However, fighting between Pesh Merga (Kurdish irregulars with ties to KDP) and the Revolutionary Guards continued. Yunesi subsequently resigned and blamed the continuation of the crisis on the center's lack of understanding for Kurdish problems. Immediately after the overthrow of the Shah, the Kurds, equipped with a variety of weapons including tanks, took some of the major cities in the area. The center's initial accommodation gave way to a forceful crackdown against its opponents in Kurdistan. The KDP was banned in August 1979 and Qassemlou lost his seat on the 73-member Council of Experts.[97] Khomeini ordered the army and the Revolutionary Guards to crush the Kurdish rebellion and asked the Kurdish rebels to lay down their arms. The central government offered amnesty to those who surrendered.[98]

Many Kurds boycotted the referendum on Iran's new constitution, even though Khomeini had declared that voting for the document was a religious duty. The situation in Kurdistan improved in the immediate aftermath of Iranian occupation of the American embassy in Tehran. The KDP declared support for "Khomeini's struggle against imperialism." There were reports of a compromise between the two sides, involving the re-legalization of the KDP and the withdrawal of Revolutionary Guards from some Kurdish areas.[99] However, fighting resumed quickly between the opposing sides. Because of the disturbances in the area the March 1980 parliamentary elections were not held in many parts of the country.

Conflict in Kurdistan is continuing. The prospects for regional autonomy appear very much to be tied with political conflict at the center. This has been recognized by the main Kurdish group, KDP, whose leadership is seeking alliance with other of Khomeini's opponents, recognizing that the fate of the periphery will depend on events within the center. The Mujahedeen appear willing to accept KDP's proposal for autonomy for Kurdish areas. But the prospects for the overthrow of the Khomeini regime in the near future do not appear promising.

The same pattern holds true for the other active ethnic groups. In Iran's Baluchistan-Sistan province, several groups emerged as the revolt against the Shah was unfolding. These groups reflected a configuration of diverse forces produced by the state and nation-building efforts of the center and by socioeconomic changes taking place in the area. One major group has been the Muslim Unity Party (Etehadol Moslemin). It supported the new regime in Tehran; opposed independence for Baluchistan; but insisted on the need for quarter-Baluch participation in local administration. This party also called for teaching the Baluch language in local schools and the rights of Sunni Baluch in Shi'i-dominated Iran. The leader of the Muslim Unity Party, Muulaui Abdol Aziz, was a member of the Assembly of Experts drawing up the new constitution, a reflection of the regime's initial efforts to appease the minorities.

When the "Islamic Constitution" made Shi'ism the state religion (Article 13) and Persian the exclusive language in schools, it led to demonstrations, boycotts, and clashes with governmental forces in Baluch areas. Khomeini sent his special envoy, Ibrahim Yazdi, to Baluchistan to ascertain local demands and survey the economic problems in the area. Some Baluch tribal leaders were demanding that a Baluch be appointed the region's governor-general.[100] Later the government agreed to amend the Constitution to give greater recognition to Sunni rights, and especially to allow the establishment of Sunni courts in Sunni areas. This concession ended the opposition from the Unity Party.

There are a number of other groups active in Baluchistan. Some tribal chiefs are royalist and pro-West. According to the Iranian press, those attacking the polling center during the referendum on the new constitution were shouting "long live the Shah."[101] Several other groups, mostly leftists, stepped up their activities in the region. These include the Mujahedeen, Fedayeen, Tudeh, and Peykar. There are also at least two Baluch nationalist organizations in Baluchistan: one is the Baluchistan Liberation Front and the other the Baluch Volunteer Force.

The 1979 revolt also brought to the surface the conflict between Azerbaijanis and the central government. The Azerbaijan problem is important because this region is adjacent to the Soviet Union and the population is the largest minority group in Iran. Between 1907 and 1918, the area was under Russian influence as a result of a 1907 agreement between Britain and Tsarist Russia which partitioned Iran into two spheres. Azerbaijan fell again under the Soviet influence when the Soviets occupied the area in 1942. The Soviets were reluctant to move out of the area after the end of the Second World War. In late 1945, a Soviet-supported Autonomous Republic of Azerbaijan was established. Finally the Soviets withdrew their forces in 1946, and the Azerbaijan Republic collapsed.

The Azerbaijanis were comparatively well represented in the Iranian military and the state apparatus. They also constituted a major element of the economic elite, and large numbers of Azerbaijanis live in Iranian cities. Turkish-speaking, the Azerbaijanis, like most other Iranians, are Shiites.[102] Many Azerbaijanis played important roles in the constitutional movement, in support of Mossadeq and in the struggle against the monarchy. The Shah's government had prohibited the use of the Azeri language in both education and media. Like the Kurds and the Baluch, the Azerbaijanis, too, pushed for greater autonomy. After the overthrow of the Shah, the opposition to the center in Azerbaijan focused on support for Ayatollah Shariatmadari. The main political party in the region at the time was the Muslim People's Republican Party (MPRP) headed by Abdolhassan Rostamkhani. MPRP supported Shariatmadari's opposition to the fundamentalist concept of rule of the Faqih. Although ethnic factors were important, it was the issue of the Faqih that was critical in the boycott of the referendum on the Constitution in the region. After the referendum boycott, the Pasdaran attacked Shariatmadari's home, which led to major demonstrations against the government in Azerbaijan.

The government sent a delegation to assess what could be done to defuse the situation, but this effort was unsuccessful. Several clashes between Pasdaran and MPRP supporters followed. On January 11, 1980, the MPRP headquarters was attacked and four party members were killed. Subsequently eleven other MPRP members were executed. Toward the end of the month, air force personnel at Tabriz air base were arrested and charged with planning a coup and providing arms to MPRP members. Four officers were executed. Under pressure from the center, Shariatmadari withdrew his support for MPRP and the party was dissolved. He himself kept a low profile for much of 1980 and 1981. He has since resurfaced but has lived under virtual house arrest since his name was linked to Sadiq Qutbzadeh's alleged plot against the regime. It is an indicator of the state of relations still existing among the clerics, and possibly a testimonial to the importance the government ascribes to Shariatmadari, that he was not arrested and executed like Qutbzadeh. Azerbaijanis are well represented in the current leadership. After the break with Shariatmadari the control of the province was given to an Azerbaijani who was close to Khomeini, Ayatollah Assatollah Madani.

Other ethnic groups active against the center since Khomeini's takeover of the government have included the Qashqais and the Turkman. Unlike the other groups, the Qashqais are not seeking greater autonomy from the center but instead want greater influence over politics in Tehran. They have sought ties with ideological groups hostile to Khomeini, especially those with ties to the monarchists. The Turkmans are more left-leaning.

Although it will be extremely difficult for ethnic nationalists to secede from Iran unless the center disintegrates, ethnic politics is likely to remain a source of weakness and a threat to the legitimacy of the state. The ethnic nationalists are likely to remain assertive, and their activities might even increase. Most will continue to seek greater autonomy, while others might push for outright independence. Iran's political regime will face difficult choices in devising policy toward ethnic groups, since a weak and a highly interventionist center encourages greater instability in center-minority relations. Therefore a policy with greater prospects for success appears to be one that is characterized by moderate state building, a strong center willing to take measures against those threatening to undermine the system, and flexibility and tolerance on issues important to the everyday life of the ethnic groups. Those issues include language, territory, cultural heritage, local elites, and symbols of autonomy. The strategy followed by the central government will depend on which groups dominate the state apparatus at the center.

Opposition to the Regime and Internal Factionalism

Whether a political regime can deal effectively with the crises and challenges is not only a function of its own characteristics but also of the strength and tactics of the opposition. The stronger the opposition and the more willing it is to use diverse tactics, including confrontation with the regime, the greater the political instability in the country. Of course, popular and effective governments will have weak and vulnerable opposition. The Khomeini regime has been faced with significant opposition, which has increased over time. However, it has shown substantial capacity to withstand conflicts.

The social strata supporting the regime after the overthrow of the monarchy were diverse and included young workers and peasants, merchants, artisans, the clergy, professionals, middle-class and urban women. The conflict between the Bazargan government and the fundamentalists supporters weakened the regime's support among modern middle-class opponents of the Shah. The trend was further reinforced with the dismissal of Bani-Sadr. A large number of professionals have fled the country. The proposed state monopoly of foreign trade and manipulation of foreign exchange controls antagonized many Bazaar merchants who had financially backed the opposition to the Shah. However, the subsequent rejection of the foreign trade nationalization bill by the Council of Guardians and the pragmatic and conservative trend in regime economic policies have decreased Bazaari fears. The women who initially supported the revolt have become polarized into two groups, those supporting the regime and those opposed to it. Industrial workers have been polarized. The IRP has tried to mobilize the workers' support for the regime. As on other major economic issues there is major disagreement within the IRP on policy toward labor. A proposed labor law has been debated for some time.

The political groups opposed to the regime have included groups associated with the Shah's regime, some of its former modernist allies, and radical leftist groups. We have seen that these groups are fragmented. Among those, the most persistent and violent has been the Mujahedeen organization.[103] It has been the object of sustained attack by the regime. Along with Bani-Sadr and the KDP leader Qassemlou, the Mujahedeen leader Massoud Rajavi has established the National Council of Resistance in Paris. Despite its losses the Mujahedeen remains more than a nuisance for the Islamic Republic.

Another group on the left that might cause problems for the regime is the pro-Soviet Communist Party, Tudeh. It had a minimal role in the 1978–79 revolt.[104] It has a small following but is well organized. Many of its members returned home after the Shah was overthrown. It sought to win favor with Khomeini by supporting his regime. Tudeh leader Nureddin Kianuri characterized Khomeini as representing "the cause of anti-imperialism and social justice."[105] Even when it criticized the government or some factions within the IRP, it did so by alleging that they were "not following the Khomeini line." Tudeh hoped to encourage the regime to eliminate those forces regarded as hostile to itself and to Moscow. Apparently, it believed that the elimination of Western-oriented political groups would enhance the prospects that it might "inherit the revolution." Tudeh probably hoped that secular and modernist forces dissatisfied with the regime would turn to Tudeh. Reportedly Tudeh tried to infiltrate the military, the Revolutionary Guards, and the bureaucracy. Several other opposition groups charged that Tudeh had been successful in its efforts and were alarmed by what they perceived as the party's high representation in the government.[106] One of the factions of the Fedayeen guerilla organization (Aksariat) joined Tudeh.

Initially, the Khomeini government showed tolerance for Tudeh; its newspaper, *Mardom*, was allowed to be published when papers belonging to other leftist groups were already banned. However, the party nevertheless was the object of suspicion by large segments of the Iranian

political and intellectual elite and the population because of its close relations with the Soviets. The government, too, was critical of Tudeh, although some IRP factions have denounced it more energetically than
others. On July 9, 1982 *Mardom* was banned; some of Tudeh's offices
were ransacked and many of its members were purged from government
positions. Early in 1983, the party general secretary, Kianuri, and several
other leaders were jailed, and finally the party was banned and more than
1,000 of its members jailed. A clash between IRP and Tudeh was inevitable because of different attitudes on many issues and IRP desires for
total control and elimination of rivals. As we have seen, several other groups
including westernized modernists, Islamic leftists (Mujahedeen-e-Khalq),
and more radical leftists had been attacked and weakened. Tudeh's turn
had to come eventually. Tudeh by itself does not present a formidable
threat to the regime in the near future. However, given Tudeh ties with
the Soviets, its role in Iran's future will have to be analyzed in the context
of Soviet policies toward Iran as well as Iranian internal politics. We shall
do this in our next chapter. There are a number of smaller leftist groups
active against the regime as well. These include the Aqaliat faction of the
Fedayeen organization, Peykar, Ranjbaran, etc. None of these presents
any serious challenge to the regime.

Beside groups on the left, there are several other opposition elements
consisting of significant political movements as well as isolated personalities, secularists, and traditional nationalists. Among these is the royal
family. The son of the Shah, Cyrus, was sworn in as Reza Shah II in
Cairo. The groups supporting him broadcast into Iran from a radio station in southern Egypt.[107] His supporters believe that he would reign
like a European constitutional monarch should he return to the Pahlavi
throne. Others believe that he might accept becoming a figurehead in a
right-wing military government. Those supporting Reza Shah include some
of the generals of the Imperial Iranian Armed Forces. The most prominent of these are Gholam Ali Oveyssi and Bahram Aryana.[108] They are
said to be organizing military operations against the Khomeini regime
inside Iran. They have ties with some traditional Kurdish leaders and used
to have significant ties with Iraq before the outbreak of the war between
those two countries. The Tehran government has accused Oveyssi of
providing Iraq with top secret information on the Iranian military, including documents dealing with gaps in the radar system around Tehran.

There have been reports that Aryana's military units are located in Eastern Turkey. This has been denied by the Turkish government. Reportedly Aryana and Oveyssi maintain ties with the Iranian officers inside the country, and might play a role in organizing a military coup in Tehran. Another former officer, with no compromising ties with Iraq, is Admiral Ahmad Madani. He was the governor of Khuzistan after the Shah's overthrow and also ran unsuccessfully for the country's presidency against Bani-Sadr. Subsequently he won a seat in the Majlis election. Since then he has gone into exile.

The military has been weakened by the recent events in Iran and has been preoccupied with the war against Iraq. The size of the armed forces has been reduced from more than 400,000 under the Shah to some 200,000. The Khomeini regime distrusts the military. Initially, it purged many officers, installed religious representatives at all levels of the military, and built a countervailing force, the Revolutionary Guards. The potential for a coup in the future, however, remains, as coups are generally very chancy affairs. It is likely that a military coup with or without ties to former officers like Madani would face considerable domestic and even external opposition.

There are a number of other political leaders opposed to the regime. One is Shahpur Bakhtiar, the Shah's last prime minister and head of the National Movement of the Iranian Resistance. Once he was the most prominent of Iranian opposition leaders abroad, but his popularity has suffered, even among the monarchists, because of his relations with the Iraqi government. These relations continued even after the outbreak of war with Iran, and there are rumors that he played a role in causing the war. He has not made it clear whether he favors the return of the monarchy to Iran. He has called for the overthrow of Khomeini, the establishment of martial law, and the organization of elections. It is clear that he has maintained contacts with the royal family, although this may have declined owing to differences over the question of Iraq.[109]

It is difficult to estimate the degree of the popular support for the opposition groups. The political regime has taken several steps toward institutionalization of its power and has used its control of the state apparatus to weaken and break the backs of several opposition groups. But complete consolidation has not occurred. State control has not extended over the entire country, and significant oppositional activities persist.

However, if the regime maintains its high degree of coercion against the opposition groups and retains the support of the urban masses, those opposed to the regime might become exhausted or decimated. On the other hand, small-scale opposition attacks may go on, and areas of the country may remain outside effective government control for some time.

A major test for the regime would come when Khomeini leaves the stage. The IRP-dominated government is worried about the succession problem. Efforts are being made to resolve the issues in order to avoid increasing internal conflicts. The country's Constitution provides for one successor or for selecting a leadership council made up of three to five senior clerics to take Khomeini's place. In December 1982 an Assembly of Experts was elected to select either one person or a council to replace Khomeini. But replacing him will be difficult. Support for Khomeini might not be transferred to his successor(s), who might lack his stature and popularity. Reportedly, Khomeini himself would like Ayatollah Husein Ali Muntaziri to succeed him, although he has not endorsed him publicly.[110] Muntaziri, who is related to Khomeini by marriage, does not share Khomeini's following. He is almost deaf, and his religious credentials are considered inadequate. According to the Constitution, the Faqih must be a mujtahed: not only qualified to interpret Islamic law, but also with impeccable credentials and unimpeachable reputation. He must also enjoy the confidence of the majority of the people. Conflicts within the IRP are likely to affect both whether one person or a group of successors are selected.

There are many conflicts among the Iranian clerics and within the ruling Islamic Republican Party, not unusual in totalitarian parties. However, the exact nature of these conflicts is not always clear. Many of the important political leaders are difficult to categorize accurately. However, certain groupings can be discerned. Among the clerics in general the main source of disagreement has been over the principle and extent of clerical domination and adminsitration of the state. According to the dominant group (the IRP) and Khomeini, in the absence of a divinely inspired Imam (according to Twelver Shi'ite tradition the last of these disappeared in A.D. 874 and will reappear at the end of time), sovereignty is vested in the qualified religious leaders, as they are the authoritative interpreters of the Shariah. Khomeini further argues for the selection of one leader or a leadership council to be the supreme guide(s). This principle was op-

posed by several other clerics, the most prominent of whom was Ayatollah Shariatmadari, who was popular and had considerable influence in
Azerbaijan and Khurasan. Several other religious leaders, such as Ayatollah Qomi, Ayatollah Shirazi, and Ayatollah Zanjani, also objected to the
concept of a Vilayat-e-Faqih,[111] and to the style of government of the
Islamic Republicans. Since 1979, the position of these clerics within the
power elite has steadily weakened as the IRP, which follows the Khomeini line, gained in strength. In the country as a whole the non-IRP clergy
remain very important and could play a significant role in legitimizing an
alternative regime or helping some against others in the IRP.

Even within the IRP there are different degrees of commitment to the
principle of the Vilayat-e Faqih. Besides, IRP members disagree over important issues such as the extent of economic restructuring of society and
Iranian foreign policy that indicate the possible formation of distinct
groupings. At the current time they still appear to be somewhat ambiguous, but they may develop into factions in the future. If internal IRP
conflicts escalate they might affect the future political coalitions in Iran,
especially once Khomeini is no longer there to transcend their conflicts
by his claim to personal loyalties. Several attempts have been made to
identify factions within the IRP. The common categorizations speak of
radicals and conservatives, pragmatists and ideologues, moderates, radicals and extremists, and Hujatis (Hujatiya) and Maktabis.[112]

Attitude towards the Soviet Union and the West, domestic economic
policies, extent of commitment to the export of the revolution have been
used as indicators for identifying and categorizing the above groupings.
While there is little doubt about the existence of major disagreements
within the IRP, because of scarcity of available data about the IRP, identifying all possible factions and their relative size is extremely difficult.
These categories, therefore, have to be approached with caution.

One influential categorization has been the distinction between Hujatis and Maktabis within the IRP. The latter are assumed to favor a more
radical domestic economic program and are strongly committed to the
rule of the religious scholar and cleric involvement in the political process. Apparently, the Hujatis oppose radical economic programs, especially government control of commerce and radical land reform. They are
not enthusiastic supporters of the principle of rule by the Faqih. Under
the Shah they began as an anti-Bahai society but at the same time sought

to spread the idea of Islamic Republicanism. They are also more anti-Communist and anti-Soviet than the Maktabis, even though the latter group also express hostility to the Soviets. The Soviets seem to be following this categorization. Broadcasts from Baku have been attacking the Hujatis, calling them "an instrument of the U.S. and counterrevolutionary."[113] Another analyst has identified three groupings within the IRP.[114] One grouping is identified as "radicals" who are less hostile to the Soviets than the other two factions. They favor more radical internal economic policies. There is some overlap between this group and the Maktabis. Another faction is identified as "moderate"; its members are less radical on domestic reforms and are more hostile to the Soviets and less hostile to the West than the radicals. They have pushed for closer relations with those Islamic countries having friendly ties to the West. There might well be some overlap between this group and the Hujatiya. The third group, identified as "extremists," argue for distance from both the West and the Soviets and in general are closer to the radicals on domestic programs. There are other, smaller groups, such as the Militant Clergy Association, also active within the IRP. Placing individual IRP leaders in each of these categories is extremely difficult. In spite of disagreements, in the face of threats to the regime they have cooperated. This might well continue into the future. It is possible, however, that with Khomeini's death, the internal disagreements might become more serious and the internal power struggle might lead to the domination of the political system by one faction in the party that eliminates others. In conformity with other totalitarian regimes, the struggle could take a violent and protracted form.

At the domestic level, the requirements for political stability can vary from regime to regime. Like many other totalitarian systems, the regime in Iran would have to meet the following requirements to gain and maintain greater degrees of stability:

1. A successful method of finding a successor to the supreme leader;

2. The resolution of internal conflicts within the ruling party, and specification of its role;

3. The management of conflicts among important regime institutions, especially the armed forces and the guards;

4. Minimum basic support (or compliance) for the regime from the public and the critical elites;

5. Minimum assimilation of techno-managerial elite for interest aggregation and help in delivering services to critical elements of the population;

6. A minimum neutralization of the opposing intelligentsia, and significant ability to prevent conflicts in other spheres of society from becoming elements of conflict against the regime;

7. Control of the state apparatus by the regime and its sustained willingness to use state resources against its opponents when other measures have failed (this is a pivotal factor);

8. A degree of success in dealing with economic problems and difficulties, including the development of a coherent program;

9. An ability on the part of the regime to extend the state authority and overcome its major internal problems.

Without success in meeting these criteria, Iran is likely to be condemned to instability for the foreseeable future. What will follow such instability is difficult to estimate, although we have tried to identify the principal protagonists. Should the fundamentalist-dominated government overcome its current problems and consolidate, Iran is likely to become a strong one-party political system.

CHAPTER SIX

The Islamic Republicans and the World

Since the overthrow of the Shah domestic issues, the consolidation of power, and Iran's relations with the rest of the world have all required the attention of the new regime. The opposition to the Shah's foreign policy was one of the motivating factors behind the revolt against him.

While there have been some continuations in foreign policy between the old regime and the new one, there have been dramatic changes. In contemplating the prospects for the next decade for Iran's foreign policy, one cannot exclude the possibility of further major changes. Both the goals and the means Iran uses might change again. Some of these possible changes are of more than theoretical interest; they could lead to greater conflict in the region and even under some circumstances, a superpower war.

As in domestic politics, a review of the foreign policy pronouncements and policies by Khomeini and his followers shows a striking similarity to totalitarian regimes in their consolidation phase. The foreign policy counterpart to domestic policy characteristics of these regimes have been identified as:

1. Internationalist ideology; a call to world rebellion, especially against those states they do not like;

2. Maintenance of conditions of external stress, in part because of domestic political considerations;

3. Rejection of many aspects of traditional patterns of diplomatic behavior and protocol: substantial use of subversion; emissaries calling on

local population in target countries to rebel against their government; imprisonment of diplomats; the use of brutal and violent language in dealing with adversaries;

4. Glorifying struggle;

5. A belief in the inevitability of one's victory.[1]

Many of the above items can be found in a variety of regimes: but in high intensity and in combination and mutual reinforcement they ideal-typically characterize the foreign policy of totalitarian regimes in their consolidation phase. As we shall see, Khomeini's foreign policy conforms to them fairly closely.

The Ideological Framework of the New Iranian Foreign Policy

Iranian foreign policy under the new regime has not always been clear or consistent, and there is evidence of genuine foreign policy differences within the IRP. However, some general ideological preferences and principles can be discerned. They are articulated in statements and works of Khomeini himself, in the new Iranian Constitution, in the program of the ruling party, and in some important foreign policy declarations, and can be subsumed under four general points: Islamic internationalism, hostility toward the superpowers, a persistent opposition to Israel, and Third Worldism.

Islamic Internationalism

While the Shah emphasized Iranian nationalism, the new regime emphasizes Islamic internationalism, rejecting Iranian nationalism in favor of pan-Islamism. Khomeini has emphasized the "oneness" of the Muslim world, and has denounced its division into many countries as the work of "imperialists" and "tyrannical self-seeking rulers."[2] These divisions are regarded as "artificial."[3] Some statements by Khomeini and other Iranian leaders point to a vision of Iran as the Prussia of the Muslim world and indeed the world as a whole through the export of "the Islamic Revolution." Khomeini and other hard-line Islamic Republicans speak at times as if they believed they had a mission to transform humanity. They are not satisfied merely with staying in power and suppressing their critics but believe in the inevitable spread of "liberating Islamic ideology." The desire to spread Islamic Republicanism has become intertwined with Iran's traditional propensities toward regional domination and seeking great power status. The emphasis on Islamic Republicanism has given Iran's ambitions a powerful ideological underpinning. In a speech on the occasion of the first anniversary of the overthrow of the Shah, Khomeini said, "We will export our revolution to the four corners of the world because our revolution is Islamic, and the struggle will continue until the cry of *La ilaha illa 'llah* (there is no God but Allah) and *Muhammad rasul-ullah* (and Muhammad is His messenger) prevails throughout the world."[4] On many occasions Khomeini has called for "worldwide Islamic revolution." Messianic visions have been a characteristic of totalitarian systems. They also serve a useful domestic purpose by marshaling the fanatical devotion that such systems require, especially in their consolidation phase.[5] As in the case of other totalitarian systems, the Iranian one has a sense of self-righteousness in its dealings with others.

In his work before his return to Iran, Khomeini had emphasized that establishment of an Islamic Republic was critical for the independence of the Muslims. Islamic government would distance itself from the dominant powers, while without such a government the Muslims almost necessarily would remain subordinate to the non-Muslims who dominate the international system. The establishment of such a government, Khomeini had argued, was important for achieving Muslim unity.[6] Once an Islamic Republic was established, its defense would become the responsibility of all Muslims, for unless it spread, Islamic Republicanism would not be possible. This clear assignment of the vanguard role to Iran has a nationalistic quality and does not represent a fundamental foreign policy departure on the part of this regime. Though the vocabulary and the style were very different, regional leadership was also sought by the Shah.

However, the fundamentalist regime is characterized by considerable ambiguity on how this goal is to be achieved. We will examine the actual policies in a subsequent section, but even the declarations by Islamic Republican leaders exhibit strong differences in emphasis. These differences indicate important disagreement on tactics, and perhaps at times a calculated strategy of confusing potential adversaries. Although the various elements of the movement share the goal of "world Islamic government," it appears that some factions, the pragmatic ones, would like Iran to become a model for others, while the more radical ones would like to turn Iran into a center for subverting other governments. Some emphasize the inevitability of conflict while others profess a desire for coexistence with "non-Islamic" governments. Khomeini at times has emphasized one and at other times the other possibility, perhaps reflecting disagreement among his advisers. As evidence of a desire to seek good state-to-state relations with non-Islamic governments, Khomeini has said: "We do not believe in exporting the revolution through armed force."[7] The IRP program states that the "revolution will spread" because Iran will establish a "perfect" state that others would seek to emulate; therefore it encourages "intellectual relations with other nations in order to spread the liberating Islam."[8] Regardless of such remarks, a number of regional states have felt threatened by Iran's regime, and are apprehensive about the ideological proselytization and subversion that have been an important element in its foreign policy. How to cope with the threat posed by Khomeini has been one of the most serious concerns of many Gulf states and those with substantial interests in the region over the past few years.

While both Khomeini and the Constitution emphasize "Islamic unity," the IRP states as its goal encouraging Islamic states to leave "Western and Eastern military pacts" and make the Islamic world "a great and independent power."[9] It does not state how this is to be achieved. IRP also demands independence for the "world's Muslims and Islamic territories under foreign occupation, especially independence for occupied Palestine and Afghanistan."[10]

Although the Iranian ruling party endorses political, economic, cultural, and military unity among all Muslims, "with equal rights for all without one group or nation gaining domination over others,"[11] the program provides a system of ideological differentiation. Three types of governments in the Islamic world are distinguished, and the IRP recommends different policies toward them. The preferred category, not surprisingly, is composed of states that are governed by Islamic principles. With these states, IRP will seek a "brotherly relation" and propose greater unity. The second category consists of those Islamic countries that do not have Islamic governments, but whose governments nevertheless have the support of the people and are "truly national governments." Relations between these states and the IRP will be "good," and Iran is to "seek expansion of relations with these states as well as common positions on international political issues on the condition that truly Islamic movements are free to operate and are not suppressed."[12] To the third group belong those states that "do not have a national base and are imposed on the people."[13] Such governments are assumed to be dependent on outside powers and to serve their interests. IRP promises to support any "Islamic group" opposing these governments and to encourage members of the first and second categories to do likewise.

As we shall see, the criteria used to assess whether a government has popular support are unclear. Aside from ideology, other factors appear to play an important role in forming a modified hierarchy of preferences. The IRP emphasizes that in providing assistance to other Islamic movements, it will take into account whether this will contribute to consolidation of "the Islamic Revolution in Iran." Priority will be given to movements with higher chances of success over those with lower chances or no immediate prospects.[14] The party program also calls for peaceful resolution of border disputes among Muslim countries through negotiations or appeal to Islamic courts. Apparently, the IRP would like the establishment of an international Islamic Court. It also calls for the establishment of an Islamic Common Market and unified positions on world economic issues, and international political gatherings in defense of "Muslim needs." In such cases, all three categories of Muslim states could work together.[15]

Hostility Toward the Superpowers

In attitudes toward the superpowers, there are both similarities and fundamental differences between the Islamic Republicans and the Shah. The fundamental difference is in attitude toward the U. S., while there is considerable similarity in regard to the Soviet Union. Despite his suspicions about the U. S. and his post-overthrow resentments, under the Shah close U. S.-Iranian relations were the central dimension of Iranian foreign policy. Alliance with the U. S. was accompanied by—in fact was in many ways the product of—hostility and fear toward the Soviet Union. The Islamic Republicans, especially Khomeini and the Maktabi radicals in the IRP, are extremely hostile to the U. S. Already in Paris, Khomeini had told us that all of Iran's problems came from the United States.[16] He accused the Shah of being the lackey of the U. S. and serving Washington's interest. He said the Shah had received his appointment (*vazifah*) to rule Iran from Washington. (Perhaps referring to the allied replacement of Reza Khan by his son in 1941 and the U. S. role in Mossadeg's overthrow in 1953). He observed that the U. S. interfered in Iran's internal affairs, blamed the U. S. for the Shah's repression, and charged that Iranian forces were taking orders from the Americans. He also accused the United States of exploiting Iran's resources and destroying Iranian values and culture.[17] His views were shared almost universally in the opposition, regardless of other ideological disagreements among the groups and factions.

After the overthrow of the Shah, many agreements with the U. S. and other Western countries were canceled. The Bazargan government was interested in normal state-to-state relations with the U. S., but for reasons that will be explored later, relations between the two countries became very hostile, especially after the occupation of the U. S. embassy and the cutoff of diplomatic relations between the two countries. Khomeini and his hardline followers have been articulate in designing names for the U. S., such as "the Great Satan (Devil)," "Criminal America," the "world-devourers," etc. "America" is used as an invaluable, highly emotive category. Dissidents are "agents for Washington," the evil designs of the U. S. necessitate constant vigilance and greater central control, and the struggle against the U. S. requires sacrifices and explains shortages and cutbacks.

While relations with the U. S. have thus changed fundamentally since the days of the Shah, there has been greater continuity in the case of relations with the Soviet Union. Like the Shah, the Khomeini government remains suspicious and fearful of the Soviet Union. The enormous deterioration of the U. S. position has even resulted in some relative improvement for the Soviet Union. However, while the brunt of Khomeini's attacks have been against the U. S., the Soviets have not been spared. As in the case of the Shah, Iran's relations with Moscow have undergone fluctuations since 1979. Iran has sought not to become too dependent on the Soviet Union. Already in 1964 Khomeini had said "America is worse than Britain, Britain is worse than America. The Soviet Union is worse than both of them. They are all worse and more unclean than each other." [18]

The central documents of the new political system commit Iran to nonalignment. Principle 146 in the second chapter of the new Constitution forbids the establishment of any kind of foreign military bases in the country, "even if these bases are used for peaceful purposes." [19] Principle 192 in chapter 10 asserts Iran's nonalignment "with respect to the dominating powers." Principle 153 excludes the possibility of any type of agreement that allows a foreign power "to dominate the natural resources, or the economic, cultural, military, and other affairs of the country." Principle 154 declares Iran's commitment to "protect the struggle of the weak against the arrogant in any part of the world." Khomeini himself has called on other nations to follow Iran's example in dealing with the superpowers, especially the United States. In 1980 on the anniversary of the overthrow of the Shah and while the American diplomats were being held he declared:

> . . . I give a warning to the East and Africa, and to all those countries
> under domination and oppression to unite in order to curtail [stop] the
> hands of the criminal American government. The hands of the U. S.
> government and other superpowers are stained in the blood of our youth
> and other oppressed and combatant peoples of the world. We will fight
> these powers and struggle. [20]

The IRP program has a similar tenor. It declares that "our revolution will not be reconciled with any oppressive or domineering powers" and will "pay attention to the dangers that the Great Satan and social imperialism pose to our revolution and our nation. . . ." [21] It encourages the completion of "our cultural revolution . . . in order to root out the psychological and intellectual influence of the Great Satan America, and the Satans cooperating with it such as Britain and other European imperialists, and social imperialism. . . ." [22] The IRP declares its opposition to any "economic relations which can serve as a bridge for the return of the oppressive powers" and favors the overthrow of "imperialist and social imperialist economic, political, and military domination of Islamic countries, especially in the Persian Gulf." The IRP commits itself to "spread Islam as a humane, revolutionary, and liberating ideology among the oppressed of these nations [the superpowers], especially the workers, American Indians, and blacks."[23] The party program asserts a willingness to expose superpower "plots," especially those of "world-devouring" America, and to similarly identify and expose their "fifth column" to the people of the area.[24] The IRP also regards international organizations as "void of any real value" in solving political and military problems and charges them with serving "the interests of superpowers and domineering blocs." Iran may participate in international organizations, while at the same time seeking to expose their real nature. As far as non-Islamic countries are concerned, the IRP declares its readiness for mutually beneficial relations and states its desire for economic, technical, and industrial relations with those countries.[25] These points illustrate the mix of ideological and pragmatic considerations that characterizes the regime's approach to foreign affairs.

Persistent Opposition to Israel

Another dramatic change in foreign policy perspectives has been in the attitude toward Israel. The Jewish state occupies a special position in radical or Maktabi thinking, a position which is as central as that of the U. S. Already before his return to Iran, Khomeini had called Israel the enemy of Islam, accused Israel and the Jews of distorting the Koran, and called on the Muslims to unite and destroy Israel.[26] Earlier, he had referred to the Jews in Iran as a "cancer." In Paris, Khomeini's supporters—particularly the modernists—had been careful to distinguish between "Jewish" and "Zionist," and the Shah's ties with Israel were portrayed as an element of his foreign dependence and servility vis-à-vis the enemies of Islam. Besides serving American interests, the Shah was accused of serving Israeli interests and of appointing many Jews to high government positions in Iran. In one place Khomeini rhetorically asks the question, "Is the Shah Jewish?" In an attempt to demonstrate the close Israeli-Iranian relations and mobilize Muslim public opinion against the Shah, Khomeini had published a picture supposedly showing the Shah together with Israeli Labor Party leader Shimon Peres. In fact the picture was that of the Shah with Venezuelan President Perez in an OPEC meeting. On January 1, 1979, Khomeini told us that Israeli troops were firing at Iranian demonstrators.

Khomeini's charge that close relations existed between the Shah and Israel was correct, even though many of his related charges lack credibility. Several Israeli leaders secretly visited the Shah in Iran, and Iranian leaders paid similar visits to Israel. The two countries cooperated in weapons production, in intelligence gathering, in several covert operations such as support for the Iraqi Kurds, and in many economic fields. The Israelis modernized Iran's arms industry, which produced small arms and ammunitions and was later to play an important role in the conflict with Iraq. Although officially the two countries did not have diplomatic relations, Israel maintained political, military, and economic representatives in Iran. Iran also provided Israel with oil. The Shah supported moderate Arab governments, especially Egypt and Jordan, and encouraged Israeli concessions to reach a peaceful settlement of the Arab-Israel disputes.[27] In his meetings with Israeli Foreign Minister Dayan and Defense Minister General Weizmann in July 1977, Iran's Vice-Minister of War, General Toufanian, expressed the Shah's "apprehension concerning policies and objectives of the new Israeli Administration" and wanted Israel "to project its desire for peace and not for war."[28]

Even before Khomeini's return, the Bakhtiar government had stopped oil shipment to Israel. After his return, the Israeli mission in Tehran was occupied and turned over to the Palestine Liberation Organization (PLO). Hostility to Israel has been a persistent theme of Iranian leaders' public pronouncements. Iran continuously affirms its objective as being the destruction of the state of Israel, and its operations against Iraq, at times, have been described as measures leading to Iran's participation in the liberation of Jerusalem. In a message to Muslim pilgrims to Saudi Arabia in 1979, Khomeini said that it was every Muslim's duty "to prepare himself for battle against Israel."[29] While the Shah supported the "moderate" Arab governments, the new Iranian regime supports the "radical" Arab states, especially Syria. Iran has spearheaded the effort to throw Israel out of international organizations, including the UN. It has broken diplomatic relations with Egypt because of its peace treaty with Israel and has condemned the Fez resolution and both the Reagan and Fahd peace plans. Iran has thus become a force against compromise with Israel. In this area as in the others, however, the pragmatic component has made itself felt. In spite of the rhetoric, Iran's relations with the PLO have undergone significant changes since 1979 and there is evidence of secret arms purchases from Israel. Now it is the Mujahedeen who criticize the reigning Iranian government of collaboration with Israel.

Third Worldism

Khomeini and his Maktabi followers have described international politics as "struggle between the oppressed nations on the one hand and the superpowers and their allies on the other."[30] They regard Islam and in particular "revolutionary Islam" as represented by the current Iranian regime as the appropriate ideology for the world's oppressed. Khomeini has allowed himself to be styled the leader of the world's "deprived" or "dispossessed" (Mustaz'afin). At the international level, they support "Third World causes" on economic and political issues and "liberation movements" as far away as El Salvador and Chile. The fundamentalist regime has also emphasized that it prefers economic dealings with Third World nations to economic ties with the West. In fact Iran's trade with the Third World countries has expanded substantially since the Shah's overthrow. Under the Shah more than 80 percent of Iran's imports and exports were with the Western industrial countries. Less than 20 percent of Iranian exports went to the Third World countries and less than 10 percent of its imports came from these countries. In 1981 almost 45 percent of Iranian exports and 23 percent of its imports came from the Third World.[31] Although these percentages are likely to change as Iran improves trade relations with the Western industrial countries, they are likely to remain at significantly higher levels than was the case under the Shah.

Having described the general principles of Islamic fundamentalist foreign policy, we shall now examine how the new regime has resolved contradictions between simple theory and complex reality. While ideological principles shape Iranian perceptions, after assuming control of the state, like any new regime, the Islamic Republicans in Iran have been obliged to go beyond the largely abstract self-definition and formulate policies dealing with the real world. We shall focus on Iranian policy toward the superpowers and the region. Although we still do not know enough about Iran's inner policy-making process with regard to important foreign policy decisions, on the basis of available evidence and within a larger framework, a useful analysis of adaptation of ideology to reality is possible.

U. S.-Iran Relations

In the period immediately after the overthrow of the Shah, Iran's foreign policy reflected the "dual" state of government in Iran already discussed with reference to domestic politics. This bifurcation was especially true of policy preferences and attitudes toward the United States. The Bazargan government favored a gradual improvement in U. S.-Iranian relations, while the fundamentalists were in general more hostile. Over time, as we shall see, those favoring normalization became the victims of the fundamentalist drive for monopoly of power and were eliminated. Ironically, U. S. policies toward Iran during this period played the role of a catalyst in bringing this about—the demise of those who were inclined to be friendlier toward them, and the success of those more hostile.

The main features of U. S. policy pertaining to Iran during this period were the following: [32] First of all, U. S. policymakers, like U. S. academics, were taken by surprise by events in Iran. Almost until the last moment, the uprising was seen as something the Shah, as the decisive ruler of an essentially stable country, could deal with. For information about the strength and organizational capabilities of opposition groups, especially the fundamentalists, Washington depended on the SAVAK. Surprisingly, Washington did not even know about the Shah's lymphoma, and therefore could not assess how it might affect his behavior during the crisis. Also, the administration was preoccupied with other issues. Not until the beginning of November was a cabinet-level meeting on Iran held. Even once attention was focused, which was after important phases in the crisis had passed, Washington did not have a coherent strategy. A section of the American government, including the U. S. Ambassador to Iran, William H. Sullivan, and powerful forces within the State Department increasingly favored a strategy of slow abandonment of the Shah while seeking accommodation between the military, where American influence was paramount and which was seen as being the only institution preventing the Shah's overthrow, and moderate elements of the opposition, especially the Liberation Movement of Iran (LMI). According to this approach, the Shah and his senior officers would leave the country. Advocates of this strategy believed that Khomeini would have to support such a compromise because of the power of the military. This school believed that Khomeini's prime goal was the removal of the Shah and that negotiations could bring about a compromise acceptable to all concerned. Another section of the government wanted continued U. S. support of the Shah in order to help him reestablish law and order by suppressing the opposition. A military coup was envisioned as the last-ditch measure for stopping a revolt if all else failed. Apparently this approach was favored by the assistant to the President on National Security, Zbigniew Brzezinski.

The policy finally followed was an ambiguous one, having some elements of each of the above approaches but lacking internal consistency. For example, although the dispatch of an emissary to Khomeini was canceled, contact with high-level members of the LMI increased, especially in January 1979. Among those with whom the American embassy in Tehran had the most sustained contact and discussion was Abbas Amir-Entezam, who subsequently became Bazargan's deputy premier. He had been referred to the embassy by Richard Cottam, a professor of political science at the University of Pittsburg who had been an official at the U. S. embassy in Tehran in the 1950s. LMI leaders in frequent meetings with the Americans before Khomeini's return emphasized three points.

First, they continuously pleaded with the embassy to prevent a military coup and to restrain the army from attacking demonstrators. In a January 8 meeting with U. S. embassy officials Entezam argued that the military "cannot turn against the people if the U. S. opposes it."[33] After the Shah's departure, LMI leaders feared a military coup would bring him back and wanted U. S. assurances that this would not happen. The U. S. officials told the Iranians that the "U. S. was opposed to the idea of military coup, did not think it was a long-term solution to Iran's problems."[34] Many LMI leaders were grateful for U. S. restraint of the military.[35] They also wanted the U. S. to arrange for an understanding between the military and the opposition so that the latter would not support the Bakhtiar government and the Regency Council, which they did not expect to survive long.

Second, they wanted the embassy not to oppose Khomeini's return to Iran. They wanted to impress on the embassy that unless he returned, violence would probably increase, as many had come to Tehran already in January to welcome him and were restive. They also emphasized that the Tudeh Party was gaining strength and making inroads into the labor movement. It was important that the "Islamic Movement" rapidly develop its program and take over the state. Amir-Entezam also believed that Khomeini's entourage in Paris was more radical than the LMI. Khomeini's return would "cut out the middle men," i.e., his Paris staff, allowing for moderate solution of problems. The U. S. told LMI leaders that it had told the military on January 21 not to oppose Khomeini's return.[36]

Third, in return the LMI leaders had assured the embassy that Khomeini did not want to harm the military,[37] an institution of great importance to the Americans, and that the future government would want close military relations with the U. S. They expressed their fears about the Soviet Union, and would want U. S. protection without a formal treaty.[38]

Washington had also started contact with Khomeini's advisers in Paris. Several of these could be categorized broadly as modernist, although there were significant differences among them and some were far more radical than others. The U. S. had the most sustained contact with Ibrahim Yazdi, who was more moderate than other Paris-based advisers, although even he was more radical them many of the LMI leaders in Iran. (In dealing with the Americans, opposition figures could be ranged along a scale of hostility; Bazargan and Amir-Entezam were relatively receptive, Yazdi was somewhat more ambivalent, followed by the more hard-line position of Qutbzadeh and Bani-Sadr and culminating in Khomeini's position of great hostility. The subsequent fate of these individuals has been reflective of the foreign policy radicalization: Bazargan and Yazdi removed from power, Amir-Entezam jailed as a suspected U. S. spy, Qutbzadeh killed for plotting to overthrow the government, and Bani-Sadr chased into exile.)

Yazdi was not so fearful of the armed forces as the LMI leaders. He was also less friendly toward the United States. Already on December 13, he had told Americans that if the army was ordered to treat the opposition harshly, it would not hold together. He also reported that Khomeini had authorized his supporters to acquire arms and to be prepared for armed struggle if necessary at later stages. He also said that Khomeini was confident of support in the armed forces and warned that if "U. S. support of the Shah continued, the U. S. would suffer the same fate as the Shah in Iran." Although Khomeini wanted to avoid a confrontation with the military, Yazdi argued it was possible that he might declare a holy war against the Shah that might also lead to attacks against the Americans.[39] Unlike the LMI leaders in Tehran, Yazdi dismissed both the Tudeh and the Soviet threats and promised that Khomeini would purge and reeducate the armed forces.[40] In his public speeches in Paris and in his interviews to others and ourselves, Khomeini was more radical than Yazdi. This was not fully appreciated at the time, even by modernists in Iran, who assumed that Khomeini himself was "moderate" and blamed his "extreme" position on the bad influence of his more secular advisers.

After Khomeini's return to Iran on February 9, Bazargan was appointed prime minister, and soon afterward the Bakhtiar government was overthrown. The various conflicts within Iran affected the country's policies toward the U. S. As we have seen, the overthrow of the Shah was followed by a substantial degradation of the power of the central government. One sign of this change was the emergence of many komitehs. On February 14, some groups of Iranians (most of whom, according to Ambassador Sullivan, were members of the Marxist Fedayeen) attacked the American embassy and the ambassador's residence.[41] American consulates in Tabriz and Isfahan were also attacked, and the Iranian employees at Kapkan, one of the two American intelligence gathering facilities, held at least 22 American technicians in protective custody because they had not been paid.[42] There had also been reports of looting at the other station at Behshahr.[43] At the public level, hostility toward the U. S. was widespread, and hence there was a sharp decline in contact between Iranians and Americans. Popular hostility to the U. S. was fueled in part at least by the fact that the official media and the fundamentalist clerics portrayed the U. S. as hostile to the goals of the new regime, responsible for assassinating some of the new leaders and for promoting instability in the ethnic minority areas. Even with positioning of new guards inside the embassy, shooting in and near the embassy compound had become a common occurrence by the spring of 1979. Several Iranians working for the U. S. government and companies had been arrested by revolutionary komitehs without government reaction.

At the official level, Bazargan's provisional government wished for cooperative relations with the U. S. However, what was desired was to be qualitatively different from what had been the case with the Shah. He had been one of the main purchasers of U. S. military equipment, but the Bazargan government did not want to continue this pattern, probably in part because his expenditure on arms had been one of the more public grievances against him.[44] The new regime also nationalized several foreign firms, including some American ones. It withdrew from CENTO, which led to the collapse of that organization. It also opposed U. S. policies in the Arab-Israeli region.

The most important contact figure between the new government and the Americans continued to be Amir-Entezam.[45] In frequent conversations with American officials he told them that his government wanted U. S. cooperation in obtaining spare parts for military vehicles and, especially, a promise of U. S. noninterference in Iranian affairs.

One persistent source of suspicion in relations between the two countries was the Iranian fear of American intervention in domestic affairs. Radical modernists and fundamentalist including Khomeini blamed the U. S. for many of the instabilities that characterized Iranian domestic politics.[46] The same was true of the official media, especially the radio and T.V. directed by Sadiq Qutbzadeh.[47] Although the Bazargan government did not go along with the invective of the attacks by others and in fact expressed frustrations with them, they feared U. S. designs to overthrow the government. In April Amir-Entezam told American officials that his country had "problems" and "seriously urged" the U. S. not to interfere.[48]

The Americans who desired good relations with the new government in Iran sought to impress upon the modernists in the government, and through them upon Khomeini himself (with whom they did not have direct contact), that Washington accepted the results of the "Iranian Revolution." They also told provisional government leaders that the U. S. sought to normalize relations with Iran at a "steady pace" and was committed to Iran's "independence, stability, territorial integrity and economic progress."[49] The American chargé, C. W. Naas, told Entezam in April that "we currently are doing nothing and in the future we will do nothing to destabilize the country."[50]

U.S. Senate resolutions criticizing Iran because of the executions by revolutionary committees led to demonstrations against the American embassy. Fundamentalist leaders, who wanted to reduce relations with the U. S. in any case, took the Senate action and negative American press coverage of Iran as evidence of U. S. hostility and interference in Iran. They characterized U. S. concern about violations of human rights in Iran as suspect in view of previous U. S. support of the Shah. Washington, they argued, had no moral authority to pass judgment on Iranian actions.[51] On May 23, the American embassy, after taking note of "increasing anti-Americanism" and "emotionally charged" circumstances, wanted the government to take the necessary measures to assure a peaceful atmosphere. Since demonstrations were planned for May 24 and 25, it wanted greater government effort to protect the embassy. The provisional government had come to the embassy's defense after the attack on February 14, had regretted the attack, and had expressed its willingness to reimburse Washington for the damage.[52] It had also placed guards inside the embassy for its protection. In May, because of increasing fear for the security of its personnel and facilities, the embassy regarded this protection as inadequate. It also sought to assure the government that the Senate resolutions did not reflect administration policy.[53]

Despite the increase in public hostility to the U. S., encouraged by fundamentalist leaders, the government—especially Bazargan and Entezam—wanted U. S. assistance in dealing with domestic instabilities in Iran and in meeting external threats. On several occasions both men expressed a willingness to share intelligence information. The U. S. had already provided Entezam with a paper on Afghanistan which he found "useful." He was particularly concerned about foreign—especially Iraqi, PLO, and Libyan—plots against Iran.[54] Entezam had expressed his worry about the PLO office in Ahwaz, but said he could not do anything about it, as it reflected the wishes of Khomeini. Washington was reluctant to give military information to the Iranian government, which it feared could not protect American military secrets. It had also decided to consider previously provided information as compromised. The embassy recommended providing information on subversive activities against Iran as a useful move that could lead to closer cooperation.[55] Some papers were prepared for Entezam and delivered to him on June 18, 1979. (Former political officer John Stemple in Tehran and CIA officer George Cave visited Entezam after he had been appointed Ambassador to Sweden.) Entezam wanted briefings on domestic threats to the government on a regular basis. He assured the Americans that the recipients of information would be Bazargan, Yazdi, Entezam, and one senior Iranian intelligence officer. The two sides also argued that sensitive information should be provided orally.[56] CIA's Robert Ames came to Iran on August 21 for the first briefing. The embassy recommended that in the briefing, "as far as possible we should try to perusade the Iranian government that their internal problems have foreign support, but that the U. S. is in no way involved in this. Naturally, this will be difficult; however, we have to try to convince them in a sustained way."[57]

However, while the government was seeking better relations with Washington, fundamentalist hostility to the U. S. continued. The government was being criticized for being too friendly to the United States. In September, Khomeini declared that America was "the number one enemy of the deprived and oppressed people of the world."[58] It is possible that the radical momentum would not in any event have permitted the normalization of relations with the U. S., and that more substantive U. S. support for the "Iranian Revolution"—such as arms supplies to the modernists—would only have hastened the discrediting of more moderate elements by making them vulnerable to charges of Shah-like dependence on Washington. As we have seen, the fundamentalists wanted rapid disassociation from the U. S.

In any event, issues such as spare parts for military equipment, perceived absence of demonstrable U. S. good-will gestures, and the possibility of the Shah's admission to the U. S. served to justify increased modernist dissatisfaction with U. S. policies. In August, Bazargan told the American chargé he was disappointed that U.S. promises of cooperation and support "have not been backed by actions," that the U. S. "had not responded in any positive way" and had only paid "lip service" to good relations with Iran. Foreign Minister Yazdi, who attended the meeting, charged that the American press was "slandering" Iran.[59] Later he accused the U. S. media of organizing a "conspiracy" against Iran.[60] The Iranian view of the U. S. remained paradoxically inflated: as fundamentalist attacks on the government mounted, Bazargan's accusations of insufficient U. S. support increased, and all parties concerned assigned to the U. S. the blame for their external and internal problems. Yazdi charged in October on the basis of "reliable information" that U. S., Israel, and Iraq were involved in the Kurdish problem. He also accused the CIA of plotting to overthrow the government (perhaps "without the knowledge of high ranking political leaders").[61] Entezam, who had the closest ties with the U. S., charged that Washington had not dealt with "the Revolution on the basis of equality and respect," but was "playing a waiting game," and would "pay a high price for this."[62]

After the occupation of the American embassy, relations between the two countries deteriorated sharply. The Bazargan government fell. The role of more radical modernists (such as Bani-Sadr and Qutbzadeh) and fundamentalists in the state apparatus increased. The nature of issues in the U. S.-Iranian discussion also changed, and hostility to the U. S. became more "institutionalized." Compared with radical Maktabi fundamentalists, Qutbzadeh and Bani-Sadr were more sensitive to the need for avoiding confrontation with the U. S. until they, too, were passed by in the course of the radicalization process.

Conflict over Issues of Mutual Interest

Although it was clear to everyone that the former intensity of military and security cooperation could not be reestablished, the U. S. nevertheless hoped—on the basis of the stated intentions of the modernists prior to the overthrow of the Shah and of the continuing influence of the Iranian military—that some sort of mutual security interests would be perceived by the new regime. However, soon after Khomeini's return the military began to disintegrate, a process which continued after the establishment of the Bazargan government.[63] Khomeini and his hardline supporters were hostile to the military which had been so intimately linked to the U. S. and the Shah. They favored an increasing role for the Revolutionary Guards. The disintegration of the military establishment reduced the U. S. leverage over a critical institution responsive to its goals. At the same time, large quantities of weapons fell into the hands of those who were in varying degrees hostile.

Still, Washington hoped that the consolidation of the Bazargan government and geopolitical necessities (such as the Soviet and Iraqi threats) would eventually bring about new ties. These American expectations were reinforced by signals from the Bazargan government.[64]

The Bazargan government told the Americans it would not buy any new weapons systems, but wanted technical assistance and more spare parts, especially for their helicopters.[65] They emphasized that the supply of spares would be an important gesture of good will toward the new regime and dismissed the U. S. explanation that U. S. laws were causing the delay or that Iranians had to make arrangements for transporting the spares as indicators of Washington's ill will. Bazargan charged that Iran had $8 million worth of spare parts at Dulles airport and wanted them brought to Iran. It is clear that the U. S. government did not take any extraordinary measures to speed up spare-part deliveries to Iran, perhaps hoping for crystallization of the political trends, including the emergence of a permanent government replacing the provisional one. They may also have wanted to use the spare-part leverage to exact an overall security arrangement with Iran. The Iranians argued that the U. S. successfully found ways to provide what the Shah wanted, when he wanted it. The U. S. could "easily . . . in a moment" find ways to help Tehran.[66]

On April 15, Entezam complained to the U. S. chargé Naas that Iran's "helicopters were out of spare parts and the U. S. would not give more than 1/6th of Iran's needs." Naas blamed the delay on injunctions against the shipment of goods to Iran and wanted to "get a good lawyer."[67] The same complaints were made in a May 5th meeting between Naas, Bazargan, and Entezam.[68] The Iranians urged some action on the spare parts already paid for. Other government leaders also encouraged the U. S. to be "forthcoming" on this issue.[69] By August some Iranian officials had begun to grow bitter about the U. S. response. (One of them, Foreign Minister Yazdi, was accused by the fundamentalist press of being an American agent.)

The period after the overthrow of the Shah is sometimes perceived as a time of chill, as a cessation of relations between the U. S. and Iran. In fact, the two countries were entangled in a host of practical and legal affairs somewhat reminiscent of the property settlements involved in a divorce: even if the two sides concerned would have preferred a total break, joint interests and financial problems precluded one. Between the U. S. and Iran, contracts, arrangements, joint ventures, and debts all required disentanglement.[70] As in a divorce, pragmatic interests mixed with sentiments to complicate the reaching of an agreement. In the quarrel over contract cancellation penalties, for example, Bazargan complained bitterly that these clauses were unfair, cost Iran millions every day, and should be dropped by the U. S. as a good-will gesture. The U. S. was concerned for the interests of American companies but included complaints about the wave of executions in Iran in their rejection of Bazargan's demands.[71] At the time of the Shah's overthrow, for example, Iran had about $6 billion worth of outstanding military contracts with the U. S. government.

The U. S. expected that the post-Shah government would cancel many of these contracts and worked out an understanding for terms of contract cancellation with the Bakhtiar government that according to Ambassador Sullivan "probably" saved "the American taxpayers $4 billion."[72]

Ideological and pragmatic considerations became confused and attached themselves to symbolic issues. Of these, the controversy over the Shah's admission to the U. S. was one of the most pointed. For Iran, the coming together of their two most powerful negative images—the Shah and the U. S.—almost necessarily made this issue explosive. The U. S. was aware of this but had, after a certain point, little choice.

U. S. embassy evaluation was against admitting the Shah, believing the danger to the embassy and to U. S.-Iranian relations to be too high.[73] In response to a State Department query, the chargé alerted the department that "the clerics here are in the ascendency, and that I fear worsens the public atmosphere as regards any gesture on our part towards the Shah."[74] The embassy referred to recent Khomeini comments characterizing the Shah as a traitor "who must be returned to Iran and tried publicly for fifty years of crimes against the Iranian people." Washington would have preferred to take up the issue of the Shah's status with the Iranian government once a new constitution had been approved and a permanent government (which the U. S. expected would resemble that of Bazargan) took charge. However, if "Iranian instabilities seriously increase," the State Department grudgingly acknowledged, "there may be an argument for admitting the Shah anyway."[75]

Finally, Henry Precht, the Director of the Office of Iranian Affairs in the State Department, went to Tehran to advise Bazargan and Yazdi of the Shah's arrival in New York. Government officials were bitter about the U. S. decision, believing that it would once again bring them into conflict with the forces of radicalization that were gaining strength.[76]

Their assessment, of course, turned out to be quite accurate. In fact, the takeover of the embassy was accompanied by the demise of the government.[77] This example illustrates a pattern characteristic of situations of extreme social turmoil. Single issues are the "hold" for a sequential process of radicalization, which in retrospect can be seen to have occurred in jolting moves from one often quite superficial "issue" to another. The more moderate forces, conscious that the impetus had not been spent, demonstrated great apprehensiveness during the entire time of their power each time they were obliged to move against the current of radicalization. They hoped the U. S. would aid them both with material support and by helping them avoid having to take moderate stands or make obvious compromises. And they were apprehensive because they knew that *any* issue could become that one that marked the moment at which the momentum of radicalization overtook them.

The takeover of the embassy, although unlikely to have been planned by Khomeini, was an opportunity to weaken those opposed to Khomeini's concept of Islamic Republicanism and bring about greater fundamentalist control of state institutions. Subsequently, he gave his blessing to the takeover. Iranian foreign policy toward the U. S. after the taking of hostages conformed more closely to the ideological preferences of the fundamentalists. Although a small group of more radical modernists including Bani-Sadr and Qutbzadeh were less hostile, Iranian policy as a whole became one of confrontation with the U. S. At the same time Iranian statements about the hostages reflected the differences in the Iranian governing circle and became an instrument in the power struggle. The fundamentalists used the hostage crisis and later the Iran-Iraq war to mobilize Iranians in support of the regime and weaken its opponents. For days emotional crowds demonstrated daily around the embassy, chanting "death to the Shah" and "death to Carter." Fundamentalist leader Ayatollah Yahya Nourie called for a "jihad against the U. S."[78] Khomeini himself called the embassy a "base for espionage and conspiracy against Iran"[79] and termed the U. S. a source of "nothing but evil."[80]

Fundamentalists called the Shah's admission to the U. S. an "insult to the Iranian national honor and Islamic Revolution"[81] and rejected any compromise. In conversations with *Time* magazine, which selected him as Man of the Year in 1980, Khomeini demanded the extradition of the Shah, compensation for damages caused by the Shah, and U. S. repentance of its past mistakes in Iran. Khomeini even implied that the Americans should get rid of President Carter and select a "suitable President."[82] He rejected American arguments that the Shah had been admitted into the U. S. for humanitarian reasons and charged that "humanitarian considerations do not enter the American government's thinking at all . . . Washington is prepared to do anything, kill 200,000 people in an atomic raid in order to gain some profit. No one can believe that these officials were humanistically motivated in giving the Shah an entry visa."[83] Khomeini argued that the Shah had been abducted by the Americans "to make sure that he will not divulge their secrets."[84] Qutbzadeh and Bani-Sadr became increasingly worried about the costs to Iran of holding the 52 Americans hostage.

The hostage crisis became a major defeat for the Carter Administration. The American strategy was to increase the cost to Iran of holding American hostages. The means adopted included economic sanctions such as suspending purchasing of Iranian oil, freezing Iranian government banking assets in the United States, and imposing international trade embargoes against Iran. Washington also tried to exert pressure on the Iranian government through various diplomatic channels, including the United Nations and the International Court of Justice. It sent Iranian diplomats home and sought to identify and process Iranians who were illegally in the U. S. Washington increased its military capability in the area, hoping to affect Iranian behavior and to provide itself with greater military options, and gave the Iranians strong warning of retaliation if any of the hostages should be tried or harmed. At this stage apparently approval had been given by Khomeini for the hostages to be tried in the revolutionary courts for espionage. Apparently Tehran took the American threat seriously enough to abandon this plan, demonstrating an element of pragmatic calculation in spite of the unrelenting rhetoric.

The two countries also carried out unsuccessful secret negotiations on the hostage crisis before the attempted rescue mission of April 24–25, 1980. The failure of negotiations was at least in part due to the internal political conflicts in Iran between radical modernists such as Bani-Sadr and the fundamentalists organized in the IRP. As we have seen, increasingly the latter group got the upper hand. The domination of the political system by the fundamentalists decreased the value of the hostages in the domestic conflict and led to the establishment of greater ideological cohesion within the government, making successful negotiations easier. Besides, American-led embargoes were hurting Iran economically. Beginning in August negotiations between the two countries made rapid progress before being delayed by the Iraqi attack. However, with Algerian mediation, an agreement was finally reached.

The Reagan Administration inherited a situation in which U. S. influence in Iran was almost non-existent. It did not even have an embassy in that country anymore, and economic relations between the two countries had declined dramatically. Several issues confronted Washington: (*a*) whether to seek rapprochement with the Khomeini regime; (*b*) whether to support some of Khomeini's opponents; (c) whether to adopt a wait-and-see position until Khomeini left the stage; or (d) whether one should choose some combination of the above. Midway through the administration's first term, no clear strategy on these issues had become apparent. It appears that Washington regards Iran as a pivotal state in the region, and wants to avoid actions that might push Iran closer to the Soviets or preclude the possibility of better U. S. relations with Iran in the future. However, it has not always been clear what those actions could be. The United States has avoided supporting Iraq in its conflict against Iran, even though a number of its friends in the region have urged such support. Balancing this has been the intermittent U. S. fear of the Iranian threat to friendly Gulf states and oil exports from the area. Washington clearly would like to contain the Iranian "revolution." To decrease the fear of abandonment on the part of local allies, the U. S. has sought increased military cooperation and joint military exercises. Washington has also increased its capability for "rapid" deployment in these countries.

Iran has continued to remain hostile to the United States, and the accusation of serving American interests continues to be effective in discrediting domestic and foreign opponents.

Some improvement in trade has taken place, especially Iranian purchases of American foodstuffs and American purchase of Iranian oil. However, trade relations are unlikely to return to pre-1974 levels in the near future. The main beneficiaries of the shift in Iranian trade patterns have been other industrial countries and the Third World. The U. S. administration has placed some hopes in internal IRP differences over the issue of relations with America. However, on the basis of available evidence, it is hard to speak about this subject with any confidence. It is possible that as an IRP regime consolidates, at some future date it might become more amenable to normal state-to-state relations with Washington. But this is likely to be preceded by improvement in Iran's relations with U. S. allies in Western Europe and with Japan.

The Islamic Republic and Moscow

The overthrow of the Shah under Islamic auspices was apparently as much of a surprise to Moscow as it had been to Washington. The Soviets, too, were conceptually unprepared for a revolt of this type. According to standard Soviet analysis, political movements led by Islamic ideology were essentially anachronistic and reactionary. Since then, several Soviet analysts have sought to revise earlier views and to reconcile the Iranian development with orthodox Marxist-Leninist ideology.[85] But the events in Iran still present explanatory dilemmas for the Soviets, and ideological criticism has continued.[86] After initial hesitation about the opposition to the Shah, Moscow in the fall of 1978 came out in support of it. Either the Soviets believed that the fall of the Shah was inevitable and wanted to be on the winning side, or they preferred to encourage the emergence of a different regime, or more likely a combination of the two. Despite substantial economic and other relations, Moscow obviously could not be pleased with the Shah, a close ally of the U. S. whose military buildup and regional policies were largely aimed at containing Soviet influence. Khomeini and his promise of nonalignment may have seemed a desirable alternative. They might also have believed that the manifest hostility of the opposition groups to the U. S. would lead them to seek closer ties with the other superpower. Finally, it is also possible that Soviet observers misjudged the situation. They may have believed the religious movement to be merely the vehicle for more "progressive" social forces and expected the figurehead Khomeini to give way to the left.

In September 1978, Moscow began to agitate against the Shah and especially the United States. Soviets blamed the Iranian crisis on "American plundering" of Iran, and on U. S. interference in Iran's internal affairs.[87] On November 18, 1978, Brezhnev warned Washington that "any interference, let alone military intervention in the affairs of Iran—a state that has common frontiers with the Soviet Union—would be regarded by the U.S.S.R. as a matter affecting its security interests." Because of this declaration, Moscow subsequently claimed that it had protected "the Iranian Revolution."[88]

In their Persian broadcasts to Iran, Moscow reminded Iranians that the weapons being used against them were American,[89] and that the Americans were their real enemies.[90] They accused Washington of treating Iran like a colony and of not recognizing the right of Iranians to choose their own government.[91] The Soviets encouraged Iranian oil workers to continue their strike, and urged the Tudeh Party to join a coalition with other opposition forces in Iran. Tudeh publications praised Khomeini and the religious movement, calling them "revolutionaries" and "friends of the oppressed people."[92]

Once the Shah had been overthrown, Moscow praised Iran's new regime, especially its decision to withdraw from CENTO and to remove U. S. monitoring posts. Moscow sought to encourage the new government to deepen its break with Washington,[93] and to reorient its economic and security relations.[94] Soviet analysts described the successful uprising as a positive development because of its anti-imperialist character,[95] and even emphasized the positive role that traditional elements in society can play. According to one analyst: "Social progress in the East is unthinkable unless the vast body of traditional elements is involved in it."[96] Brezhnev and other leaders emphasized their desire for "good neighborliness" between the two countries, and for intensification of economic and security ties.[97] However, as early as 1979, other Soviet analysts saw Iranian developments as having a counterrevolutionary trend serving the interests of the bourgeoisie and the professional middle class. This trend, it was argued, included "Muslim figures" who "displayed a tendency to neutralize and to isolate left-wing forces."[98]

Since the overthrow of the Shah, the Soviet Union and its Iranian friends have emphasized several themes, although the relative weight put on some points have changed over time. First was a continuous propaganda effort to encourage and intensify Iranian hostility to and dissociation from the United States. While the U. S. sought to absolve itself of any responsibility for Iran's internal conflicts, the Soviets were busy blaming the conflicts on Washington. The U. S. was charged with responsibility for "bomb explosions,"[99] for the Iraq-Iran war, and for preventing greater Iranian military victories by encouraging Arabs to join the war against Iran.[100] NVOI (National Voice of Iran) broadcasts from Baku warned the Iranians that U. S. forces were in the area as part of Washington's aggressive designs on Iran.[101] The Saudi refusal to accept Iranian demands to lower its oil production was blamed on Washington's monopolist interest.[102] The hostage crisis offered new opportunities. While Soviet leaders told Western audiences that "we support the international convention requiring respect for diplomatic immunity," in their broadcasts to Iran they tended to encourage the hardline radical position. Iranians were told that the Shah had more than $20 billion in the United States, that the hated SAVAK was a branch of the CIA, that Washington sought to return the Shah to power, and that American leaders (including former Secretary of State Henry Kissinger) took bribes from the Shah.[103] Moscow also offered alternate transit facilities to the Iranians in case of an American blockade, hoping to increase Iranian dependence on the Soviets. Clearly Moscow's least preferred choice is Iran's return to close ties with the U. S.

A second priority was to strengthen the left. Efforts were made to identify anti-Soviet Iranian officials as agents of the "Satanic" U. S. who should be "eliminated."[104] Moscow also sought to encourage greater regime tolerance of and cooperation with the pro-Soviet forces, especially the Tudeh Party, and encouraged the adoption of radical economic policies.

Third, the Soviet Union sought to discourage Iranian economic ties and cooperation with regional states friendly toward the West. The Tudeh radio, NVOI, declared that "friends of the United States cannot be friends of the Islamic Republic."[105] Moscow has seemed especially worried about improvements in Iran's economic relations with Turkey and Pakistan.[106] Both countries were charged with plotting against Iran and with taking Iran back into CENTO through a "back door" of economic dependence.[107] Moscow has also sought to discourage friendly relations with Peking after learning that Iran was showing interest in purchasing Chinese arms.[108]

Fourth, the Soviet Union tried to decrease Iranian hostility to Soviet regional policies, especially its invasion of Afghanistan, while encouraging Iran to seek a better economic, political, and military relationship with the Soviet Union and its allies and friends. From the beginning, the Soviet Union sought to present itself as the supporter of the new regime and to offer aid.[109] In meetings with Khomeini and others, the Soviet envoy in Tehran reportedly offered Moscow's assistance in many areas.[110] Tehran was urged to "take advantage of these offers," and those opposing closer ties were attacked as counterrevolutionaries.[111] Some economic exchange did result from these efforts, but not to the extent that the Soviet Union may have desired. In spite of a relative shift in favor of the Soviets compared to the U. S., Iranian relations with the USSR have shown surprising continuity between the Shah's policies and those of his successors. After the initial Soviet pleasure over the removal of the Shah and the anti-American dimension of the popular movement, a Soviet assessment of real gains would have to present a mixed picture. The 1983 ban on the Tudeh Party and the expulsion of 18 Soviet diplomats from Tehran was a significant setback in Soviet-Iranian relations, indicating increasing unhappiness by both sides with each other's policies. The reasons for Iranian hostility toward the Soviets have included: fear of Soviet intervention and expansionism; Soviet regional policies; ideological commitment to nonalignment and hostility to all great powers; and disagreement over economic issues such as the price of Iranian natural gas purchased by the Soviets.

Fear of Soviet Intervention

After the overthrow of the Shah, both modernists and fundamentalists feared external interference. Bazargan warned both the Soviets and the Americans not to interfere in Iranian affairs. The same warning was repeated by Khomeini.[112] Moscow denied any involvement in Iran's internal problems; however, Moscow provided Tudeh with financial support and a "clandestine" radio station (NVOI). With Soviet backing, Tudeh strategy was to express support for the regime while encouraging radical fundamentalists to eliminate those forces regarded as hostile to the Soviets who might be possible alternatives to the Khomeini regime. Tudeh supported the ouster of the Bazargan government, the removal of Bani-Sadr, the execution of Qutbzadeh, and the regime's attacks against the Mujahedeen. Tudeh apparently felt that the Western-oriented political groups were their main rivals, and that their elimination would increase the prospects for the pro-Soviet left to "inherit the revolution." It hoped that secular forces dissatisfied with the regime would turn to Tudeh. Part of this strategy appears to be Tudeh's infiltration of the military, the Revolutionary Guards, and the bureaucracy.

Tudeh's close identification with Moscow made it the object of much suspicion by wide segments of the Iranian political elite. Initially the Khomeini government showed greater tolerance toward Tudeh. Subsequently, the regime moved against it, banning the party and jailing more than 1,000 of its members. Tudeh leaders have confessed that they spied for the Soviet Union.[113]

Besides supporting Tudeh, Moscow had maintained ties with ethnic minorities, which disturbed the regime. Soviet policy has undergone changes with regard to Iran's ethnic minorities. Initially after the Shah's overthrow, Moscow apparently sought to strengthen its friendship in the minority regions. Subsequently, fearing that it might push the Iranian government toward the West, it encouraged moderation toward the regime. However, this policy has changed again. According to Entezam, immediately after the Shah's overthrow, "Soviet overflights were a real problem." In one case, the government gave permission for overflight of Mazandaran at 21,000 feet. Instead, planes came at 4,000 feet and en route to the Persian Gulf dropped at least one large packet to dissident Kurds. The Soviets had also made requests for Baluchistan overflights which were not approved.[114] As foreign minister, Qutbzadeh had complained that "substantial amounts of Russian arms not used by the armed forces of neighboring countries" had been found in Kurdistan. He also accused Moscow of sending money and photographs of Iranian military positions to the Kurds.[115] Entezam reported that his government had located and confiscated eight 50-watt transmitters placed at various locations by the Soviets to "broadcast subversive material."[116] A pro-Soviet faction emerged in the Kurdish Democratic Party, and KDP leader Qassemlou has characterized the Soviets as his "friends." Tehran has charged that KDP leaders went to Moscow in 1979 to obtain military and financial assistance.[117] Moscow has sustained ties with Azerbaijan, without overtly encouraging its secession.[118] In June 1980, Iran expelled a Soviet diplomat on charges of spying. Qutbzadeh accused Moscow of interfering in Iranian affairs. The Iranian government closed the Soviet consulate in Rasht and urged Moscow to reduce the number of its diplomats in the country. In a message to Soviet Foreign Minister Gromyko, Qutbzadeh accused the Soviets of shipping arms to the Kurds and demanded an end to Soviet espionage activities against Iran.[119] Iranian hostility was reinforced by Soviet refusal to accept Iranian demands for the cancellation of the 1921 "Treaty of Friendship" between the two countries. This treaty, signed between the two countries in 1921, gives Moscow the right to intervene in Iran if a third country threatens to attack the Soviet Union from Iran or if Iran becomes a base for "anti-Soviet aggression." Iranians have feared that Moscow might use the treaty "as a pretext to launch aggression and attacks" against their country.[120]

Ideological Hostility

Ideological hostility to the Soviet Union has been widespread. Although the U. S. has been the main target of criticism for the fundamentalists, Moscow has not been forgotten,[121] and the slogan "neither East nor West" has been followed. Khomeini has attacked the Soviets on many occasions. For example, in a speech on the occasion of the Persian New Year in March 1980, he warned his listeners: "Dear Friends! Be fully aware that the danger represented by the Communist powers is no less than that of America."[122] Slogans of "Death to America" have at times been accompanied with chants of "Death to the Soviet Union" at national ceremonies and in the presence of government leaders.[123] Government-controlled broadcasting has presented unflattering reports[124] of Soviet involvement in various parts of the world. NVOI has attacked the "Voice and Vision" (radio and T.V.) of Iran as the "mouthpiece of international capitalism" for its attacks against the Soviet Union.[125] It has also attacked Iranian leaders who place Moscow on "the same level" as the United States.[126]

The Soviets and their allies have blamed the anti-Soviet statements from Iranian leaders on "liberals," "American agents," "pseudo-clerics," and counterrevolutionaries. Qutbzadeh, a vigorous critic of the Soviets, was attacked as an "American agent" and accused of straining relations between Iran and the Soviets in the interests of imperialism and on Brzezinski's orders.[127] Similar charges were leveled against Bani-Sadr and Yazdi.[128] More recently, the object of attack has been the Hujatiya faction of the IRP.[129] However, the Soviets and their supporters have been cautious in attacking Khomeini. This has continued after Tudeh was banned. When a particular individual or group is attacked, the main charge is the violation of the Imam's line.[130] Since Khomeini himself has on occasion attacked the Soviets, this appears to be part of an effort to avoid antagonizing the Islamic movement while at the same time exploring the possibility of using incipient division within it.

Economic Problems

Khomeini told us in Paris that while the U. S. was exploiting Iranian oil resources, the Soviet Union was exploiting Iranian natural gas. Because of strikes, Iranian natural gas exports had already been disrupted during the upheaval against the Shah's regime. Soon after the new regime was established, conflict between the two countries developed over what price Moscow ought to pay for the gas, although Iran began to sell gas again in April 1979. However, the Iranians continued to push for a fivefold increase in gas prices from 76¢ per 1,000 cubic feet to $3.80, which was at the world market level.[131] Moscow refused, which led to Iran's shutdown of shipments in March 1980. Moscow insisted on paying only $2.66 per 1,000 cubic feet. The Khomeini regime also canceled the second Iran Natural Gas Trunkline (IGAT-2), which was expected to be completed in 1981 and was to deliver more gas to the Soviets.[132] In a complex agreement, the Soviets were expected to deliver equivalent amounts of gas to Western Europe. Moscow was to levy some transit charges which Iran would pay in gas. Moscow tried hard to prevent the cancellation of the project, which would have increased Iranian economic ties with the Soviet Union. More recently the Iranians have talked about shipping their natural gas to Western Europe through Turkey. Moscow has tried unsuccessfully to prevent improved economic relations between Tehran and Ankara.

Because of decline in gas exports to the Soviets, total Iranian exports to the Soviets have decreased. According to IMF data, Iranian exports to the Soviet Union declined from $64 million in 1978 to $33 million in 1981. However, imports from the Soviet Union and its allies have increased significantly, from $767 million in 1978 to $1.1 billion in 1980. In 1980 imports from the Soviet bloc countries formed 8.8 percent of Iran's total imports; the figure was 3.9 percent for 1978.[133] Moscow benefited from the American economic blockade of Iran during the hostage crisis. Transit of Iranian imported goods through the Soviet Union increased. However, Tehran has been careful not to become too dependent on Moscow. Nevertheless, the Soviets have been relied on for the completion of several projects.

Conflict over Regional Policies

Two regional crises have affected Iran's relations with the Soviet Union. One is the Soviet invasion of Afghanistan, and the other is the Iran-Iraq war. Like the Shah, the Khomeini regime was concerned about the Marxist-

Leninist regime in Afghanistan even before the invasion. Like Moscow, the Khalq regime in Kabul had expressed support for the Khomeini-led revolt against the Shah, even though the regime itself was being challenged by opponents some of whom had ideological preferences similar to Khomeini's. Later, relations between the two countries deteriorated. Already before the Soviet invasion many Iranian fundamentalist, traditionalist, and modernist leaders had expressed opposition to the Soviet-dominated government in Kabul and warned Moscow against interference there.[134]

Despite its problems with the U. S. because of the hostage crisis, Iranian leaders were vocal in their condemnation of the Soviet invasion of Afghanistan. Qutbzadeh as foreign minister characterized the invasion as "a hostile measure not only against the people of the country but all Moslems of the world."[135] Bani-Sadr charged Moscow with hostile designs on the entire region and demanded immediate and unconditional Soviet withdrawal.[136] Khomeini, too, has on many occasions condemned the Soviet invasion.[137] Iran boycotted the Moscow Olympics and has taken a hard line against the Soviets in international meetings such as the Islamic Conference, the nonaligned meetings, and the U. N. General Assembly. Iranian media often discuss the Afghan crisis and portray the Soviets as an aggressive imperialist power. The Iranian foreign minister refused to participate in U. N.-sponsored talks in Geneva in the summer of 1982. The condemnation of the Soviet move has been a persistent theme in Iranian declarations, even after the eruption of the Iran-Iraq war was added to Iran's conflict with the United States.

Soviet statements to Iran on Afghanistan, unlike those to Pakistan, rather than being threatening, have taken the tack that Tehran has "misunderstood" Soviet motives. NVOI has sought to persuade Iranians that like those fighting against the Tehran regime, Afghan partisans are counter-revolutionaries.[138] The Afghans are also charged with having worked together with Israel and the United States, both unpopular in Khomeini's Iran.[139] Iranian official reporting on Afghanistan is characterized as "distorted."[140] It has also called on Iran to return Afghan refugees to Afghanistan.[141] At times, Soviet-controlled broadcasts have attacked key IRP leaders for supporting the Afghan partisans.[142] Afghanistan is portrayed as a people's democracy with a legitimate government, and NVOI has urged Iran to seek normalization of relations with Kabul immediately.[143]

Another regional crisis affecting Soviet-Iran relations has been the Iran-Iraq war, which has been going on since September 22, 1980. It posed major dilemmas for the Soviets. On one side was Iraq, a country with which Moscow had a treaty of friendship and which was a major purchaser of Soviet arms. However, relations between the two had become somewhat strained over Afghanistan, Baghdad's treatment of the Iraqi Communist Party, and the Iraqi-Syrian conflict. On the other side was Iran, a major strategic prize where Moscow was cautiously seeking greater influence, and where Americans had suffered a major defeat. Given the importance of the Gulf to the industrial world, it is unlikely that the Soviet Union did not consider the global ramifications of the conflict. It feared that if it supported Iraq, Iran might move back toward the West. Not supporting Iraq could lead to further deterioration of relations. Supporting Iran could lead to greater Soviet influence there at the price of hurting Soviet relations with the Arab countries.

Moscow's official position was one of neutrality. Moscow and its allies in their public statements emphasized that the war should stop, since only "imperialists" would benefit from it. However, Moscow's actual policies favored Iran. Apparently, Moscow had decided that Iran was the more important country and that its potential gain or loss would lead to fundamental change in the geostrategic environment. To demonstrate good will toward Iran it stopped arms shipments to Iraq, while maintaining economic ties. The Soviets offered to sell arms to Iran and signed a treaty of friendship with Syria, Iraq's rival and Iran's ally.

Moscow's policy on this issue brought only limited success. Iran apparently bought some arms from the Soviets (Iranian officials deny purchasing weapons from the Soviets), and more from Soviet friends such as Libya, Syria, and North Korea. But at the same time, Tehran purchased arms from Israel, and on the international illegal arms market, which is evidence of a highly pragmatic attitude on the part of Iranian leaders. Iran was not willing to move very close to the Soviets. As Iran began to do better in the war, and perhaps out of frustration with lack of progress in relations with Iran, the Soviet Union changed policy. NVOI and Moscow's local friends attacked Iran's move into Iraqi territory in the spring and summer of 1982.[144] The Soviets, like Washington, do not want Iran to spread its ideology to the neighboring countries. They might even fear that a successful spread of the Iranian ideology in the region, besides affecting their position negatively in Afghanistan, might influence their own rapidly growing Muslim population.

On the whole, however, the IRP's policy toward the Soviet Union will continue to conform to its basic principle of avoiding alliance with any of the major powers. Future relations between the Soviet Union and Iran will be influenced both by developments in the region and by Iran's internal developments. There are reports of divisions within the IRP over the issue of ties with the Soviets. As we have argued, on the basis of available data it is difficult to identify IRP groupings accurately. In general it has been assumed (by the Soviets, among others) that the conservative Hujatiya faction is the most hostile to the Soviet Union. Despite the apparent commitment of the various IRP factions to nonalignment, it is possible that some might be more willing to accept expanded economic and military relations with Moscow. If this is true, the evolution of the power struggle between various IRP factions could affect, although not very dramatically, Iran's policy toward the Soviets.

The Islamic Republic and the Region

The Dual Government Phase

It is difficult to classify the differences between fundamentalists and modernists in attitudes and policy preferences toward the region. The two groups shared many overlapping concerns, but there were differences between the two and within each group, especially among the modernists. We can observe these complexities by examining the formulation of Iran's policy on several regional issues during the dual-government phase of Iranian development.

The Palestinians

Both modernists and fundamentalists support the Palestinians, and both opposed the Shah's close ties with Israel. Many of those active in opposition against the Shah, including the fundamentalists, the moderate modernists, the Mujahedeen, and the Fedayeen, had ties with the PLO, especially with its dominant faction, Fateh. Soon after Khomeini's return to Iran, large numbers of Palestinians of whom Yasser Arafat was the most prominent came to Iran, and the PLO opened offices in Iran, including the Arab-speaking region of the country, Khuzistan. The PLO also participated in training the Pasdaran.[145]

However, shortly afterwards, differences developed between the modernists and the fundamentalists and among the modernists themselves on the desirability of ties with the PLO. Moderate Iranian leaders in the government without past ties to the PLO became suspicious of PLO activities in their country. They feared a PLO role in Khuzistan conflicts and were also displeased with the PLO's ties to the Mujahedeen and Fedayeen, fearing that the PLO was training these leftist groups in the use of weapons. Deputy Premier Entezam told the Americans that his government was unhappy about the PLO office in Ahwaz,[146] complained about "plots" by George Habash (leader of the Popular Front for the Liberation of Palestine—PFLP) to destabilize Iran,[147] and wanted Washington to share any information it might have on Palestinian activities against his government.

During this period, the fundamentalists and modernists such as Qutbzadeh and Yazdi (both had spent time in Lebanon and had ties with the PLO) favored closer relations with Arafat's faction, and Khomeini, too, came out in support of the PLO. In fact, Entezam told the Americans in May 1979 that his government could do nothing about suspicious PLO activities because Khomeini was sympathetic to them.[148] The Palestinian cause was of such importance that Khomeini announced the break in ties with Egypt, after the signing of the Egyptian–Israeli peace treaty, without first consulting the Bazargan government.

"Export of Revolution"

Iran's official attitude toward export of the "revolution" to other Islamic states was also a subject of disagreement. The overthrow of the Shah unleashed powerful energies and increased the relative power of groups with various "internalistic" tendencies.

The fundamentalists in general favored encouraging similar revolts in other Islamic countries, especially in the Persian Gulf states. As we have seen, the IRP program commits Iran to supporting Islamic movements everywhere. Khomeini himself denounced the Gulf monarchies as "atheist" governments. Fundamentalist publications attacked Iraq's Ba'thists, the Gulf Emirates, and Saudi Arabia as dependent on the U. S., and some fundamentalists issued warnings to Bahrain that unless it established a regime similar to Iran's, Tehran would impose it on them by force.[149] Fundamentalist clerics were sent to the surrounding countries to mobilize opposition to their governments. Khomeini himself used Islamic gatherings such as the hajj to call on the world's Muslims to rebel against "tyranny" and "imperialism." Fundamentalists may have believed that spreading similar revolts to other states in the region was not only a moral responsibility but also a necessary prerequisite for the security and longevity of their own regime in Iran.

The modernists did not have a coherent approach of their own. On this issue, too, they suffered from internal conflicts. Some shared the fundamentalist emphasis on spreading "Islamic Revolution" and agitating against other states in the area. This was particularly true of Qutbzadeh and Bani-Sadr. As the head of Iranian radio and T.V., Qutbzadeh allowed inflammatory broadcasts to the Gulf States in Arabic (as foreign minister, Qutbzadeh advocated a more moderate policy). This was done in direct opposition to the wishes of other government leaders, including the prime minister and Foreign Minister Ibrahim Yazdi, who wanted good relations with neighboring countries.[150] The disagreement may have been due not just to ideological differences but also to the fact that those in governing positions dealing with foreign affairs were obliged to be more pragmatic. The prime minister and foreign minister emphasized the importance of correct relations with neighboring states and of concentrating on finding solutions for the many pressing domestic problems. They might also have feared retaliation by neighboring states in the form of assistance to forces hostile to the government. Both Iraq and Iran had already begun their mutual accusations of interference in each others' affairs.

The Iraqi regime felt particularly vulnerable because the majority of its population was Shi'ite while the elite is dominated by a Sunni clan. Iran feared Iraqi involvement in anti-regime activities in Khuzistan and Kurdistan. Iraq apparently maintained ties with Shahpur Bakhtiar and several former Iranian military leaders now opposed to Khomeini. Yazdi, who prior to the success of the revolt in Iran had characterized Iraq as being ripe for a similar development, met Iraq's Sadam Hussein in Havana during the nonaligned summit in the fall of 1979 and sought his assurances not to interfere in Iran, and declared that Iran will not "export its Revolution." The Foreign Minister was bitterly attacked by fundamentalists for his meeting with Hussein.[151] Over time the Iraqi regime too became convinced that the fundamentalists were assuming real power in Iran and that they represented a major threat to Iraq's domestic stability and regional ambitions.

Regional Policy During the Consolidation Phase

The Islamic Republicans' foreign policy toward the region shows many characteristics of a totalitarian regime in its consolidation phase. In the hope of achieving their goal of globalizing Islamic Republicanism, Iran has rejected many traditional tenets of diplomatic behavior, thus frightening many neighboring states. The regime's emissaries and propaganda machinery have called on the people of the area to rebel against their governments. They have given assistance to many opposition groups and they have used Islamic and regional gatherings to mobilize support for their position.

However, actual policy has not always conformed entirely to declarations, and there have been important changes in Iran's policy during this period that indicate a degree of pragmatism. Like the Shah, the fundamentalists, too, have sought regional dominance for Iran and exclusion of outside powers from the region. However, they have changed many aspects of Iran's pattern of alignment and have employed different instruments. They shifted the alignment of Iran from conservative and moderate Arab states to radical ones. Iran withdrew its forces from Oman. As far as the non-Arab neighbors are concerned, after an initial period of hostility, relations with Turkey and Pakistan improved significantly during 1982. This shift may reflect factionalism within the IRP, or a desire to maintain balanced relations between states friendly to the U. S. and those friendly to the Soviet Union, or other pragmatic considerations.

On the "Export of Revolution"

With the elimination of the Bazargan government, the relative balance shifted in favor of more radical elements. This greater radicalism reflected itself in the issue of "exporting" the revolution. Speeches by fundamentalist leaders, including Khomeini and Montazari, emphasized this goal, particularly in regard to Pakistan, Turkey, and the Gulf.[152] Apparently Khomeini believed that spreading the revolution was necessary in order for the Iranian regime to survive. In March 1980 he told Iranians, "We must strive to export our revolution throughout the world, and must abandon all ideas of not doing so, for not only does Islam refuse to recognize differences between Muslim countries, it is the champion of all oppressed people. Moreover, all the powers are intent on destroying us, and if we remain surrounded in a closed circle, we shall certainly be defeated."[153] Qutbzadeh as foreign minister wanted improved ties with many states in the area, including Pakistan and the Arab states of the Gulf. He feared that the country's isolation from the West and the region might push it toward close ties with Moscow. He came under severe attack by the fundamentalists. They argued that isolation was good for Iran and that Pakistan was ripe for an Islamic Revolution. Qutbzadeh was dismissed in August 1980.

The change in Iran had the greatest effect on Iraq—ultimately, of course, leading to the war between the two countries. Historically, relations between the two countries have often been characterized by rivalry and conflicts over issues such as sectarian politics, modern nationalisms, regional rivalry, and territorial and border disputes.[154] In recent times conflicts have been most intense when rival ideologies ruled Tehran and Baghdad. In addition, there have been conflicts over material interests, such as the contested Shatt-al-Arab river.

The overthrow of the Shah provided risks and opportunities to Iraq in its relations with Iran. The Ba'thist regime was denounced often by Iranian fundamentalist leaders. The hostility to Iraq might have been due to a number of reasons. Khomeini, who had spent many years in exile in Iraq before being forced to leave by Iraqi authorities, might have been resentful about his poor treatment there. He was also unhappy with the treatment of Shi'ites, including their clerics, by the Baghdad government. The government had executed a close colleague of Khomeini, Ayatollah al-Bakr al-Sadr, in 1980. In addition, the fundamentalists may have judged Iraq to be a pivotal country for their ambitions. Besides having a Shiʿite majority under Sunni rule, Iraq may also have seemed attractive because of its critical regional position—a victory of pro-Khomeini forces would dramatically increase the likelihood of success in the Gulf. Tehran, therefore, started a propaganda war against the Iraqi regime and asked the Shiʿite majority to overthrow their government. There are some indications that Pasdaran might have trained Iraqi citizens in the use of weapons and sent them back to Iraq.

On the other hand, the Iraqi government, too, apparently saw an opportunity for itself in the Iranian upheavals. The country was isolated from traditional allies such as the U. S. and from much of the international community, especially after the taking of American hostages. The internal conflicts of the country and the collapse of Iran's armed forces led many outside analysts and perhaps the Iraqis as well to conclude that the military balance had changed decisively to their advantage. This weakening of Iran, and the isolation of Egypt after its peace treaty with Israel, seem to have led Baghdad to believe that it could easily defeat Iran and overthrow the Khomeini regime, thereby destroying the threat of Islamic Republicanism and establishing Iraq's hegemony in the region in one fell sweep. The massive invasion began on September 22, 1980, but this action was preceded by Iraqi support for Kurds and a variety of other groups hostile to Khomeini.[155]

Despite initial military successes, fundamentally the Iraqi strategy failed. Although Iran suffered from many political and military problems, it mustered formidable resistance to the invasion and eventually even moved into the offensive. However, Iran suffered considerable human and economic losses, and as the war continued differences emerged between President Bani-Sadr and the fundamentalists over strategy and over terms of peace. Apparently Bani-Sadr wanted the army to conduct the war, while the fundamentalists assigned a central role to the Pasdaran. And while Bani-Sadr was willing to accept an unconditional Iraqi withdrawal, the fundamentalists insisted on the overthrow of the Baʿthist regime.[156] As in his attacks on domestic opponents, Khomeini declared that "the war against Iran is a war against Islam, it is a war against the Koran, it is a war against the prophet of God."[157] Khomeini and other Iranian leaders also believed that Iraq's actions were in collusion with the United States.

Another aspect the Iraqis had neglected to consider was that their invasion might have positive domestic consequences for Iran and actually contribute to the regime's stability by providing a rallying cause and an explanation for shortages and other domestic problems. In addition the fundamentalists used the war to reorganize the armed forces, expand the number of Pasdaran, and move against many opposition groups. At the regional level Iran moved closer to Syria and Libya. On the other hand, the other Gulf states, fearing the spread of Iran-type revolts elsewhere in the region, moved cautiously to support Iraq. They formed the Gulf Cooperation Council aiming at economic, political, and security cooperation of the small Gulf states and Saudi Arabia. Iraq also received support from Jordan and Egypt. In order to counter Iran's appeal on the basis of Islam, Iraq has tried to give the conflict an Arab versus Persian connotation.

With the elimination of modernists from positions of significant power, factional politics within the IRP became the relevant conflict within the ruling elite. Apparently some groups favor more restraint, while others favor continuing the war until Iranian demands, including reparations and the overthrow of the Baghdad regime, are achieved. The dominant faction favors the establishment of an Iranian-style Islamic government in Iraq. In a June 21,1982 speech Khomeini sided with those favoring Iranian invasion of Iraq. He depicted Iranian "liberation of Iraq" as a step in Iranian plans for the liberation of Lebanon and Israel, pointing to larger Iranian aspirations. However, with substantial outside help the Iraqis have managed to defend their own country, and there has been no massive Shi'ite uprising against the regime.[158] Iran's effort to topple the Iraqi regime, however, is likely to persist, with the methods emphasized depending, especially in post-Khomeini Iran, on the configuration of the relative power of various factions within the IRP.

While Iraq has been the main target, the Islamic Republic has also promoted uprisings in a number of other states in the area. The attempted coup in Bahrain in December 1981 by a multinational group has been blamed on Iran. Tehran radio has continued to encourage Islamic revolts in Egypt and Saudi Arabia. Pasdaran has reportedly been training groups from several Islamic states. Iran has also used the annual Muslim pilgrimage to mobilize support for Iranian goals. Both in 1981 and in 1982 this led to conflict between Iranians and the Saudi police.[159]

However, pragmatic considerations have been evident in dealings with Pakistan and Turkey. Iran's current policies toward these countries are similar to what was advocated by modernists such as Qutbzadeh. During 1982, economic relations with both countries improved significantly, and at the same time both remained officially neutral in the Iran-Iraq war. Pakistan has been active in efforts to mediate a settlement. Pakistan, concerned that Tehran might incite the country's large Shi'ite population, has made a number of friendly gestures to Iran. For example, it has allowed its territory to be used for refueling and overflights of planes carrying military equipment to Iran.[160] Pakistan will be purchasing Iranian oil and in turn will export food items and other goods to Iran. A similar change has occurred in relations with Turkey, which initially was severely attacked by the fundamentalists.[161] The two countries have apparently been graduated from IRP's category three (un-Islamic, no national base) to category two (government non-Islamic but with a popular base) without any significant change having occurred in their domestic politics. This again demonstrates the high degree of pragmatism in Iran's application of the categories. The changes may reflect IRP's recognition that it needed to diversify its regional relations, maintaining a balance between pro-Soviet and pro-Western states in the area, while targeting the Gulf for the spread of Iranian influence and ideology. Totalitarian regimes are capable of such adaptations of their radical ideology to Realpolitik. This need not indicate an abandonment of IRP's goals, but may merely be evidence of more sophisticated tactics in regional politics.

"Muslims contra Muslims"

During the consolidation phase as in the earlier period, Iran's most immediate loyalties have been to the Shi'ites. Fundamentalist subversion has focused on the Shi'ites more than on other sects, and Iran has continued to assign itself the role of protector of Shi'ite interests.

Sunni fundamentalists (Ikhwan-ul-Muslimin, Jamaat-i-Islami etc.) complain that the IRP is closer to nonfundamentalist Shi'ites than to Sunni fundamentalists.[162] For example, Pakistan's Jamaat-i-Islami had expected closer ties with the IRP. Not much has come of this expectation.

This preference has also reflected itself in Iran's policy toward Iraq and

Syria. Both countries are ruled by Ba'thist parties. However, in the case of Iraq a Sunni class dominates the Shi'ite majority, while in Syria a Shi'ite (Alawite) clan dominates the Sunni majority. Iran has denounced the Iraqi Ba'thists but has had close and friendly relations with Ba'thist Syria. It has called on Iraqi Shi'ites to rebel against their government, but when the Sunni fundamentalists in Hama rebelled against their govenment, Tehran supported the Syrian regime.[163] Iran's support of the Syrian regime in the face of its brutal suppression in Hama, including the massacre of thousands, has strained relations between Shi'ite and Sunni fundamentalists in the region.

The Palestinians

Despite its ideological hostility to Israel, Iran's new rulers have been pragmatic enough to buy some arms from Israel. Israel's aim has been to prolong the conflict by helping prevent a total defeat of either side.

As far as the PLO is concerned, its position in Iran has worsened compared with the period immediately after the overthrow of the Shah. The fundamentalists became growingly displeased with the PLO when their efforts to get them to emphasize Islamic themes in programs and propaganda were unsuccessful. The PLO's continuing ties with Mujahedeen and Fedayeen and conflicts between the PLO and Lebanese Shi'ites all added to the strain. As the domestic conflict in Iran escalated, and after the eruption of the Iran-Iraq conflict, the PLO decreased its overt contacts with the Iranian government. Although officially neutral, Arafat appears to have moved cautiously toward supporting Iraq.

However, despite these developments, Iranian leaders continuously reaffirm their dedication to the destruction of Israel. Iran is the only non-Arab country to attend meetings of the "Arab Steadfast Front," i.e., states following a hard line toward Israel. It has pushed for expulsion of Israel from the U. N. and opposed the U. S.-sponsored Israel-Lebanon agreement. The leaders of the Islamic Republic apparently are seeking to attach themselves to the symbolic issue of an irredenta by linking their foreign policy to the emotionally laden question of Palestine.[164] The operation aimed at pushing the Iraqis out of Khoramshahr was named "Operation Jerusalem," and fundamentalists have declared the defeat of the Iraqi regime as only the first step toward the liberation of Jerusalem.[165] Regardless of the vicissitudes of Iran-PLO relations, public opposition to Israel will remain a persistent theme of IRP foreign policy.

The Afghans

Iran's public posture has continued to be one of opposition to the Soviet presence. However, while loud in protest, it has been cautious in actual policy. Tehran has not provided substantial aid to the resistance groups. Initially both traditionalist and fundamentalist opposition groups were allowed to open offices in Iran. By the end of 1982, only the fundamentalist parties Hezbi-Islami and Jamaat-i-Islami still had offices in Iran. In the aftermath of the deterioration of Soviet-Iran relations, Tehran has given more publicity to the Afghan cause and has declared its opposition to talks with the Karmal government in Kabul.

Summary

Although the foreign policy of the Islamic Republicans has conformed to the model of totalitarian foreign policy in the consolidation phase, its future is uncertain. Khomeini's death and the evolution of the conflict with Iraq could lead to major changes. There appear to be two opposing tendencies on foreign policy within the IRP. One side tends to be pragmatic, the other more ideological; the first is inclined to coexistence but not necessarily reconciliation with other regimes in the region, while the other side believes in active export of the Iranian rebellion to other countries; one side wants to focus more on domestic issues, building a strong and attractive Islamic Republic that others would seek to emulate, while the others see Iran in the center directing armed rebellion against target countries, even supporting such rebellion with Iran's own armed forces.

The death of Khomeini could have various consequences. It could intensify the rift between factions of the IRP to the breaking point—rifts which Khomeini, through his stature, the force of his personality, and his ability to settle conflicts by making the decisions personally, has so far been able to minimize. There has been little room for criticism and debate, a situation which increases the likelihood of errors. His successors, if they control their differences and continue the consolidation process, may permit more criticism and discussion in the decision-making process. Which faction emerges as the dominant one will critically affect Iran's foreign policy and the security of the region. The victory of the more uncompromising could involve Iran and some of the countries of the region in persistent military conflicts, and Iranian successes could bring about a radical realignment of the states in the region. On the other hand, the rise to dominance of more moderate elements might lead to greater emphasis on coexistence and on building a model polity, with a more abstract formulation of the goal of spreading "the Government of God."

CHAPTER SEVEN

Prospects for Iran

Although the fundamentalists in Iran have survived longer than many political observers would have thought likely, and although they have made strides in consolidating their power, the outcome remains undetermined, and a range of consequences can be plausibly envisioned. Each of these outcomes would have far-reaching societal consequences for Iran and the region, and will affect the theoretical evaluation of what occurred in Iran.

Three broad categories of outcomes present themselves. Within each of them, important variations are possible and each contains the possibility of specific events that cannot be foreseen.

The Consolidation of Fundamentalist Republicanism

Once the clerics had chosen the route of direct rule, and taken some successful steps toward its institutionalization, they gained the advantages accruing to any power-holder vis-à-vis the opposition. Even if their consolidation effort is successful, however, consolidation can take different forms and be achieved to differing degrees. Complete consolidation would be characterized by the extension of state control over the entire country, control of the state apparatus by the ruling elite, and an agreed procedure for the resolution of conflicts within the ruling party. At present the regime is faced with many real tensions and unsolved problems, including major rifts within the ruling elite itself. Iran could still experience major convulsions, before complete consolidation occurs. Lesser degrees of consolidation could also be achieved and maintained over time.

In other words, consolidation has to be viewed as a process, and this process could go in several directions. The fundamentalist regime can maintain its high degree of coercion of the opposition; the opposition may become exhausted or decimated, economic problems may be dealt with in a satisfactory manner, and the extension of state legitimacy and control may continue until higher levels of consolidation are attained. On the other hand, continuous small-scale opposition attacks may go on, some areas of the country may remain outside the center's control, the komitehs may continue to exercise partial authority independent of the center's wishes, and conflicts might become more open among various IRP factions; but the regime may still command sufficient strength to maintain control of the central government apparatus. If, despite these many conflicts, complete consolidation occurs, then Iran will become a strong one-party system and a totalitarian government. In a consolidated state the Islamic Republic is likely to have the following characteristics:

—one-party rule and party monopoly of political power and organization;
—an increasingly pragmatic approach superceding the previous moral absolutism;
—continuous use of political power to bring social changes;
—political centralization;
—an economic policy determined by which faction of the IRP wins (one faction favors greater economic centralization, others have different preferences);
—institutionalization of bureaucratic hierarchy;
—more regularized decision-making;
—greater cohesion within the party;
—increased role of professionals in running the state, although in advisory roles;
—decrease in use of terror;
—greater responsiveness to the aspirations of more social elements.

Internal factionalization of the ruling elite, and the struggle for leadership within the party, and the personality and policies of the leader (Faqih) or the oligarchy, will then acquire greater significance in decision-making and will increasingly become a focus of academic inquiry. The kinds of questions asked by analysts studying Iran will come to resemble the work on the Soviet Union or China: Can the system survive, must it liberalize and how much, must it adapt itself more to the dominant international order in order to last, how much dissent exists internally, how important is the military as a political actor, and so on. In the case of a continuation of the state of partial consolidation with unrest on the periphery, sustained opposition activity, and ongoing economic and authority problems, the questions focused on by academia will include issues external to the regime: the capability of the opposition, the possibilities of disintegration of the center and cooperation between members of the elite and factions of the opposition, and the prospects for a military takeover to end the disorder (either in the sense of an Iranian Napoleon or of a Reza Khan).

Some of these eventualities already bring us to the second possible group of outcomes.

Another Overthrow

If the regime fails to manage or resolve the problems outlined above, and the opposition maintains its activities and gains ground, then the fundamentalists might be removed from power. At present the Mujahedeen, though weakened by the coercive methods of the regime, appear to be the strongest of the opposition groups. Popular mobilization against the fundamentalists of the kind that overthrew the Shah appears unlikely, first, because this regime seems more willing to use massive violence against opponents in a sustained and relentless way than the Shah was when the crisis peaked; second, because it is hard to imagine a scenario in which the masses could be rallied against the fundamentalists by an idiom powerful enough to compete with the religious movement. It is also unlikely that the central institutions would shift their allegiance to the opposition, since coordinating such a shift would require more freedom of action than the opposition can possibly have in Iran today. The most likely scenario for a Mujahedeen takeover is premised on neutralization of the masses, some degree of support both on a popular and on an institutional level, and a period of civil war leading to a Mujahedeen victory. While problematic, such an outcome might be possible if the traditionalists, disturbed over the continuing disorder and displeased with the sociopolitical model of the fundamentalists, enter into an alliance with the modernists, both radical and moderate, on the basis of a consultative role for the clergy as envisaged by the 1905 Constitution. Some crucial elements within the institutions would also have to support a change.

Intervention of the Military

Several of the opposition groups, especially the monarchists and the secularist forces on the left, such as the Tudeh Party and the Fedayeen, are too weak and lacking in popular support to pose a direct challenge to the fundamentalists. They could come to power only if sponsored by the military. The regime itself has been fearful of the military and has developed the Revolutionary Guards to counterbalance them. Any successful coup attempt would be premised on the neutralization or cooperation of the Pasdaran; otherwise, a protracted conflict would ensue between the guard and the army from which either could emerge victorious, with different consequences. A strong military leader or a military group could undertake this independently, or they could act as agents of some other group—the monarchists, the secular left, the modernists, or some combination thereof. If they acted successfully and alone, a military dictatorship of uncertain duration could be expected to result; otherwise the form of government would depend on the nature of the coalition, but an extended period of authoritarian rule appears likely in any of these cases. Their weakness as independent actors must by now be apparent to all the opposition groups; therefore it appears likely that all of them will attempt to engage in infiltration of important state institutions, especially the military and the Pasdaran.

One factor that complicates any analysis in an already convoluted situation is the crucial role that could be played by external actors. Given the importance of Iran, the documented tendency of the great powers to become involved, and the inclination of the internal protagonists to seek outside support, the configuration of external linkages might be a determining factor in the outcome of the internal power struggle in Iran. Whether Islamic Republicanism in Iran, in the long run, proves to be a viable form of social and political organization remains to be seen. However, regardless of what happens there, Islamic Republicanism will remain a powerful political force in the region, unlikely to be ignored in the near future.

NOTES

1. CRISIS IN IRAN, CRISIS IN DEVELOPMENT THEORY

1. J. M. Balfour, *Recent Happenings in Persia* (Edinburgh and London: Blackwood, 1922), p. 288.

2. Samuel Huntington, "The Change to Change," *Comparative Politics* (April 1971).

3. Ali Mazrui, "From Social Darwinism to Current Theories of Modernization: A Tradition of Analysis," *World Politics* (October 1968), 21(1).

4. Alex Inkeles and David Smith, *Becoming Modern: Individual Change In Six Developing Countries* (Cambridge: Harvard University Press, 1974).

5. Gabriel Almond and James Coleman, eds., *The Politics of the Developing Areas* (Princeton: Princeton University Press, 1960), p. 64.

6. Dankwart A. Rustow, "The Politics of the Near East," in Almond and Coleman, *The Politics of the Developing Areas*, p. 387.

7. Lucian Pye, *Aspects of Political Development* (Boston: Little, Brown, 1966), p. 10.

8. Ibid.

9. Inkeles and Smith, *Becoming Modern*.

10. Gabriel Almond, *Political Development: Essays in Heuristic Theory* (Boston: Little, Brown, 1970), p. 37.

11. Daniel Lerner, *The Passing of Traditional Society: Modernizing the Middle East* (Glencoe, Ill.: Free Press, 1958).

12. Inkeles and Smith, *Becoming Modern*.

13. Ibid.

14. Clifford Geertz, *Islam Observed* (New Haven: Yale University Press, 1968) and Geertz, ed., *Old Societies and New States* (London: Macmillan, 1963); David Apter, *Ghana in Transition* (Princeton: Princeton University Press, 1972); Sylvia Thrupp, ed., *Millennial Dreams in Action* (The Hague: Mouton, 1962); Bernard Lewis, *The Middle East and the West* (Bloomington: Indiana University Press, 1964). See also Hans Kohn, *Nationalism in the Middle East* (Washington, D.C.:

Middle East Institute, 1952); George Antonius, *The Arab Awakening* (New York: Capricorn, 1965).

15. See George Kahin, Guy Parker, and Lucien Pye, "Comparative Politics of Non-Western Countries," *American Political Science Review* (1955), 49:1024 ff.; Edward Shils, "The Concentration and Dispersion of Charisma—Their Bearing on Economic Policy in Underdeveloped Countries," *World Politics* (1958–59), vol. 2; Lucian Pye, "The Non-Western Political Process," *Journal of Politics* (1958), vol. 20. See also P. J. Vatikiotis, "The Military in Politics—A Review," *Journal of Conflict Resolution* (1965), vol. 9; Hisham Sharabi, "Parliamentary Government and Military Autocracy in the M.E.," *Orbis* (Fall 1960); Eric Nordlinger, "Soldiers in Mufti—The Impact of Military Rule Upon the Economic and Social Change in Non-Western States," *American Political Science Review* (December 1970); Majid Khadduri, "The Role of the Military in M.E. Politics," *American Political Science Review* (1953); no. 47.

16. Samuel P. Huntington, "The Change to Change," *Comparative Politics* (April 1971), 3:283–322.

17. Reinhard Bendix, "Tradition and Modernity Reconsidered," *Comparative Studies in Society and History* (April 1967), 9:293–346.

18. Lloyd and Suzanne Rudolph, *The Modernity of Tradition* (Chicago: University of Chicago Press, 1967).

19. Joseph Gusfield, "Tradition and Modernity: Misplaced Polarities in the Study of Social Change," *American Journal of Sociology* (January 1966), 72:351–62.

20. S. N. Eisenstadt, "The Changing Vision of Modernization and Development," in Wilbur Schramm and Daniel Lerner, eds., *Communication and Change: The Last Ten Years and the Next* (Honolulu: University of Hawaii Press, 1976).

21. Huntington, "The Change to Change," p. 322.

22. On this point, see also the critique of Baldev Raj Najar, "Political Mainsprings of Economic Planning in the New Nations—The Modernization Imperative vs. Social Mobilization," *Comparative Politics* (April 1974), pp. 341–66. The author makes the point that "most of the models, frameworks and typologies of political systems—from Gabriel Almond and David Apter through Samuel Huntington and others to Edward Shils and Aristide Zolberg—exclude the international system from consideration" and that the "prevailing model in mainstream development literature is still that of the autonomous, closed political system."

23. Dieter Senghaas, *Dissoziation* (Frankfurt: Suhrkamp, 1978).

24. For some examples, see Michael Bohnet, ed., *Das Nord-Süd Problem— Konflikte Zwischen Industrie und Entwicklunsländern* (Munich: Piper, 1971) and especially Behrendt, "Die Zukunft der Entwicklungslander als Problem des Spätmarxismus," pp. 86 ff.

25. Cheryl Payer, *The Debt Trap: The IMF and the Third World* (New York: Monthly Review Press, 1975); Jonathan David Aronson, ed., *Debt and the Less Developed Countries* (Boulder: Westview Press, 1979).

26. A good review of this direction in theory is provided in Dieter Senghaas,

ed., *Peripherer Kapitalismus—Analysen über Abhängigkeit und Unterentwicklung* (Frankfurt: Suhrkamp, 1974).

27. As, for example, by Ivan Illich in "Aus Durst wird Coca-Cola—Hilflose Entwicklungshilfe" [The Answer to a Drought Is Coca Cola], *Neues Forum* (February 1970), in which the author concludes that "the ploughshares of the domiant can do as much damage as his swords."

28. Stephen Weissman, ed., *The Trojan Horse* (San Francisco: Ramparts Press, 1974).

29. Tony Smith, "The Underdevelopment of Development Literature: The Core of Dependency Theory," *World Politics* (January 1979), pp. 249–61.

30. Lee Paul Baran, *The Political Economy of Growth* (New York: Monthly Review Press, 1962); Colin Leys, *Underdevelopment in Kenya* (Berkeley: University of California Press, 1974).

31. Aidan Foster-Carter, "From Rostow to Gunder Frank: Conflicting Paradigms in the Analysis of Underdevelopment," *World Development* (March 1976), pp. 174 ff.

32. Walter Rodney, *How Europe Underdeveloped Africa* (Washington, D. C.: Howard University Press, 1981).

33. For a collection of them, see Joyce Ladner, ed., *The Death of White Sociology* (New York: Random House, 1973), and Edward Said, *Orientalism* (New York: Pantheon, 1978)

34. For an overview see Metin Tamkoç, *International Civil War* (Ankara: Middle Eastern Technical University Press, 1967).

35. A good criticism of this assumed solidarity on the part of the student movement is provided by Habermas, *Die Linke Antwortet Jürgen Habermas* (Frankfurt: Europäische Verlagsanstalt, 1968).

36. Immanuel Wallerstein, "The Rise and Future Demise of the World Capitalist System: Concepts for Comparative Analysis," *Comparative Studies in Society and History* (January 1974), p. 391.

37. Ibid.

38. Patrick Clawson, "The Internationalization of Capital and Capital Accumulation in Iran and Iraq," *Insurgent Sociologist* (Spring 1977), (2):67.

39. See Ira Gerstein, "Theories of the World Economy and Imperialism," *Insurgent Sociologist* (Spring 1977), (2):9 ff.

40. Clawson, "The Internationalization of Capital," p. 71.

41. For a series of writings attempting to reconcile Marxism and dependence, see Ronald H. Chilcote, *Dependency and Marxism: Towards a Resolution of the Debate* (Boulder: Westview Press, 1982).

42. On the Iranian economy under the Shah, see Charles Issawi, "The Iranian Economy 1925–1975: Fifty Years of Economic Development," in George Lenczowski, ed., *Iran Under the Pahlavis* (Stanford: Hoover Institution Press, 1978), pp. 129–66; Fred Halliday, *Iran: Dictatorship and Development* (London: Penguin, 1979), pp. 9–19; Firouz Vakil, "Some Macro-Economic Considerations," in Abbas Amirie and Hamilton A. Twitchell, eds., *Iran in the 1980s* (Tehran: In-

stitute for International Political and Economic Studies, 1978), pp. 111–45.

43. Abdul Kassim Mansur (pseud.), "The Crisis in Iran: Why the U.S. Ignored a Quarter Century of Warning," *Armed Forces Journal International* (January 1979), pp. 26–29.

44. James Bill, "Iran and the Crisis of '78," *Foreign Affairs* (January 1979), p. 333.

45. Ervand Abrahamian, "Structural Causes of the Iranian Revolution," *MERIP Reports* (May 1980); Amin Saikal, *The Rise and Fall of the Shah* (Princeton: Princeton University Press, 1980); Shahram Chubin, "Repercussions of the Crisis in Iran," *Survival* (May–June 1979).

46. Marvin Zonis, *The Political Elite of Iran* (Princeton: Princeton University Press, 1971), p. 44.

47. Quoted in Mansur, "The Crisis in Iran," p. 28.

48. Leonard Binder, *Factors Influencing Iran's International Role* (Santa Monica: RAND Corporation, RAND-5968-FF, October).

49. Ibid, p. 1.

50. Ibid, p. 20.

51. Marvin Zonis, "Iran: The Politics of Insecurity," quoted in Binder, *Factors,* p. 48.

52. For an example of this ongoing neglect, see also James Bill, "The American Analysis of Iranian Politics," *Iranian Studies* (1977), 10 (3).

53. Saikal, *Rise and Fall.*

54. Lenczowski's article "Political Process and Institutions in Iran: The Second Pahlavi Kingship," is a paean of praise, lauding the Shah's "intelligent appraisals" and "ingenious approaches," describing his book *Mission for My Country* as containing "eloquent passages," ridiculing Iran's "dissident intellectuals" as being "intoxicated with the liberty and permissiveness of the West," and justifying the arms buildup and the activities of SAVAK as being "necessary under the circumstances." Lenczowski, *Iran under the Pahlavis.*

55. Many diagnosed secularism as proceeding smoothly. Richard Cottam believed it to be "most unlikely that religious influence on Iranian nationalism would ever again reach the proportions it exercised in 1951–52." Richard Cottam, *Nationalism in Iran* (Pittsburgh: University of Pittsburgh Press, 1964), p. 156. Shahram Chubin and Sepahr Zabih in 1974 reflected mainstream social science in their assessment that "the general values of [Iranian] society today largely coincide with the Shah's own predilections." Shahram Chubin and Sepahr Zabih, *The Foreign Relations of Iran* (Berkeley: University of California Press, 1974), p. 300.

56. *Area Handbook for Iran* (Washington D.C.: Government Printing Office, 1971).

57. Abbas Amirie and Hamilton A. Twitchell, eds., *Iran in the 1980s* (Tehran: Institute for International Political and Economic Studies, 1978), p. 30.

58. Rouhollah Ramazani, "Iran's 'White Revolution': A Study in Political Development," *International Journal of Middle East Studies* (1974), 5:124–39.

59. In 1977, for example, Robert Looney published a prognostic study of the Iranian economic and social situation in which he described the positive potential of Iran to overcome its problems but warned that "unless Iran can control its urge to spend on military arms, the forecasts made concerning the country's improving prosperity by the end of the century" would be invalidated by the increase of social tensions arising from the growing disparity between urban and rural regions and between a small group of beneficiaries and a mass of impoverished Iranians. Robert Looney, *Iran at the End of the Century* (Lexington, Ky.: Lexington Books, 1977), pp. 101–2.

60. Amirie and Twitchell, *Iran in the 1980s*, p. 37.

61. Bahman Nirumand, *Iran: The New Imperialism in Action* (New York: Monthly Review Press, 1969), p. 8.

62. Ibid., pp. 187–88.

63. Yahya Armajani, "What the U. S. Needs to Know About Iran," *Worldview* (May 1979).

64. Richard Dekmejian, "The Islamic Revival in the M.E. and North Africa," *Current History* (April 1980), p. 173: Aryeh Shmuelevitz, "The Iranian Crisis," *New Outlook* (January–February 1979), p. 35; Theda Skocpol, "Rentier State and Shi'a Islam in the Iranian Revolution," *Theory and Society* (1982), 11:267.

65. Richard Falk, "Trusting Khomeini," *New York Times*, February 16, 1979, p. A-17.

66. Martin Woollacott, "Does Khomeini Understand?" Ibid. In this editorial, the author argues that Kohmeini is not the "Mad Mullah of colonial demonology." From this sensible reminder he went on to argue that "he can best be described as a traditional religious intellectual who made great efforts to adapt his thoughts to changing events."

67. In *Monthly Review* (February 1979), p. 1, the editors noted that "Iran is once again proving the profound truth" of an observation made by one of the journal's authors and prominent writers of the school, Samir Amin, that "the periphery is a world in which class relationships are in a state of upheaval."

68. *Monthly Review* (February 1979), p. 17.

69. Ibid., p. 16.

70. Ibid., p. 19.

71. The borderline between propaganda and theory is thinly drawn in some of the leftist journals. *The World Marxist Review,* a pro-Soviet journal, published without comment or addition the article of Noureddin Kianouri, secretary of the Tudeh Party in Iran, in which he asserts that the "working class in Iran now numbers over 3 million and is an organized and politically conscious force," receiving training and education from his party. Religion and the religious movement are not even mentioned in passing in the forecast for the future. Instead, it is claimed that the fundamentally progressive and politicized state of the masses is illustrated by the fact that "not a single instance of anti-Soviet or anti-socialist" crowd activity took place. *World Marxist Review* (April 1979), 22:4.

72. Peter Waterman criticizes this tendency. The debate within his school on

the question of the revolutionary consciousness of the workers, and of their significance in societies where they really are only a minority, is "inspired more by revolutionary rhetoric than by class analysis." Otherwise, one would have to confront the fact that where social agitation and "revolution" occur, they are carried on by the peasants, as in Vietnam. "Workers in the Third World," *Monthly Review* (September 1977), 29:64.

73. See, for example, Annemarie Stein, *Iran—Neue Diktatur oder Frühling der Freiheit* (Hamburg: J. Reents-Verlag, 1979), pp. 141–208.

74. Waterman, "Workers," p. 63.

75. Ervand Abrahamian, "Political Forces in the Iranian Revolution," *Radical America* (June 1979), 13(3):54.

76. Ibid., p. 55.

77. For an interesting study of the reception given to the institutions of modernity in Europe when they were first introduced, and of the slow process by which newly emerging groups and classes transformed the dominant cultural and church-structured attitudes to work, time, knowledge, and government, see esp. Bernhard Groethuysen, *Die Entstehung der bürgerlichen Welt- und Lebensanschauung in Frankreich—Das Bürgertum und die katholische Weltanschauung* (1927; Frankfurt: Suhrkamp, 1978), vols. 1 and 2. Medieval clergy attitudes toward the introduction of secular schooling and even literacy in general, toward interest, toward individualism, and toward the emerging view of God, the world, and government as held by the developing middle class are strikingly similar to some of the current positions taken by Islamic traditional clergy. What is different is the relationship of state, clergy, and emerging new classes to each other.

2. WHY ISLAM?

1. For a criticism of this development, see Shaheen Dil, "The Myth of the Islamic Resurgence in South Asia," *Current History* (April 1980), pp. 165 ff. The author concludes with the warning that "Just as American foreign policy makers ignored the possibility that political power may have a religious basis, they are in danger of ignoring the political basis of what appears to be religious power." See also Mohammad Ayoob, "Two Faces of Political Islam: Iran and Pakistan Compared," *Asian Survey* (June 1979), pp. 535 ff. Ayoob concludes that "no attempt is made [by Western analysts] to understand and analyze the different, very divergent social and political goals for which the vehicle of Islam has been chosen and is being used by various leaders, groups and parties. . . . Saudi attempts at enforced puritanism . . . Pakistani attempts to legitimize military rule through the medium of Islam, and the Iranian effort to transform an unjust socioeconomic order through the political weapon of Islam are all viewed as part of the same grand design" (p. 535). The criticism is somewhat sweeping, but it contains an element of truth.

2. For a critique of this expectation, see esp. Wilhelm Mühlman, *Rassen-Eth-*

nien-Kulturen (Neuwied: Luchterhand, 1964); Alexander Touraine, et al., *Jenseits der Krise* (Frankfurt: Syndikat, 1976) and Joseph Rothschild, *Ethnopolitics* (New York: Columbia University Press, 1981).

3. Radio speech, October 1, 1981. On this question, see also Harald Müller, "Stabilität in der Dritten Welt," in Studiengruppe Militärpolitik, *Aufrüsten um Abzurüsten* (Reinbek: Rowohlt, 1981), p. 21.

4. Gamal Abd al-Nasser, *Philosophy of the Revolution* (Washington, D.C.: Public Affairs Press, 1955).

5. See Malcolm Kerr, *The Arab Cold War* (Oxford: Oxford University Press, 1970); see also Muhammad Khalil, *The Arab States and the Arab League* (Beirut: Khayat's, 1962); Walid Khalidi, ed., *From Haven to Conquest* (Beirut: Institute for Palestine Studies, 1971).

6. Some useful information on this can be found in Hazim Nuseibeh, *The Ideas of Arab Nationalism* (New York: Van Nostrand, 1966).

7. George Antonius, *The Arab Awakening* (1946; New York: Paragon, 1979), pp. 101 ff.

8. Ali Shari'ati, *On the Sociology of Islam* (Berkeley: Mizan Press, 1979), p. 115. Shari'ati's model of society in one of the lectures reprinted in this booklet divides society into two poles, the "pole of Cain" and the "pole of Abel." The pole of Cain is made up of king, owner, and aristocracy. "These three manifestations," he writes, are "referred to in the Quran as mala', mutraf and rahib, meaning, respectively, the avaricious and brutal, the gluttons and the overfed," and the official clergy as "the long-bearded demagogues." Shari'ati's other works include *Shi'i Yek Hizbai Tamam* [Shi'i Is a Complete Party] (n.p., 1976); *'Ali Tanha Ast* [Ali Is Alone] (n.p., 1978); *Bazgasht* [Return] (n.p., 1978); *Abu Zarr* (n.p., 1978); *Islam Shenasi* [Islamology] (n.p., 1973); *Tamadon va Tajadod* [Civilization and Progress] (n.p., 1974); and *Entezar* [Expectation] (n.p., 1978).

9. Ali Shari'ati, *Marxism and Other Western Fallacies: An Islamic Critique* (Berkeley: Mizan Press, 1980), p. 38.

10. Michael Fischer, *Iran: From Religious Dispute to Revolution* (Cambridge, Mass.: Harvard University Press, 1980); see also Said Amir Arjomand, "Traditionalism in Twentieth Century Iran" (unpublished paper prepared for the Social Science Research Council, Conference on Social Movements in the Contemporary Near and Middle East, May 1981).

11. Sharough Akhavi, *Religion and Politics in Contemporary Iran* (Albany: State University of New York Press, 1980), p. 114.

12. Sayyid Abul A'la Maududi, *Towards Understanding Islam*, trans. by Khursid Ahmad (Cedar Rapids, Iowa: Unity Publishing, 1980), p. 131. A useful overview of the political patterns that had emerged in Iran is provided in Nikki Keddie, *Iran: Religion, Politics, and Society* (London: Frank Cross, 1980).

13. The IRP platform clearly states that a nation made up of people all living according to the precepts of Islam but not ruled by an Islamic government is not an Islamic nation, while a nation ruled by Islamic government in which some people do not live piously *is* an Islamic nation.

14. Nikki Keddie, *Roots of Revolution* (New Haven: Yale University Press, 1981), p. 214.

15. This is well argued in Michael Fischer, "Persian Society: Transformation and Strain," in Hossein Amirsadeghi, ed., *Twentieth Century Iran* (London: Heinemann, 1977). Fischer has the distinction of being one of the few analysts who never discounted the importance of religion in the political order in Iran. See also his book *Iran: From Religious Dispute to Revolution.*

16. Fischer, *Iran,* p. 191.

17. See especially Keddie, *Iran,* and Arjomand, "Traditionalism."

18. Arjomand, "Traditionalism," p. 43.

19. Norman Calder reviews the practice of early (pre-Ghayba) Shi'ism of declaring a ruler unjust in order to unseat him and replace him with a preferred candidate, who was identified as one or another descendant of Ali. He describes the stance of the ulama as one of "accommodation," but this term implies passivity. Calder, "Accommodation and Revolution in Imami Shi'i Jurisprudence," *Middle East Studies* (January 1982), 18(1).

20. On the one hand, assaults on the legitimacy of kings appear to have been a basic element of Shi'i conflict behavior. A European living in Isfahan reported in the seventeeth century that "The Persians are divided amongst themselves regarding who has the right to the . . . 12th Imam's place, and to be sovereign in both spiritual and temporal matters. . . . 'How could it be possible,' say the men of the Church, 'that these . . . impious kings, drinkers of wine and carried off by passion, be the Vicars of God . . . ?' " Quoted in Nikki Keddie, "The Roots of the Ulama's Power in Modern Iran," in Keddie, ed, *Scholars, Saints, and Sufis* (Berkeley: University of California Press, 1972). On the other hand, the position of the ulama was not unassailable either. There was disagreement over what functions of the Imam they were authorized to carry out in his absence, especially the collection of tax and the call to jihad. See on this Joseph Eliash, "Misconceptions Regarding the Juridical Status of the Iranian Ulama," *International Journal of Middle East Studies* (February 1979), 10(1):11 and Calder, "Accommodation."

21. See Majid Khadduri, *Arab Contemporaries,* (Baltimore: John Hopkins University Press, 1973).

22. In Keddie, *Roots of Revolution,* p. 206.

23. Reprinted in *Islam and Revolution: Writings and Declarations of Imam Khomeini,* trans. by Hamid Algar (Berkeley: Mizan Press, 1981), p. 170.

24. Ibid., pp. 170, 171.

25. Akhavi, *Religion and Politics,* p. 163.

26. Quoted in ibid., pp. 110–16.

27. "The Granting of Capitulatory Rights to the U.S.," Speech, Qum, November 4, 1964, in *Islam and Revolution,* p. 183.

28. Akhavi, *Religion and Politics,* p. 169.

29. Ibid., p. 162.

30. Khomeini, *Islamic Government,* trans. by the Joint Publications Research Service (New York: Manor Books, 1979).

31. Conversations with regular visitors to Neauphle-le-Château, December 1978/January 1979.

32. "Briefing" overheard on December 29, 1978.

33. Our interview, Paris, March 1982, published in AZ, "Die späte Reue des Bani Sadr," March 17, 1982 and the *Middle East* (June 1982).

34. Again, it is Said Amir Arjomand who goes furthest in ascribing purely opportunistic motives to the ulama ("Traditionalism"). However, it is not necessary to disclaim all ideological sincerity on their part to recognize the ability of the ulama to participate in the tactical and strategic activities of competitive politics. They have clearly misrepresented their aims, undergone tactical coalitions and compromises, and changed position in midstream when that seemed more opportune. The ability to demonstrate flexible responses in the face of social changes marks the behavior of religious Islamic elites in other contexts, too, and is not at all specific to Iran. Gregory Massell describes the efforts of Soviet Central Asian religious leaders to respond to Soviet reforms not only through doctrinaire opposition and coercive measures, but also through some adaptation: offering positive inducements to women who re-veiled, and opening Islamic girls' schools for the first time in the history of their area. Gregory Massell, *The Surrogate Proletariat* (Princeton: Princeton University Press, 1974).

35. See Shaul Bakhash, "Popular Pamphleteering and Crowd Mobilization in the Iranian Revolution: 1978" (Social Science Research Council, May 1981) and Arjomand, "Traditionalism."

36. See Rupert Emerson, *From Empire to Nation* (Cambridge, Mass: Harvard University Press, 1960), p. 291. Carl Friedrich, ed., *Authority* (Cambridge, Mass.: Harvard University Press, 1958); Edward Shils, "Tradition and Liberty: Antinomy and Interdependence," *Ethics* (April 1958), pp. 158 ff.; Carl Friedrich, "Political Leadership and the Problem of Charismatic Power," *Journal of Politics* (1961), vol. 23; K. J. Ratnam, "Charisma and Political Leadership," *Political Studies* (1964), vol. 12; Edward Shils, "The Concentration and Dispersion of Charisma—Their Bearing on Economic Policy in Underdeveloped Countries," *World Politics* (1958–59), vol. 11; Claude Ake, "Charismatic Legitimation and Political Integration," *Comparative Studies in Society and History* (October 1966), esp. pp. 3–6. See especially the important collection of articles edited by Clifford Geertz, *Old Societies and New States* (London: Collier-Macmillan, 1963).

37. See Fischer, *Iran*, ch. 3 and Akhavi, *Religion and Politics*, ch. 4.

38. Morris Janowitz, *Political Conflict—Essays in Political Sociology*, (Chicago: Quadrangle, 1970), p. 142.

39. For example, Bani-Sadr's father was an ayatollah; Talighani's son became a Marxist.

40. For an excellent study of the left, including the Tudeh Party, in Iran, see Ervand Abrahamian, *Iran Between Two Revolutions* (Princeton: Princeton University Press, 1982).

41. The original version was published in 1976 or 1977. The new edition (1980) is cited in note 9 above.

42. There is also a reverse side to this phenomenon: the ideological dependence of much of Western leftist thought on the "Third World" and a postulated though often vague solidarity with its anti-imperialist struggle. On this, see *Die Linke Antwortet Jürgen Habermas* (chap. 1) and Albert Menni, *Der Kolonisator und der Kolonisierte* (Frankfurt: Syndikat, 1980).

43. On this, see also Edward Shils, "The Creation and Dispersion of Charisma," *World Politics* (1958–59), vol. 2, which speaks of an "anti-chrematic" value complex, that is, one which scorns considerations of gain, material advantage, and pragmatism.

44. Ali Shari'ati, *Red Shi'ism* (Tehran: Shari'ati Foundation, 1979).

45. Khomeini, *Islamic Government*, p. 80.

46. Clifford Geertz, *Islam Observed* (New Haven: Yale University Press, 1968).

47. *Selection and/or Election (Vesayat va showra)*, trans. by Ali Asghar Ghasseng (Tehran: Hamdami Foundation, 1979), pp. 11, 12.

48. Ibid., p. 14.

49. Or, in the formulation of Barry Rubin, "Bazargan and the National Front helped them [Khomeini and supporters] remove Bakhtiar; Yazdi conspired against Sanjabi; Ghotzbzadeh eliminated Yazdi; Bani Sadr undermined Bazargan" etc. Barry Rubin, *Paved with Good Intentions* (Oxford: Oxford University Press, 1980), p. 303.

50. Abul-Hasan Bani-Sadr, *Work and the Worker in Islam* (Tehran: Hamdami Foundation, n.d. [probably summer 1980]).

3. IRAN—WHAT HAPPENED?

1. Gerschenkron describes the work of comparative analysis as the "application to empirical material of various sets of empirically derived hypothetical generalizations and in testing the closeness of the resulting fit, in the hope that in this way certain uniformities, certain typical situations, and certain typical relationships among individual factors in these situations can be ascertained. None of these lends itself to easy extrapolations. All that can be achieved is an extraction from the vast storehouse of the past of sets of intelligent questions that may be addressed to current materials." Alexander Gerschenkron, *Economic Backwardness in Historical Perspective* (Cambridge, Mass.: Harvard University Press, 1962), p. 6.

2. Joachim Spiegel, *Soziale und Weltanschauliche Reformbewegungen im Alten Agypten* (Heidelberg: Kerle Verlag, 1950), p. 10.

3. Michael Walzer, *The Revolution of the Saints* (New York: Atheneum, 1976), p. 1.

4. Samuel P. Huntington, *Political Order in Changing Societies* (New Haven: Yale University Press, 1969), p. 204.

5. Hannah Arendt, *On Revolution* (New York: Viking Press, 1965). p. 35.

6. See Eric Voegelin, *Anamnesis* (Munich: Europäische Verlagsanstalt, 1966).

7. Arendt, *On Revolution*, p. 26.

8. Ibid., p. 35.

9. An excellent book dealing with this issue is Leonor Ossa, *Die Revolution — Das ist ein Buch und ein freier Mensch* (Hamburg: Furche, 1973).

10. Arendt, *On Revolution*, p. 27.

11. Charles Tilly, "Does Modernization Breed Revolution?" *Comparative Politics* (April 1973), pp. 425–47.

12. Ibid., p. 427.

13. A coup, Tilly argues, can lead to changes as far-reaching and significant as those commonly associated wth a revolution; so can wars, and some bandits establish regional autonomy and follow their own alternative social, political, and economic system. "Does Modernization Breed Revolution?" pp. 444–47.

14. Crane Brinton, *The Anatomy of Revolution* (New York: Vintage, 1965).

15. See Robert Graham, *Iran—The Illusion of Power* (New York: St. Martin's Press, 1979), pp. 90–121 and Barry Rubin, *Paved with Good Intentions* (Oxford: Oxford University Press, 1980), p. 194.

16. Robert Looney, *Iran at the End of a Century* (Lexington, Ky.: Lexington Books, 1977), p. 102. On overspending, failure to achieve significant growth in non-oil-related industries, and maldistribution along with inflation that had reached 30 percent by 1977, see Amin Saikal, *The Rise and Fall of the Shah* (Princeton: Princeton University Press, 1980), pp. 184–86.

17. In Graham, *Illusion of Power*, pp. 90 ff.

18. Saikal, *Rise and Fall*, p. 151.

19. It has been estimated that only 15 percent of the population benefited from the oil revenues. Saikal, *Rise and Fall*, p. 186.

20. Religious subsidies were cut from $80 million to $30 million, thus increasing the ulama's incentive to turn to the Bazaaris for alternate funding and encouraging one aspect of the coalition that was to make possible the ousting of the Shah. See Rubin, *Paved with Good Intentions*, pp. 262 ff, and Michael Fischer, *Iran: From Religious Dispute to Revolution* (Cambridge, Mass.: Harvard University Press, 1980).

21. Arthur Millspaugh, *Americans in Persia* (Washington, D. C..: Brookings Institution, 1946), p. 49.

22. Saikal, *Rise and Fall*, p. 191. And also see Khosrow Fatemi, "Leadership by Distrust: The Shah's Modus Operandi," *The Middle East Journal* (Winter 1982), 36(1):48–62.

23. See Graham, *Illusion of Power*, pp. 121–31.

24. Figures vary. James Bill and Carl Leiden give a figure of 40 percent; *Politics in the Middle East* (Boston: Little, Brown, 1979), p. 212. Graham cites lower figures: 29.2 percent for 1975/76 and 24.4 percent for 1977/78. *Illusion of Power*, p. 172.

25. "Report on Leading Personalities in Persia," Great Britain, Public Record Office, Foreign Office 371/20837, April 12, 1937.

26. Bill and Leiden, *Politics in the Middle East*, p. 211.

27. The observations in this section are based on conversations held with former high-ranking officials in the Iranian armed forces.

28. In 1971 about 50 percent of school-age children were receiving no education at all, and the provision of other services such as medical care was largely an urban pheonomenon, with the ratio of doctors/patients high in urban centers and as phenomenally low as 1/15,000 in Azerbaijan. Saikal, *Rise and Fall*, p. 151.

29. The Shah's inaction might have been due to his illness. He might have believed that given his cancer, his priority should be to pass on the throne to his son and that the sustained use of massive force against his opponents might well undermine that possibility.

30. For a more detailed version of this argument, see Bill and Leiden, *Politics in the Middle East*, p. 200; some authors argue that Mossadeq's support came from the "rising professional middle class," but that Mossadeq had the charisma necessary to rally support "across class lines."

31. On the shift of U. S. policy from initial support of his position to the eventual determination to participate in his elimination, see Richard Sale, "America in Iran," *SAIS Review* (Winter 1981–82), 3:35–37.

32. See Joachim Wach, *Religionssoziologie* (Tübingen: Mohr, 1951); Gustav Mensching, *Soziologie der Revolution* (Bonn, 1947).

33. Barrington Moore most clearly deals with the peasants as an "archaic" social phenomenon. *Social Origins*, fn. 40.

34. *The Muqaddimah*, trans. by Franz Rosenthal (London: Routledge and Kegan Paul, 1967), p. 258.

35. Eric Wolfe, *Peasant Wars of the Twentieth Century* (New York: Harper and Row, 1969).

36. Ibid., p. 295.

37. Ibid.

38. Norman Cohn, *The Pursuit of the Millennium: Revolutionary Millenarians and Mystical Anarchists of the Middle Ages* (New York: Oxford University Press, 1970).

39. In Iran, migration to the cities had moved the peasantry to an urban context, where their behavior was a much more significant political factor. In the 20 years between 1956 and 1976, the population of Tehran rose from 1.5 million to 4.5 million. See Rubin, *Paved with Good Intentions*, pp. 262 ff.

40. Barrington Moore, *Social Origins of Dictatorship and Democracy* (Boston: Beacon Press, 1966), pp. 422, 423.

41. Manfred Halpern, *The Politics of Social Change in the Middle East and North Africa* (Princeton: Princeton University Press, 1963), p. 136.

42. On this, see especially Julien Freund, in *Säkularisation und Utopie* (Stuttgart: Ebracher Studien, 1967), p. 99.

43. The Saint-Simonian school, for example, believed that "the religion of the future will be greater and more powerful than all the religions of the past . . . the synthesis of all the conceptions of mankind, and more still, of all its ways of

existence . . . it will not merely dominate the political order, but the political order, 'dans son ensemble,' will become a religious institution." In Gabriel Talmon, *Political Messianism: The Romantic Phase* (London: Secker and Warburg, 1960), p. 87.

44. T. K. Oommen, "Charisma, Social Structure, and Social Change," *Comparative Studies in Society and History* (1967–68), 10:94, 95.

45. Eugen Lemberg, *Ideologie und Gesellschaft* (Stuttgart: Kohlhammer, 1971).

46. Shils, "Tradition and Liberty, Antinomy and Interdependence," *Ethics* (April 1958), p. 162; Clifford Geertz, in David Apter, ed., *Ideology and Discontent* (New York: Macmillan, 1964), p. 64.

47. Eric Erikson, cited in Joungwan Alexander Kim, "The Politics of Predevelopment," *Comparative Politics* (January 1973).

48. In Claude Ake, "Charismatic Legitimation and Political Integration," *Comparative Studies in Society and History* (October 1966), p. 2.

49. Alois Dempf, *Sacrum Imperium* (Darmstadt: Wissenschaftliche Buchgesellschaft, 1954). See also Rudolf Otto, *Das Heilige* (Munich: Biederstein, 1947).

50. Immanuel Wallerstein makes this point repeatedly in *Africa: The Politics of Independence* (New York: Random House, 1961) and *Africa: The Politics of Unity* (New York: Random House, 1967).

51. The Shah reported that he was cured of typhoid fever by a visitation, in a dream, from Ali. Later he had a vision of Abbas, a saint. He also reports a vision of the Twelfth Imam. Mohammad Reza Pahlavi, *Answer to History* (New York: Stein and Day, 1980), p. 57.

52. Iranian monarchists today still forward this view of the king as a symbolic rallying point and hope that the young shah, by remaining as unaffiliated as possible with the currently contending parties, will be turned to as a symbol of unity when everything collapses. Our interview, Princess Azadeh and other leaders of the monarchist faction, Paris, March 1982.

On the lack of commitment of the masses to their leaders once they fall from power, even if they appear to have been charismatic leaders, see Jean Lacoutoure, *The Demigods* (New York: Knopf, 1970), which cites instances of mass indifference to the overthrow of heroes.

53. See the FBIS for typical broadcasts, especially FBIS-MEA-79-L30, July 5, 1979, vol. 5, no. 130, reporting broadcasts of the National Voice of Iran. This point is also made in Hannah Arendt's *Origins of Totalitarianism*.

54. J. L. Talmon, *The Origins of Totalitarian Democracy* (1952; London: Sphere Books, 1970) and *Political Messianism—The Romantic Phase* (London: Secker and Warburg, 1960.

55. Talmon, *Political Messianism*, p. 20.

56. However, the Shah's attempt to personalize power under a dynastic claim added a nonpragmatic component.

57. Shah Pahlavi, *Answer to History*, p. 57.

58. See the important study by Edgar Salin, *Civitas Dei*, (Tübingen: Mohr,

1926) for an excellent review of totalitarian political values in Christian social thought.

59. ". . . There are no more than two kinds of human society, which we may justly call the two cities. The first consists of those who wish to live after the flesh, the second of those who wish to live after the spirit." St. Augustine, *Civitas Dei* (New York: Penguin, 1972). For an elaboration, see Robert Nisbet, *History of the Idea of Progress* (1969; New York: Basic Books, 1980), ch. 2, "The Early Christians."

60. "The leading ulama, the mujtahids (unlike their Sunni counterparts under the Ottomans) . . . maintained a state of potential and actual criticism of the regime. . . . " Marshall G. S. Hodgson, *The Venture of Islam* (Chicago: University of Chicago Press, 1974), 3:35.

61. Ibid.

62. On this question, see also Norman Calder, "Accommodation and Revolution in Imami Shiʿi Jurisprudence: Khumayni and the Classical Tradition," *Middle East Studies* (January 1982), 18(1).

63. In *Kitab al-Bay,* a five-volume work published in Iraq circa 1970, Khomeini elaborated on the necessity of the leadership of one faqih, and the obligation of the other scholars to follow his leadership, an idea that Calder believes to be "probably without precedent in the Imami tradition" ("Accommodation," p. 16).

64. Talmon, *Origins.*

65. Yvonne Yazbeck Haddad, in her article "The Qurʿanic Justification for an Islamic Revolution: The View of Sayyid Qutb," *Middle East Journal* (Winter 1983) 37(1), proceeds as if the Manichean world view, the division into the forces of good and the forces of evil, and the notion of a "kingdom of God" to be established on earth were the unique and original notions of Islamic authors.

66. Talmon, *Political Messianism,* p. 423.

67. Talmon, *Origins,* p. 161. In making this point, Talmon writes that the ideal of totalitarian democracy is "not the voluptuous happiness of Persepolis, but the bliss of Sparta."

68. Bani-Sadr says his economic planning, which included food purchases from abroad in order to alleviate shortages, was violently opposed by Khomeini, who accused him of sabotaging the revolution by trying to cheat the people of the "experience of deprivation." Interview with us, March 1982.

69. Moore, *Social Origins,* p. 427.

70. For one exposition of this view, see Norris Hetherington, "Industrialization and Revolution in Iran: Forced Progress of Unmet Expectations," *Middle East Journal* (Summer 1982), 36(3).

71. Lee Karl Polanyi, *The Great Transformation* (Boston: Beacon Press, 1957), esp. pp. 240–58.

72. On this, see also the exchange in *World Politics* between Henry A. Turner, "Fascism and Modernization" (1972) 24(2), and James Gregor, "Fascism and Modernization: Some Addenda," (1974), 26(3).

4. PREJUDICE AS A CULTURAL WEAPON:
ORIENTALISM VS. OCCIDENTALISM

1. For the Islam/West case, the obvious source is the progenitor of the term and initiator of the current debate, Edward Said, with his books *Orientalism* (New York: Pantheon, 1978) and *Covering Islam* (New York: Pantheon, 1981).

Some of the more general functions of prejudice are discussed best in the literature on racism against blacks in the U. S. and on the functions of anti-Semitism in European fascism. See, for example, Michael Banton, *Race Relations* (New York: Basic Books, 1967); John Hodge, Donald Struckmann, and Lynn Dorland Trost, *Cultural Bases of Racism and Group Oppression* (Berkeley: Two Riders Press, 1975); Peter Rose, ed., *Slavery and its Aftermath* (New York: Atherton Press, 1970); Stanley Elkins, *Slavery: A Problem in American Institutional and Intellectual Life* (1959; Chicago: University of Chicago Press, 1976). On prejudice as a cognitive problem, a barrier to perception and learning, see also Karl Deutsch, *Nationalism and Social Communication* (New York: Wiley, 1953). On prejudice as a tool of fascism, vast bodies of literature exist, and the discussion centering around Theodor Adorno's *The Authoritarian Personality* remains one of the most useful entry points because it rallied so many different schools of thought into clarifying their views on the origins of this phenomenon.

2. Peter Berger and Thomas Luckmann, *The Social Construction of Reality* (Harmondsworth, Eng.: Penguin, 1966).

3. Carl Schmitt, *The Concept of the Political,* trans. by George Schwab (New Brunswick, N.J.: Rutgers University Press, 1976).

4. August Nitschke, *Der Feind* (Stuttgart, 1964), p. 17.

5. The best study of how social science worked to rationalize conquest has been done by the noted anthropologist Wolf Lepenics, *Soziologische Anthropologie* (Munich, 1971).

6. A more detailed analysis of this ideological effort is presented in Cheryl Benard, *Die Geschlossene Gesellschaft und ihre Rebellen* (Frankfurt: Syndikat,1982).

7. Theodor Adorno, *Negative Dialektik* (Frankfurt: Suhrkamp, 1975), p. 32.

8. This will be the effort, Adorno goes on, of "an imposed order to represent itself as a natural one." Ibid. On this issue see also Jürgen Ritsert, *Denken und Gesellschaftliche Wirklichkeit* (Frankfurt: Campus, 1977), esp. pp. 83 ff.

9. Norbert Elias, *The Civilizing Process* (New York: Urizen Books, 1978), pp. 68–69.

10. Said, *Orientalism* (cited in note 1). See also the critique by Sadik Jalal al-'Azm, "Orientalism and Orientalism in Reverse," *Khamsin* (1981), 8:5 ff.

11. Hamid Naficy, "Cinema as a Political Instrument," in Michael Bonine and Nikki Keddie, eds., *Continuity and Change in Modern Iran* (Albany: State University of New York, 1981).

12. Prejudice relies for its effectiveness on the fact that it is not localized, but diffuse, filtering through many levels of conscious and unconscious thought and reinforced by multiple agents, from jokes and childrens' counting rhymes to im-

ages in advertising and film, popular aesthetics, and adages to pseudo-scientific theories and models.

An instructive source, for example, would be the substratum of popular thought toward Islam on the part of those European societies that had most closely experienced Islam as a military threat. Children in Austrian elementary schools still sing a verse intended to influence them against drinking coffee, a substance thought in some curricular Austrian past to be a narcotic. The origin of this verse has not been traced, and only the archaic spelling of the word in the rhyme (*caffe* rather than today's *kaffee*) attests to its age. In this verse, small children sing that they "don't want to be weakened in brain and body" like some "Musulman" who can't "free himself from this drug." Austrian tradition contains numerous churches and squares with plaques commemorating the atrocities of Muslim armies and the valiance of the resistance; there are also linguistic reminders of the Islamic presence, names of towns and streets and additions to the diet that stem from this time, such as the Austrian appellation *Fisolen* (from *fasulya*) for string beans (in German they are called *Bohnen*) or the technique for making strudel dough.

13. On this, see Hanno Kesting, *Herrschaft und Knechtschaft* (Freiburg: Romback, 1973).

14. C. J. Wills, M.D., *Persia as It Is—Brief Sketches of Modern Persian Life and Character* (London, 1886); Hermann Norder, *Under Persian Skies* (London: H. F. and G. Witherby, 1928); Edward Granville Browne, *A Year Amongst the Persians* (1893; Cambridge: Cambridge University Press, 1927), featuring a picture of the author "In Persian Dress"; Col. C. E. Stewart, *Through Persia in Disguise* (London: George Routledge and Sons, 1911); Wilhelm Litten, *Persische Flitterwochen* (Berlin: Georg Stilke, 1925); Curtis Harnack, *Persian Lions, Persian Lambs* (London: Victor Gollarct, 1965).

15. This particular notion is the product of the pen of C. J. Wills, who coyly hints at great intimacy with harem procedures through his office as a medical doctor. His approach is by no means exclusive to Britain. Engelbert Kaempfer, who traveled as a doctor with the Swedish trade delegation, published upon his return a book entitled *Am Hofe des persischen Grosskönigs* (1864; Basel: Tübingen, 1977), which conforms perfectly to the structure of the genre, including the hazardous infiltration of the serail by Mr. Kaempfer, disguised as a Persian gardener, and assurances that the king engaged the attentions of at least six wives per night.

16. For a sample of the style at its best, the following paragraph is more than illustrative: "There they were, lying among cushions on a carpet thick as turf, plump creatures with painted faces, swathed in brilliantly colored silks. The light was dim, softened by panes of stained glass, in this place of damnation. Perfumes of poisonous sweetness rose in spirals of blue smoke from the firepans. The most beautiful of the women writhed to Ory's feet, weeping and moaning in the Saracen tongue. She wreathed her arms about him and mingled caresses and languishing looks of diabolical power with her supplications." The hero, needless to say, runs for his life.

17. James Cleugh, *Ladies of the Harem* (London: Frederick Muller, 1955), pp. 20, 47, 193.

18. Wills, *Persia as It Is* (see note 15).

19. William Forbis, *The Fall of the Peacock Throne* (New York: Harper and Row, 1980), p. 118.

20. Ibid., p. 125.

21. Roland Barthes, *Mythologies* (London: Jonathan Cope, 1957).

22. Angela Rodkin, *Unveiled Iran* (London: Hutchinson, 1943).

23. George Curzon, *Persia and the Persian Question* (London: Longman's Green, 1892).

24. J. M. Balfour, *Recent Happenings in Persia* (Edinburgh and London: W. Blackwood and Sons, 1922), p. 54. On the cowardliness of the Persians, Balfour relates this anecdote: In 1911, a great deal of military training took place in order to prepare against a threat from Russia. At the same time, the Persian authorities appealed to the British for help against some robber bands terrorizing the countryside. Why didn't the trained men take care of the robbers, the British consul asked. Yes, the authorities admitted, many Persian men were ready to fight the Russians, but then the Russians were a long way off, while the robbers were very near (p. 35).

25. *Foreign Relations of the United States, 1950* (Washington, D.C., 1978) hereafter cited as *FRUS*.

26. The discussions over arms deliveries are reported as a kind of bartering over toys. "After exhausting the question of tank ammunition, he then accusingly asked, 'And what about mortars?' " Wiley writes. Ibid.

27. Ibid.

28. Wiley to Secretary of State, May 26, 1950, ibid.

29. September 3, 1948, ibid.

30. January 30, 1950, ibid.

31. As late as 1971, the U. S. government's *Area Handbook for Iran* (Washington, D.C.: Government Printing Office, 1971) noted that the Iranian population expects an authoritarian manner from those in power, and that the "strong Shah" is therefore a perfect government for them.

32. Ibid.

33. See also the interesting article "America in Iran" by Richard Sale. On the basis of official documents and some reports of clandestine U. S. activities in Iran during the late forties and the Mossadeq era, Sale concludes that 1953 marked the turning point in U. S. policy toward that country, the moment when populist aims were abandoned and the U. S. only desired to "secure Iran as a base of operations." *SAIS Review* (Winter 1981–82), 3:36, 37.

34. November 30, 1950, *FRUS*, vol. 5.

35. William H. Sullivan, *Mission to Iran* (New York: Norton, 1981), p. 117.

36. Ibid., p. 231.

37. "Iran: Evaluation of U.S. Intelligence Performance Prior to November

1978." U.S. House of Representatives, Permanent Select Committee on Intelligence, Staff Report.

38. An interesting study of the glamorization of Iran by popular media is presented in Richard Black's book *Der letzte deutsche Kaiser, Reza Schah* [Reza Shah, The Last German Emperor] (Reinbek: Rowohlt, 1977). The author analyzes the enormous amount of coverage given to the Iranian imperial family's real and imagined "daily life" in such popular German women's magazines as *Das Goldene Blatt* and speculates on the significance of such projections of dynastic fantasies. On the rapid shift of images, Princess Azadeh observed bitterly in an interview with us that during the high point of the crisis, French media showed her uncle as a monster with cannons for eyes and blood dripping from vampire teeth, while Khomeini, then in exile in Paris, was depicted as a mild and meek ancient philosopher. This has obviously changed as Khomeini became a demoniac figure shrouded in dark robes and sinisterly alien.

39. U. S. Embassy, Tehran, to the Secretary of State, Cable no. 3245 (Confidential), April 25, 1979. Muslim Students Followers of the Imam's Line, *Asnad-e Lanah-i Jasusi* [Documents of the Den of Espionage] (Tehran, n.d.), 18:131.

40. U. S. Embassy, Tehran, to the Secretary of State, Cable no. 12069 (Confidential), (July 24, 1979). Ibid., p. 3.

41. There is definitely a need for more work on the connection between prejudice and alienation, particularly when that prejudice takes the form of an enthusiastic and uninformed endorsement of a foreign culture. Wilhelm Litten, a German scholar who published his observations after returning to Europe in 1914, noted that there were three kinds of Europeans living in Persia: those who were "more Persian than the Persians" and who vigorously encouraged nationalism and xenophobia among their adopted brethren; those who felt contempt for Persia and wanted only to divide up the imperial spoils; and those who sincerely believed in the benefits of modernity. Wilhelm Litten, *Persien* (Berlin and Leipzig, 1920), conclusion.

42. An obvious example is Sir Richard Burton, the British diplomat, author, and Orient-addict. His horrified sister Georgina Stisted had to witness her brother's final laying to rest in a simulated Arab tent topped by a gold star and hung with camel bells. See Richard Burton, *Personal Narrative of a Pilgrimage to El-Medinah and Meccah* (London: Longman, Brown, Green, and Roberts, 1860); an effort to rehabilitate her brother in British eyes was made by Stisted in *The True Life of Capt. Sir Richard Burton* (London: H. S. Nichols, 1896).

43. Said mentions this phenomenon without acknowledging it as evidence that the Western view of the East was not nearly so closed, firm, or self-confident as he portrays it. Said, *Orientalism*, p. 225.

44. Rupert Emerson, *From Empire to Nation* (Cambridge, Mass.: Harvard University Press, 1960), p. 280.

45. The individuals who are protégés of a superpower often seem to feel that their relationship with that power is a personal one, and tend to invest it with a surprisingly high degree of subjective content. The Iranian royal family analyzed

the genuineness of President Carter's smiles and the expression on his face to gain insights into intended U. S. foreign policy, for example. Ashraf notes that in Tehran in 1978, Carter's "eyes were icy" and his "face was pale"; for her, this is directly linked to the fact that "within that very year" he sent emissaries to Khomeini to "hedge his own political bets." Ashraf Pahlavi, *Faces in a Mirror* (Englewood Cliffs, N. J.: Prentice-Hall, 1980), p. xi.

The memoirs of such rulers as Anastasio Somoza display a high degree of sentiment being projected onto "the U. S." Somoza's book is entitled *Nicaragua Betrayed* (Belmont Mass.: Western Island, 1980), but the sense of betrayal is in reality highly personal. Not without pathos, he recalls being sent to school in the U. S. at the age of ten and thinking, "I'm in the United States and I'm all by myself." The hesitation of U. S. officialdom in sending him the requested airplane to fly him to Miami for medical treatment after a heart attack was for Somoza a profound personal blow; Carter's human rights campaign and the OAS commission dispatched to survey his performance in this regard appeared as acts of personal disloyalty. One is tempted to describe such relationships as feudal, in the sense that fealty is given in exchange for protection within a relationship based on personal linkages rather than formalized diplomatic structures. An analysis of this matter, beginning with the socialization of many such leaders and their personal biographical experience, would not be without use to political science and might shed light on some otherwise surprising facets of superpower relations to Third World leaders.

46. Al-Masudi, Kitab al-Tanbih uàl-Ishraf, translation in Bernard Lewis, ed., *Islam* (New York: Harper and Row, 1974), 2:122.

47. Ibid. p. 123.

48. See Georges Duby, *Krieger und Bauern: Die Entwicklung von Wirtschaft und Gesellschaft im frühen Mittelalter* (Frankfurt: Syndikat, 1977), p. 146.

49. Al-'Iqd al-Farid, in Bernard Lewis, *Islam*, 2:206.

50. The Arabs unrightfully claim superiority on racial grounds without allowing for religious or moral achievement. In flagrant violation of the Koran, he alleges, the Arabs claim supremacy; "you [Arabs] persist in your boasting and you say, 'They [the Persians] are not equal to us, even if . . . they pray until they are bent like bows and fast until they are thin as bowstrings.'" Ibid.

51. Ibid. p. 203.

52. Marshall G. S. Hodgson, *The Venture of Islam* (Chicago: University of Chicago Press, 1974), 3:23. See also Fischer on the persecution of Sunnis, Sufis, and non-Muslims during this period; Michael Fischer, *Iran: From Religion Dispute to Revolution* (Cambridge, Mass.: Harvard University Press, 1980), p. 29.

53. Bernard Lewis, in his book *The Muslim Discovery of Europe* (New York: Norton, 1982), has compiled a fascinating collection of sources and accompanying texts dealing with this side of the cultural interaction.

54. Lewis, *Muslim Discovery*, pp. 281, 94.

55. Ibid. p. 289.

56. See Berger and Luckmann, *Social Construction of Reality.*

57. For interesting parallels in another context, see Harold Cruse, *The Crisis of the Negro Intellectual* (New York: William Morrow, 1967).

58. On these questions, see Carlton Hayes, *Nationalism, A Religion* (New York: Macmillan, 1960); Victor Alba, *Nationalists Without Nations* (New York: Praeger, 1968), and especially Eugen Lemberg, *Ideologie und Gesellschaft* (Stuttgart: Kohlhammer, 1971) and *Nationalismus* (Reinbek: Rowohlt, 1964), vols. 1 and 2.

59. Turkey went the farthest with this line, followed by Egypt. Japan served as a reference point for many authors of this persuasion, demonstrating how quickly and successfully an Asian country could master the skills of the modern West.

60. The feelings of inferiority, rejection, and envy experienced by many Arabs, Persians, or North Africans living in the Western capitals as students mirror on an individual level the sentiments of this whole group of secularists. For some, the "rejection" by Western civilization gave the real impulse to radicalization, providing a personal refutation of the belief that one could meet the West on Western terms.

61. Charles Cremeans, *The Arabs and the World—Nasser's Arab Nationalist Policy* (New York: Praeger, 1963), p. 59.

62. See also David Apter's *Ghana in Transition* (Princeton: Princeton University Press, 1972), for a useful exposition of the role of leadership.

63. One example he cites is the case of Egypt's Muhammad Heikal, who began his career as a secularist, and changed—Khadduri alleges—because the popular success of an article on the life of Muhammad showed him that the way to reach the masses was through Islam. Majid Khadduri, *Arab Contemporaries—The Role of Personality in Politics* (Baltimore: Johns Hopkins University Press, 1973).

64. See especially the excellent summary in Fazlur Rahman, *Islam* (New York: Doubleday, 1966), pp. 261–89. Al-Afghani is another example for what some authors see as a tactical shift from secularism to Islamic modernism; see Nikki Keddie's interpretation, *Iran: Religion, Politics and Society* (London: Frank Cross, 1980), p. 29.

65. See Amir Ali, *The Spirit of Islam* (London, 1939); Muhammad Abduh, in Rahman, *Islam*, p. 271; Muhammad Iqbal, *Reconstruction of Religious Thought in Islam* (Lahore, 1944).

66. "Colonialism," Qaddafi has on occasion stated, "has its origins in the [Western] struggle against Islam." *Arab News*, September 1971 (irregular publication distributed by the Libyan embassy).

67. In original Islam, Shari'ati argues, there was no division of labor; everyone "promulgates Islam, fights, farms, cultivates dates or herds camels." Each person was simultaneously "worker, warrior and intellectual." Later, however, classes appear and the clergy comes to comprise one of them. Since this official class "must . . . work to serve its class interests . . . it grafts its concerns onto the formal religion." Shari'ati, *Marxism and Other Western Fallacies* (Berkeley: Mizan Press, 1980), p. 105.

68. Shari'ati reviews and dismisses the Western belief systems of the present,

from Marxism to existentialism, and concludes that Islam is the only system of values that combines material and political with moral and spiritual goals.

69. Rahman, *Islam,* p. 284. See also his concluding chapter. Some of the observations he makes may well be based on personal experience; formerly director of the Islamic Research Institute in Islamabad, he was forced out by the fundamentalists (or, in his terminology, the revivalists.) The new director described Rahman's removal in the concise words that "his views did not fit in and so he had to leave." (Our interview, January 1982.)

70. Khomeini has frequently criticized this group of "intellectuals who speak in such a way that only their so-called intellectual friends can understand them," and who, either out of deliberate intention or from confusion, "mix up Islamic issues with Marxism." Speech, March 20, 1980, translated in *Teheran—Eine Revolution Wird Hingerichtet* (Munich: Zeit Verlag, 1980).

71. For example, members of this school will try to argue that while the cutting off of hands is clearly spelled out in the Koran as the punishment for theft, a conviction for theft requires the criminal to confess; without a confession no amount of evidence is sufficient to amputate. Modernists have succeeded in outlawing polygamy by apt interpretations of Koran passages. In Pakistan today, modernist theologians are arguing that Islam does not require two female witnesses to equal one male, as the fundamentalist rivals continue to claim, but that the initial ruling has been misunderstood all along. In fact, they say, a female witness was merely required to be accompanied to court by a second woman, so that her nerve would not fail her upon being confronted, suddenly and in a stressful context, by a courtroom full of men. Only if she was so unnerved that she could not testify did the second woman have a role to play, by supporting and encouraging her to be calm and remember what she had seen or heard. These argumentative efforts, while often displaying great ingenuity, are nevertheless largely defensive. They are attempts to counter fundamentalist efforts to push for regressive legislative changes or annulments of more liberal previous reforms.

72. In fact, coalitions between secularists and modernists are not uncommon, as for example, in Pakistan today, where organizations such as WAF, the Women's Action Forum, combine secularist and modernist membership in an effort to combat the advance of the fundamentalists.

73. For a more detailed exposition of the traditionalist view, see Mushin Mahdi, *Die geistigen und sozialen Wandlungen im Nahen Osten* (Freiburg: Rombach, 1961).

74. Both in their necessity to counter the very real arguments leveled against Islam and against them, and in their actual behavior, traditionalists usually do not live up to their autonomy claims. For example, Ahmad Gailani, an Afghan traditionalist, will insist in an interview that he cannot think of a single Western thinker who has influenced him because he "devotes himself exclusively to Islamic studies." He will hold this position despite the fact that his wife lives in London, many of his other relatives live permanently in the U.S., and he himself is a rather urbane figure who spends much time abroad seeking Western assistance and support for his political party. (Interview with the authors, January 1982.)

75. This is most obvious in the oil industry, the basis for Saudi Arabia's economic existence. It holds true also for the minute details of enforcement of traditional Islamic life styles: doctors with modern education supervise floggings to make certain that culprits do not die of them; and the system of sexual apartheid is possible only through use of high technology, including televised university lectures for the female students and electronic equipment with which they communicate their questions to the professors.

76. Sayyid Qutb, *Milestones* (Cedar Rapids, Iowa: Unity Publishing, n.d.), p. 93.

77. Ibid., p. 136.

78. Ibid.

79. Ibid., p. 138, 9.94.

80. Ibid., pp. 138, 139.

81. Musawi Lari, *Western Civilization Through Muslim Eyes* (Houston: Free Islamic Literatures, 1979). No date for the Persian original is given in this translation. The author was born in 1934.

82. Ibid., introduction. Compare with such titles as *Persia As It Is*, with equally totalistic claims of scholarship.

83. The chapter on "Love of Animals" (ibid.), which initially holds the promise of featuring one redeeming Western virtue in a bleak catalogue, is in fact an essay on the disgusting and depraved personal habits of the Europeans, based on the author's observation during his stay in Germany for medical treatment. Rahman has described the tendency of this genre of contemporary Islamic literature, of which he considers Maududi's publications to be the best illustration, to collect "the most revolting details of Western brothels supplied by Western writers" in order to hold forth sweepingly on the ruin of Western civilization. Rahman, *Islam*, p. 288.

84. Lari, *Western Civilization*, p. 58.

85. This aspect of cultural and ideological conflict has been explored by Hanno Kesting, *Herrschaft und Knechtschaft* (Freiburg: Rombach, 1973), pp. 17 ff.

86. Address, March 20, 1980. Khomeini said that "it was the will of God to free this oppressed country from the burden of tyranny and the domination of the *hegemonic* powers, especially the U.S. government. . . ."

87. Qutb, *Milestones*, p. 98. He goes on to write that "those societies which give ascendance to physical desires and animalistic morals cannot be considered civilized, no matter how much progress they may make in industry or science."

88. Quoted in Mary Flounders Arnett, "Qasim Amin and the Beginnings of the Feminist Movement in Egypt" (Ph. D. diss., Dropsie College, Philadelphia, 1965), p. 108.

89. *Kashf-al-Asrar* (1941), in *Islam and Revolution*, p. 172.

90. Quoted in *Die Zeit*, March 30, 1979 and the *New York Times*, April 22, 1979.

91. Reza Baraheni, *The Crowned Cannibals* (New York: Vintage, 1977).

92. Bahman Nirumand, *Iran—The New Imperialism in Action* (New York: Monthly Review Press, 1969), p. 170.

93. Platform of the Provisional Government of the Democratic Islamic Republic of Iran, October 1981, p. 20. Bani-Sadr formulates it more catchingly: "Khomeini forces women to cover themselves, the West forces them to uncover themselves." Interview, March 1982.

94. There is some ambiguity on this point; some fundamentalist authors take the position that nature has clearly delineated sexual roles and one must merely adhere to them, while others portray human nature as driven by lust and passion and requiring the most rigid control. Compare Sayyid Qutb for the latter version, Maududi for a version that regards women as the anarchic element in society ("women have been ordered to remain in their houses" as a consequence and are to leave it "only when necessary" and after observing "certain formalities") and Lari for the version that Islam merely codifies human nature. Qutb, *Milestones*, p. 97 ff.; Lari, *Western Civilization;* Maulana Maududi, *Towards Understanding Islam* (Cedar Rapids, Iowa: Unity Publishing House, 1960).

95. Qutb, *Milestones.*

96. See Arnett, "Qasim Amin," p. 113.

97. Interview with the authors, March 1982.

98. In 1982, by coincidence, we attended two subsequent conferences with Nawal as-Saadawi. On May 8 in Paris, at a symposium held at the Sorbonne on the occasion of International Women's Day, as-Saadawi was to speak on "Islam and Women." Warned that a recent symposium in Paris on the same topic had ended in a pitched battle between European feminists and Arab women sympathetic to fundamentalism, as-Saadawi chose to be cautious. The oppression of women in the Muslim world, she argued, was the product of capitalism and not of Islam. At this, a group of Algerian women in the audience began to attack her for being a Muslim apologist, and as-Saadawi amended her position, saying that in fact "a combination of capitalism and Islam" was responsible and both manifestations of patriarchal rule had to be combated. The next day, as-Saadawi spoke before the Women's Branch of the U.N. in Vienna. Evidently encouraged by her experience in Paris, she immediately criticized the influence of Islam and tradition as causes of women's subjugation and illustrated this through reference to her own life.

See also Nawal as-Saadawi, *The Hidden Face of Eve* (London: Zed Press, 1980). For a very instructive example of a tactical and ideological effort to reconcile anticolonialist nationalism, criticism of tradition, secularist liberalism, and fears of popular resistance against such a position, see as-Saadawi's paper for the Arab Women's Conference (Cairo, 1979).

5. THE ISLAMIC REPUBLICANS IN POWER

1. Henry Precht, "Memorandum to the Files" (Secret-Sensitive), Conversation with Dr. Ibrahim Yazdi, Adviser to Khomeini, December 13, 1978. Both sides had agreed "that neither of us would acknowledge that there had been any official contact between Khomeini and the U.S. Government." This memorandum

along with a lot of other U. S. official documents was captured by the "student followers of the Imam line" when they occupied the U. S. embassy in Tehran on November 4, 1979. Many of these documents were subsequently published by the students.

2. William Sullivan reports, for example, that "at least 3 separate komitehs were functioning [at the airport] in the precincts of the passenger terminal, in the customs area and on the loading ramps, and it was always difficult to know which one had the upper hand at any given moment." *Mission to Iran* (New York: Norton, 1981), p. 279. A similar picture is portrayed in a cable by the U. S. embassy in Tehran to the Secretary of State in Washington, March 2, 1979. Also see the cable from embassy's Air Force Attaché Col. T. E. Schaefer to DIA in Washington, no. 2653 (Secret NOFORN), March 3, 1979, describing his trip with Captain Johnson to Kapkan, where 22 Americans had been taken prisoners.

3. Interview with the authors, March 1982.

4. Islamic Republican Party, *Mavazihi-Ma* (Tehran, n.d.).

5. U. S., Central Intelligence Agency, Office of Central Reference, Mehdi Bazargan, CRM 78-16626 (Confidential), December 8, 1978. Released by the "Muslim Student Followers of the Imam's Line."

6. Eric Rouleau, "Khomeini's Iran," *Foreign Affairs* (Fall 1980), p. 9.

7. Islamic Republican Party, *Az Hizb Cheh Medanim*, 10,000 copies published by the Central Office of the IRP (Tehran, n.d.).

8. In *Ittila'at*, September 14, 1980.

9. February 28, 1979 speech.

10. Muslim Student Followers of the Imam's Line, *Ifsha-i imperialism* [Exposing Imperialism] (Tehran: Muslim Student Followers of the Imam's Line, n.d.), vol. 1.

11. Ibid.

12. *Az Hizb Cheh Medanim*, p. 17.

13. U. S. Embassy, Tehran, Telegram to the State Department, no. A-6941 (reference no. B-175166), July 1979. Because of the expansionn of the Revolutionary Council, some members of the government became council members.

14. Cable from U. S. Embassy to Secretary of State based on conversation with Bani-Sadr, no. 10827, October 22, 1979.

15. Earlier (March) Bazargan tried to convince Khomeini that unless the economy recovered the government would not survive. At this time Khomeini was persuaded. In a major speech in March, Khomeini called on all leaders, religious and lay, and on Pasdaran to help the government in overcoming economic problems. Reported in cable from U. S. Embassy, Tehran, to Secretary of State, March 8, 1979.

16. Khomeini's speech on the occasion of the anniversary of Khordad (June 5, 1979), reprinted in *Islam and Revolution: Writings and Declarations of Imam Khomeini*, trans. by Hamid Algar (Berkeley: Mizan Press, 1981), pp. 268–74.

17. Ibid.

18. *Az Hizb Cheh Medanim*, p. 33.

19. Ibid.

20. Also mentioned by Oriana Fallaci, "Everybody Wants to Be a Boss," *New York Times,* October 18, 1979, p. 16.

22. Several works deal with Iranian politics in this period. The most important ones are: James Bill, "Power and Religion in Revolutionary Iran," *Middle East Journal* (Winter 1982); *The Iranian Revolution and the Islamic Republic,* Conference Proceedings (Washington, D. C.: Middle East Institute, 1982); Nikki Keddie, *Roots of Revolution* (New Haven: Yale University Press, 1981).

23. As reported in a cable by U. S. Embassy, Tehran, to Secretary of State, Washington, no. 9710 (Confidential), September 1, 1979.

24. *Le Monde,* October 17, 1978.

25. James Cockroff, reporting his interview with Khomeini in a letter to the *New York Times,* January 3, 1979.

26. Information based on conversation between an embassy official and Entezam; see cable from U. S. Embassy, Tehran, to Secretary of State, no. A6941 (Secret), July 8, 1979.

27. There is much evidence of opposition fear of a military coup before Khomeini returned to Iran, and this fear persisted after the establishment of the provisional government. One major function of the Pasdaran was to deter a coup. The purges in the armed forces were another such safeguard.

28. According to American embassy reports, Entezam, a moderate modernist, who was Bazargan's deputy prime minister and later Iranian Ambassador to Sweden, later still jailed in Tehran, did not like Bani-Sadr: "Entezam was absolutely avid about Bani-Sadr, describing him as a menace who wants to talk and complain, but does not want responsibility." Before the overthrow of the Shah, in January 1979, Bazargan supporters such as Entezam were expressing their suspicions about Khomeini's Paris entourage. They regarded them as more radical than themselves. Cable from the Embassy to the Secretary of State, 1077/1 (Secret), January 22, 1979. Also, no. 1447/1 (Secret), January 29, 1979.

29. Interview with Bani-Sadr, Paris, March 1982.

30. Juan J. Linz, "Totalitarian and Authoritarian Regimes," in Fred I. Greenstein and Nelson W. Polsby, eds., *Handbook of Political Science* (Reading, Mass.: Addison-Wesley, 1975), 3:175–411; Giovanni Sartori, *Democratic Theory* (Detroit: Wayne State University Press, 1962); H. V. Wiseman, *Political Systems: Some Sociological Approaches,* (London: Routledge and Kegan Paul, 1966).

31. Carl J. Friedrick, M. Curtis and Benjamin Barber, eds., *Totalitarianism in Perspective: Three Views* (New York: Praeger, 1969); Sigmund Neumann, *Permanent Revolution: Totalitarianism in the Age of International Civil War* (New York: Harper, 1942); Leonard Schapiro, *Totalitarianism* (New York: Praeger, 1972); Carl J. Friedrick and Zbigniew K. Brzezinski, *Totalitarian Dictatorship and Autocracy,* 2d ed. (New York: Praeger: 1965).

32. Linz, "Totalitarian and Authoritarian Regimes," p. 191.

33. Alexander Gershenkron, *Continuity in History and Other Essays* (Cambridge, Mass.: Harvard University Press, 1968), p. 4.

34. Samuel P. Huntington, *Political Order in Changing Societies* (New Haven: Yale University Press, 1968), p. 1.

35. *Islamic Government,* in *Islam and Revolution,* p. 80.

36. IRP, *Mavazihi-Ma,* p. 26.

37. Ibid., p. 41.

38. For some anecdotal comments on this, see V. S. Naipaul's report on "Islamic City Planning," in *Among the Believers: An Islamic Journey* (New York: Vintage, 1982).

39. Khomeini's speech on April 26, 1980, Kayhani Hava'i Urdibihisht 10, 1359 (April 30, 1980).

40. Ibid.

41. In his New Year Message, March 21, 1980, he expanded on this, saying that "most of the blows our society has sustained have been inflicted on it precisely by these university-educated intellectuals, who, with their inflated notions of themselves, speak in a manner only their fellow so-called intellectuals can understand; if the people at large cannot understand them, too bad! Because the people do not exist in the eyes of the intellectuals, only they themselves exist." English translation in *Islam and Revolution.*

42. *Mavazihi-Ma,* p. 36.

43. Ibid. Even before his return from Paris, Khomeini had said he would combat the existing films which he thought were a corrupting influence. Our interview, January 1, 1979.

44. J. Linz, "Totalitarian and Authoritarian Regimes," p. 214.

45. *Mavazihi-Ma,* p. 26.

46. Ibid., p. 34.

47. Ibid., p. 41.

48. James A. Bill, "Power and Religion in Revolutionary Iran," *Middle East Journal* (Winter 1982), 36(1):33–34.

49. The clerical members of the first Council of Guardians were Ayatollah Mohammad Mehdi Amlashi, Gholamreza Rezvani, Ayatollah Mohammad Reza Mahdavi Kani, Ayatollah Ahmad Jannati, Lotfollah Safi, and Ayatollah Abulgasem Khazali.

50. *Kayhan International,* June 9, 1983.

51. Others who were elected to the Central Council include Ayatollah Mohammad Mehdi Rabbani Amlashi (member of the Council of Guardians), Abbas Va'ez Tabasi (Superintendent of Imam Reza's shrine), and Movahedi Kermani (Majlis member).

52. *Kayhan International,* June 1, 1983, p. 2.

53. Neumann, *Permanent Revolution.*

54. According to Majlis Speaker Rafsanjani, when Khomeini "makes a decision on an action he does not allow any doubt to enter his mind . . . the news and reports of various events in the country reach the Imam [Khomeini] through various means. I state here that the main decision-maker of general issues such as the war and others is the Imam himself." *Kayhan International,* June 4, 1983.

55. Alexander Dallin and George Breslauer, *Political Terror in Communist Systems* (Stanford: Stanford University Press, 1970). On Italy see Alberto Aguarone, *L'organizzatione dello stato totalitario* (Turin: Einaudi, 1965), quoted in Linz, "Totalitarian and Authoritarian Regimes," p. 219.

56. For an example of this terminology, see Khomeini's April 1979 speech, *Majmuʿa-yi Kamil,* pp. 135–36.

57. *Mavazihi-Ma,* pp. 37–38.

58. Ibid.

59. Ibid.

60. In his New Year message, March 1980, Khomeini warned everyone to "be aware that to adopt a syncretistic ideology is a great treason toward Islam and the Muslims, the bitter fruits of which will become apparent in the years ahead. Unfortunately, we see that because of the failure to understand certain aspects of Islam correctly and precisely, these aspects have been mixed with elements of Marxism, so that a melange has come into being that is totally incompatible with the progressive laws of Islam."

61. The IRP has stated a goal of 20 million militia members. *Mavazihi-Ma,* p. 52.

62. Some have also reported the existence of another organization dealing with domestic security, SAVAMA; others doubt its existence. Elaine Sciolino, "Iran's Durable Revolution," *Foreign Affairs* (Spring 1983).

63. *Iran Liberation* (July 19, 1982) 28:5, and the *Times* (London), July 1, 1981.

64. Elaine Sciolino, "Iran's Durable Revolution."

65. See Elie Kedouri, *Islamic Revolution,* Salisbury Papers no. 6, London. See also his "Khomeini's Political Heresy," *Policy Review* (Spring 1980), pp. 133–46.

66. For the Mujahedeen position, see National Council of Resistance, *Platform of the Provisional Government of the Democratic Islamic Republic of Iran* (Long Beach, Calif., 1982), p. 10.

67. Our interview, March 1982.

68. *Mavazihi-Ma,* p. 57.

69. The term, which can be translated as "the Disinherited" or "the Dispossessed," is associated with the writings of Ali Shariʿati.

70. *Mavazihi-Ma,* p. 58.

71. Our Interview, January 1, 1979.

72. See *MERIP Reports* (May 1980), 87:12. Also see *MERIP Reports* (March–April, 1982), pp. 22–25.

73. "Land must be distributed according to the Shariah," Khomeini said in his 1980 New Year address, "and only the competent courts have the right to sequester land after due investigation. None else has the right to encroach on anyone's land or orchards. Unauthorized persons in general have no right to intervent in these affairs. . . . Anyone who acts in defiance of Islamic and legal criteria will be subject to severe prosecution."

74. Except to call for distribution of land newly coming under cultivation to those who will work it themselves.

75. Central Office of Statictics, *Iran der Ayenahi Amar* (Tehran, 1360).

76. Ibid.

77. Some government officials wanted to complete some of the nuclear plants. Reportedly Deputy Premier Tabatabai told the German government in October 1979 that Iran was interested in completing the Bushir nuclear plant. Telegram from U. S. Embassy, Bonn, to the State Department, no. 19172, October 1979.

78. Iran der Ayenahi Amar.

79. National Movement of the Iranian Resistance, *Iran 1981* (London, February 1982).

80. Ibid.; *Iran der Ayenahi Amar*.

81. *Iran der Ayenahi Amar*.

82. Patrick Clawson, "Iran's Economic Problems and Islamic Economics" (paper presented to the Conference on Iranian Forces in the Gulf, Center for Strategic Studies, Georgetown University, Washington, D. C., March 10, 1982).

83. *Middle East Economic Digest* (May 6, 1983), p. 22.

84. Iranian government officials told visitors in 1982 that they had reduced the inflation rate to 18 percent. Opposition sources estimate it at 80 percent. The actual figure is probably somewhere in between. *Iran Solidarity* (May–June 1982), p. 2 (published by the Fedaii Organization).

85. *Iran Times,* May 21, 1982.

86. Fischer has described the Shah's efforts to displace the religious network of social and socioeconomic institutions with his own secular ones. Michael Fisher, *Iran: From Religious Dispute to Revolution* (Cambridge, Mass.: Harvard University Press, 1980).

87. Erhard Franz, *Minderheiten in Iran* (Hamburg: German Orient Institute, Middle East Documentation, 1981), p. 23. Other studies dealing with this problem include: S. Burky, "The Ethnic Composition of Iran," *Central Asian Review* (1960), 8(4):417–20; S. Aliyeu, "The Problem of Nationalism in Iran," *Central Asian Review* (1966), 14(1):62–70; M. Ivanov, "The Question of Nationalities in Iran," *Donya* (Spring 1971), 14:48–77; Leonard Helfgolt, "The Structural Foundation of the National Minority in Revolutionary Iran," *Iranian Studies* (1980), 13:196–214; Louis Beck, "Revolutionary Iran and its Tribal Peoples," *MERIP Reports* (1980), 87:14–20.

88. See Joseph Rothschild, *Ethnopolitics: A Conceptual Framework* (New York: Columbia University Press, 1981).

89. S. Enders Wimbush, *Iran's Ethnic Factions Threaten to Split the State,* Los Angeles: RAND Corporation, Rand/P-6477, April 1980).

90. For a more thorough analysis of this question, see Zalmay Khalilzad, *The Security of Southwest Asia* (London: IISS, 1983).

91. *Kayhan International,* May 30, 1983; see also Firuz Kazemzadeh, "The Terror Facing the Baha'is," *New York Review of Books* (1982), 29(8):43–44.

92. *Mavazihi-Ma,* p. 40.

93. On the background of the Kurdish problem, see G. Chaliand, *People Without a Country* (London: Zed Press, 1980).

94. *Tehran Times,* June 19, 1980.

95. *Arab News,* May 9, 1979.

96. He had been sentenced to death by the Shah for separatist activities. Later his sentence was reduced to 8 years in jail.

97. *Dawn* (Karachi), August 20, 1979.

98. *Tehran Times,* August 30, 1979.

99. *Tehran Times,* January 26, 1979.

100. *Tehran Times,* December 25, 1979.

101. *Tehran Times,* October 14, 1979.

102. Leonard Binder, *Iran: Political Development in a Changing Society* (Berkeley: University of California Press, 1982), p. 160; and Leonard Helfgott, "The Structural Foundation of National Minority Problems in Revolutionary Iran," *Iranian Studies* (1980), 13:195–214.

103. On the background of the Mujahedeen, see Shahram Chubin, "Leftist Forces in Iran," *Problems of Communism* (July–August 1980), pp. 15–18; Ervand Abrahamian, *Iran Between Two Revolutions* (Princeton: Princeton University Press, 1982), pp. 489–94; Mujahadeen, *Sharh-i Tasys va Tarikhehah-i Vaqa'eh-i Sazeman-i Mujahedeen* (Description of Establishment, Short History, and the Major Developments of the Mujahedeen) (Tehran, 1979).

104. Sepehr Zabih, *The Communist Movement in Iran* (Berkeley: University of California Press, 1966); U. S. Department of State, *World Strength of the Communist Party Organization* (Washington, D.C., 1973); Richard Staar, ed., *Yearbook of International Communist Affairs* (Stanford: Hoover Institution Press, 1976), p. 542; Younes Parsa Benab, "Political Organization in Iran" (Spring 1979), 3(1):30–80; Abrahamian, *Iran Between Two Revolutions;* Chubin, "Leftist Forces in Iran."

105. National Voice of Iran (clandestine), "Pro-U.S. Groups Hiding Behind Islamic Mask," *Foreign Broadcast Information Service, South Asia* (May 18, 1982), 8:1–4.

106. Interviews with Iranian opposition leaders in Paris, March 1982.

107. Ashraf Pahlavi now lives in Paris and New York. She helps finance some of the monarchist groups, but is keeping a low public profile, some say because her reputation for corruption might harm the monarchist cause. Her son, active in the movement, was assassinated in Paris. Her daughter Azadeh Shafik leads a movement called "Free Iran." The newspaper of the same name denounces the role played by the U. S., and the movement claims to view the young Shah as merely a symbolic integrative figure who will be titular head of a democratic parliamentary Iran.

108. Oveyssi was a former commander-in-chief of the Iranian ground forces. He left Iran at the time of the government of Shahpur Bakhtiar. Reportedly he wanted to organize a coup before the success of the oppositon.

109. While Bakhtiar's opponents have accused him of selling Iran to Iraq, he compares himself to Germans opposed to Hitler who cooperated with the allies. Bakhtiar is reported to have visited Iraq several times before and during the Iran-

Iraq war; allegedly his tactical plan was to allow Iraq to defeat Khomeini, to which purpose he encouraged them to attack Iran. This theory is held by both Bani-Sadr and the monarchists around Princess Azadeh. Bani-Sadr says that Bakhtiar is worse than the Shah because of his cooperation with Iraq and his instigation of the Iraqi attack against Iran. Our interview, March 1982.

110. Shahrough Akhavi, "Clerical Politics in Iran Since 1979," in *The Iranian Revolution and the Islamic Republic,* Conference Proceedings (Washington, D. C.: Middle East Institute, 1982), p. 17.

111. According to Bani-Sadr only a minority of the clerics (10 percent) support the principle of Vilayat-e-Faqih and cleric domination of and participation in the political process. Interview with Cheryl Benard.

112. There have been several attempts at identifying the various groupings within the IRP. For one view of IRP factions, see Akhavi, "Clerical Politics in Iran Since 1979," pp. 17–28. For another view see Gregory Rose, "Factional Alignment in the Central Council of the Islamic Republican Party of Iran: A Preliminary Taxonomy," in *The Iranian Revolution and the Islamic Republic,* pp. 45–53. Also see *Iran Times,* February 26, 1982.

113. NVOI, "The Mask of U.S.-Made Association Must Be Ripped Off," *Foreign Broadcast Information Service, South Asia* (Tuesday, May 18, 1982), 82-096. Gregory Rose has argued that the Hujatiya group was the dominant faction in the IRP Central Council prior to the summer of 1981 and that the Maktabis have become dominant since. He also asserts that the Hujatis were led by Beheshti and included other prominent personalities such as Jalaleddin Farsi. Rose also believes that they favor closer relations with the Soviets than the Maktabis. Rose, "Factional Alignment," p. 49.

114. James Bill, "Power and Religion in Revolutionary Iran," *Middle East Journal* (Winter 1982), pp. 22–48.

6. THE ISLAMIC REPUBLICANS AND THE WORLD

1. Carl J. Friedrich and Zbigniew K. Brzezinski, *Totalitarian Dictatorship and Autocracy* (New York: Praeger, 1965), pp. 353–66; John Armstrong, *The Politics of Totalitarianism* (New York: Random House, 1961).

2. *The Guardian* (November 1978).

3. The Iranian Constitution, in somewhat milder terms, states the same point: "According to the Koran all Muslims are of the same and one single religious community, and the Islamic Republican Government of Iran is bound to base its general policies on the coalition and unity of the Islamic nations, and it should exert continuous efforts to realize the political, economic and cultural unity of the Islamic World." Principle II.

4. Speech, February 11, 1980.

5. See Friedrich and Brzezinski, *Totalitarian Dictatorship,* pp. 353–66.

6. *Islamic Government*, in *Islam and Revolution: Writings and Declarations of Imam Khomeini*, trans. by Hamid Algar (Berkeley: Mizan Press, 1981), pp. 48–49.

7. Mohammad Dashti, *The Selected Messages of Iman Khomeini Concerning Iraq and the War Iraq Imposed on Iran* (Tehran: The Ministry of Islamic Guidance, 1981). In an earlier speech, Khomeini had been even more conciliatory: "Islam wants to be the friends of all countries of the world, and the Islamic Government wants to have relations of correct mutual understanding with all peoples and all governments, provided they, too, in return show respect for the Islamic state." *Ettela'at*, July 15, 1979.

8. Islamic Republican Party, *Mavazihi-Ma* (Tehran, n.d.), pp. 81–86.

9. Aim Number Three; *Mavazihi-Ma*, p. 82.

10. Aim Number Four; ibid.

11. Aim Number Five; ibid.

12. Ibid., p. 83.

13. Ibid.

14. Ibid., p. 84.

15. Ibid.

16. Khomeini's hostility to the U. S. policies in Iran had a long history. In 1963 he denounced the granting of capitulatory rights to the U. S. ("Our dignity has been trampled underfoot. The dignity of Iran has been destroyed. The dignity of the armed forces has been trampled underfoot.") He charged that Iran had "sold itself" and "reduced Iran to the level of a colony." Translated by Hamid Algar in *Islam and Revolution*, pp. 181–83. In 1967 he had declared, "Let the American President know that in the eyes of the Iranian nation he is the most repulsive member of the human race today because of the injustice he had imposed on our Muslim nation." Ibid., p. 186. In 1967 he argued that he had been sent into exile because of his opposition to the U. S., Ibid., p. 189.

17. Interview, December 1978.

18. *Islam and Revolution*, p. 185.

19. Since the U. S. maintained listening posts in Iran, this principle excluded the possibility of establishment of such facilities by any power.

20. Speech, February 11, 1980.

21. IRP, *Mavazihi-Ma*, p. 84.

22. Ibid.

23. Ibid., p. 85.

24. Ibid.

25. Ibid.

26. Already in 1963, when he was leading the opposition to the Shah, Khomeini in a message to the army commanders had said, "I know their [army commanders'] hearts are troubled by . . . subordination to Israel, and that they do not wish Iran to be trampled by the boots of the Jews." April 13, 1963 declaration, in *Islam and Revolution*, pp. 175–76. Later that year, he charged "that Israel does not wish the Qur'an to exist in this country. Israel does not wish the 'ulman

to exist in this country. Israel does not wish a single learned man to exist in this country." Ibid., p. 177.

27. Documents captured at the Israeli Embassy; Moshe Dayan talked about his last visit to Tehran to General Toufanian. Minutes from meeting held in Tel-Aviv between H. E. General M. Dayan, Foreign Minister of Israel, and H. E. General H. Toufanian, Vice Minister of War, Imperial Government of Iran, July 18, 1977 (Top Secret).

28. Ibid.

29. Message of September 14, 1979, in *Islam and Revolution*, p. 276. Speaker of the Majlis Rafsanjani has justified his country's demand for the overthrow of the Iraqi regime in order to prevent Arab moderates from effecting reconciliation with Israel. *Kayhan International*, June 11, 1983, p. 1.

30. Khomeini has declared, "We extend our support to any people under domination, who are struggling to gain independence and liberty. We are telling them straightforwardly that a 'right' is something which should be taken. They should first of all put an end to the domination of the superpowers of the world." Speech on the second anniversary of the victory against the Shah, February 11, 1981.

31. International Monetary Fund, *Directions of Trade 1982* (Washington, D.C: IMF, 1982), p. 208.

32. A detailed examination of U. S. policy is outside the scope of our book. Useful expositions may be found in Michael A. Ledeen and William H. Lewis, *Debacle: The American Failure in Iran* (New York: Knopf, 1981); Barry Rubin, *Paved with Good Intentions* (Oxford: Oxford University Press, 1980); William H. Sullivan, *Mission to Iran* (New York: Norton, 1981); R. K. Ramazani, *The United States and Iran* (New York: Praeger, 1982); Sephehr Zabih, *Iran Since the Revolution* (Baltimore: Johns Hopkins University Press, 1982); *Ettela'at*, March 28–30, 1979.

33. Cable from U. S. Embassy, Tehran, to the Secretary of State, no. 0431/1 (Secret), January 9, 1979, published by the Students Followers of the Imam's Line (Tehran, n.d.).

34. Ibid.

35. Mohammad Tavassoli, a leading LMI member, has thanked the embassy for restraining the army. Cable from U. S. Embassy to Secretary of State, no. 0920/1 (Secret), January 28, 1979.

36. U. S. Embassy, Tehran, to Secretary of State, no. 1077/1 (Confidential), January 22, 1979.

37. U. S. Embassy, Tehran, to Secretary of State, no. 0431/1 (Secret), January 9, 1979.

38. Secretary of State to Tehran Embassy, no. 4510, January 7, 1979 (Confidential).

39. Henry Precht, "Memorandum to the Files" (Secret-Sensitive), Conversation with Dr. Ibrahim Yazdi, Adviser to Khomeini, December 13, 1978. Walter

Zimmerman, head of the political section at the U. S. Embassy in Paris, was also in contact with Yazdi. Ambassador Sullivan describes these contacts as "nonproductive." Sullivan, *Mission to Iran.*

40. Precht, "Memorandum to the Files."

41. Sullivan, *Mission to Iran.*

42. Cable from Captain H. F. Johnson to DIA, no. 2653 (Secret NOFORN), March 2, 1979.

43. Ibid.

44. Already the Bakhtiar government had canceled approximately $7 billion in U. S. military contracts for F-16 fighters, Air Warning and Control System (AWACS) aircraft, destroyers, and RF4E reconnaissance aircraft.

45. He was described by American chargé Bruce Laingen as an "unusually polished and urbane and westernized Iranian, very much in the inner circle of the revolution here in Iran, but hardly a revolutionary in style or appearance." Letter from Laingen to the American Ambassador to Sweden, Rodney Kennedy Minott, July 10, 1974, released by the Muslim Students Followers of the Imam's Line.

46. The American officials took note of Khomeini's attacks against the U. S. Cable from the U. S. Embassy, Tehran, to the Secretary of State, no. 3688 (Confidential), April 17, 1978.

47. U. S. Embassy, Tehran, to the State Department, no. 7064/1, July 8, 1979.

48. U. S. Embassy, Tehran, to the Secretary of State, April 16, 1979 (Secret). No. not legible.

49. U. S. Embassy, Tehran, to the Secretary of State, no. 3688, (Confidential), April 7, 1979.

50. Ibid.

51. From USICA to the U. S. Embassy, Tehran, no. 16052 (Confidential), July 11, 1979. Khomeini questioned the utility of maintaining ties with the U. S., declaring that Iran did not need the United States. *Ettela'at,* no. 15858, May 20, 1979. According to Beheshti, "We had repeatedly said in the Central Council of the Party that we must try to bring our relations with the U. S. to zero as rapidly as possible." *Az Hizb Cheh Medanim,* p. 29.

52. Bazargan's letter contained in a cable from the U. S. Embassy.

53. Letter from C. W. Naas to the Prime Minister Bazargan, May 24, 1979.

54. U. S. Embassy, Tehran, to the Secretary of State, no. 5491 (Secret), May 27, 1979. On May 5, Bazargan had told Americans that if the U. S. "had any information that would help Iran defend its independence from its enemies . . . we will appreciate it if you can pass it to us." U. S. Embassy, Tehran, to the Secretary of State, no. 4679 (Secret), May 6, 1979.

55. U. S. Embassy, Tehran, to the Secretary of State, no. 5491 (Secret), May 27, 1979.

56. Secretary of State to the Tehran Embassy, no. 106729, August 8, 1979.

57. U. S. Embassy, Tehran, to the Secretary of State, no. 8946 (Secret), August 1979. Our translation from Persian publication of U. S. Embassy files.

58. In *Islam and Revolution,* p. 305.

59. U. S. Embassy, Tehran, to the Secretary of State, no. 8970 (Confidential), August 12, 1979.

60. U. S. Embassy, Tehran, to the Secretary of State, No. 11089, October 16, 1979.

61. Ibid.

62. U. S. Embassy, Stockholm, to the Secretary of State, no. 4164, October 9, 1979.

63. Ambassador Sullivan at least implicitly blamed the disintegration of the armed forces on U. S. policies. He argued that he sought unsuccessfully Washington's approval for efforts "to convince the Khomeini [Bazargan] group and the armed forces that they share a broad community of interests and should work together to eliminate the Communists. In rejecting this policy recommendation, Washington directed a series of tactical actions which succeeded in placing the religious and the military in antagonism to each other. This resulted in the consequences we consistently warned about—the disintegration of the military. . . ." Sullivan, *Mission to Iran,* p. 273. Sullivan does not say what those tactical actions were.

64. The government asked 25 military advisers to stay in Iran. It also arranged, with some difficulty because of the existing komitehs, for American Air Force officers to reach Kapkan, pay the Iranians 30,000,000 rials in back pay, and rescue the 22 American technicians held there.

65. In September 1979, Entezam complained that "1000 Iranian helicopters were grounded because of improper maintenance and unavailability of spare parts." He characterized Iran's need for spare parts as "vital." U. S. Embassy, Stockholm, to the Secretary of State, no. 3638 (Confidential), September 1979.

66. From U. S. Embassy, Tehran, to the Secretary of State, April 16, 1979.

67. From the U. S. Embassy, Stockholm, to the Secretary of State, no. 7950 (Secret), October 9, 1979.

68. From the U. S. Embassy, Tehran, to the Secretary of State, no. 4679 (Secret), May 6, 1979.

69. Meeting between U. S. Embassy official and Tehran Mayor Mohammad Tavassoli, described in a cable from the U. S. Embassy, Tehran to the Secretary of State, no. 6211, June 14, 1979.

70. Sullivan, *Mission to Iran,* p. 247.

71. See embassy report of a meeting with Bazargan; U. S. Embassy, Tehran, to the Secretary of State, no. 4679 (Secret), May 6, 1979.

72. Sullivan, *Mission to Iran,* p. 247.

73. U. S. Embassy, Tehran, to the Secretary of State, no. 7930 (Secret/NODIS/CHEROKEE), July 1979. Also see no. 10506 (same classification), September 30, 1979.

74. U. S. Embassy, Tehran, to the Secretary of State, no. 7930 (Secret/MODES/CHEROKEE), July 1979.

75. Henry Precht (Director of the Office of Iranian Affairs in the State Department) to Bruce Laingen, U. S. Chargé in Iran, August 2, 1979.

76. U. S. Embassy, Tehran, to the Secretary of State, no. 11516, October 31, 1979.

77. Bazargan met with Brzezinski in Algiers, after the Shah had been admitted to the U. S. This did not endear him to his fundamentalist opponents.

78. During the first two days of the takeover, Bazargan wanted to organize a rescue, but apparently Khomeini finally decided to support the takeover and the government fell. *Time* (European Edition), November 26, 1979, p. 15.

79. *Time* (European Edition), January 7, 1980, p. 17.

80. Ibid., p. 16.

81. *Time* (European Edition), November 26, 1979, p. 20.

82. *Time* (European Edition), January 7, 1980, p. 17.

83. Ibid., p. 16.

84. Ibid.

85. See, for example, Georgy Kim's "Ideological Struggle in Developing Countries," *International Affairs* (April 1980).

86. Y. Primakov, "Dialectic of Social Development and Ideological Struggle: Islam and Social Development Processes in Foreign Oriental Countries," *Voprosy Filosofii*, no. 5, August 11, 1980, trans. by JPRS. Alexander Bovin, *Vedeya,* September 3–9, 1979.

87. BBC, *Summary of World Broadcasts: USSR,* September 29, 1978.

88. Ibid., October 10, 1978.

89. BBC, *Summary of World Broadcasts: Radio Moscow in Persian,* December 19, 1978.

90. Ibid., and January 10 and 12, 1979.

91. Ibid., January 5, 1979.

92. *Dunia,* a Tudeh Party publication, nos. 6–7, 1357.

93. In an April 4, 1979 *Pravda* article, Moscow claimed that "during the Iranian peoples' struggle against the monarchy, the USSR resolutely sided with the Iranian Revolution and did everything to prevent outside interference in Iran's affairs and block plans for armed intervention against the revolution." *Pravda,* April 4, 1979.

94. Foreign Broadcast Information Service (FBIS), *USSR,* July 24, 1979, P.Hl.

95. P. Demchenko, "Khrusheniye Absolyutizma" [Collapse of Absolutism] *Kommunist* (February 1979), 3:83. Also see his, "Iran: Stanovleniye republiki" [Iran: The Making of a Republic], *Kommunist* (June 1979), 9:116.

96. Kim, "Ideological Struggle."

97. There were several reports of Soviet offers to sell arms to Iran: *Times,* October 6, 1980, and *Baltimore Sun,* August 23, 1980.

98. Primakov, "Dialectic." Also A. Bovin, in *Vedelya,* September 3–9, 1979.

99. NVOI, "Another Dreadful Crime by Agents of World-Devouring America," FBIS, *South Asia Service* (SAS) 82-037, February 24, 1982.

100. NVOI, "Washington's Satanic Policy," FBIS, *SAS,* 82-029, February 11, 1982.

101. NVOI, 'Reagan's Hypocrises," FBIS, *SAS,* 82-034.

102. FBIS, *SAS,* 82-093, May 13, 1982.

103. Radio Moscow Persian broadcast, afternoon of March 27, 1980, monitored by Zalmay Khalilzad.

104. NVOI, "Dismiss the Liberals and Other Dregs From Sensitive Government Organizations," FBIS, *SAS,* 82-036, February 23, 1982.

105. FBIS, *SAS,* 82-091, May 11, 1982.

106. NVOI, "Being in Harmony with Ziaul Haq's Regime is Beneath the Dignity of Our Islamic Republic," FBIS, *SAS,* 82-097, May 1982.

107. FBIS, *SAS,* 82-096, May 18, 1982.

108. FBIS, *SAS,* 82-103, May 27, 1982.

109. FBIS, *SAS,* 82-103, May 27, 1982.

110. Entezam reported the Soviet offers to the Americans; U. S. Embassy, Tehran, to the Secretary of State, October 9, 1979, no. 7950 (Secret). Also see no. 10977/1, October 15, 1979.

111. NVOI, "Justice Seekers Must Unite in a Single Rank," FBIS, *SAS,* 82-028, February 10, 1982. Also see FBIS, *SAS,* 82-039, February 26, 1982, and FBIS, *SAS,* 82-103, May 27, 1982.

112. *Financial Times* (London), June 13, 1979.

113. In a February 20, 1982 broadcast, NVOI complained that some Tudeh students had been expelled from the university. FBIS, *SAS,* 82-036, February 23, 1982. A later statement complains further about the "purges" of a large number of "true revolutionaries" from Iran's educational institutions. FBIS, *SAS,* 82-076, April 20, 1982.

114. John Stemple's report after conversations with Entezam, from Secretary of State to the U. S. Embassy, Tehran, no. 3941, August 1979.

115. Qutbzadeh's message of August 11, 1980 to the Soviet Foreign Minister was sent to Moscow on August 11, 1980. It was made available by the Muslim Student Association of the U. S. and Canada (The Persian Speaking Group), P. O. Box 6322, Albany, Calif. 94706.

116. John Stemple's report on conversations with Entezam (see note 114).

117. *Kayhan International,* June 2, 1983, p. 2.

118. *Bakinskii Rabochii,* October 9, 1981, trans. by the Joint Publications Research Service, JPRS # 79606, p. 31; referred to by Muriel Atkin, "The Islamic Republic and the Soviet Union," *The Iranian Revolution and the Islamic Republic,* Conference Proceedings (Washington, D. C.: Middle East Institute, 1982), p. 146.

119. FBIS, Iran, August 15, 1980, pp. 11–16.

120. Qutbzadeh's message of August 11, 1980, cited in note 115.

121. See FBIS, *MENA,* May 3, 1979, p. R3. Also May 9, 1979, p. R4. FBIS, *MENA,* June 27, 1979; FBIS, South Asia, November 10, 1981, January 7 and 12, 1982.

122. Translated in *Islam and Revolution*, p. 285.

123. NVOI, "A Provocative Attack at the Esteqlal Hotel," FBIS, *SAS*, 82-025, February 5, 1982. Also see FBIS, *SAS*, April 6, 1982.

124. Pro-Soviet groups complained about this. For example see, NVOI, "Dismiss the Liberals and Other Dregs from Sensitive Government Organizations," FBIS, *SAS*, 82-036, February 23, 1982.

125. FBIS, *SAS*, April 13, 1982. In another broadcast it is attacked as a "mouthpiece of Western and SAVAKist interest." FBIS, *SAS*, 82-039, February 26, 1982.

126. FBIS, *SAS*, 82-196, October 8, 1982.

127. NVOI, "Traitors Who Are the Implementors of an Anti-Iranian Trend," FBIS, *SAS*, April 15, 1982. When Qutbzadeh was on trial, NVOI urged the regime not to show mercy to this "mercenary wolf." FBIS, *SAS*, April 27, 1982. His subsequent execution was commended. FBIS, *SAS*, 82-196, October 8, 1982.

128. NVOI, "America's Strategy of Terror in Our Land," FBIS, *SAS*, 82-028, February 10, 1982; NVOI, "Ibrahim Yazdi—Agent of the U. S. CIA," FBIS, *SAS*, 82-035, February 22, 1982. The broadcast called for Yazdi's punishment.

129. NVOI, "The Mask of U.S.-Made Associations Must be Ripped Off," FBIS, *SAS*, 82-096, May 18, 1982.

130. Ibid.

131. Alvin Rubenstein, "The Soviet Union and Iran under Khomeini," *International Affairs* (Autumn 1981), p. 613.

132. *New York Times*, July 19, 1979.

133. IMF, *Directions of Trade*, p. 208.

134. *Financial Times* (London), June 13, 1979, *Dawn* (Karachi), September 20, 1979.

135. *Middle East* (London), April 1982, p. 18.

136. Ibid.

137. In his Persian New Year Message in 1980, Khomeini stated "I vehemently condemn once more the savage occupation of Afghanistan by the aggressive plunderers of the East, and I hope that the noble Muslim people of Afghanistan will achieve victory and true independence as soon as possible, and be delivered from the clutches of the so-called champions of the working class." Translated in *Islam and Revolution*, p. 287. The same language is repeated in a September 12, 1981 speech, ibid., p. 301.

138. FBIS, *SAS*, 82-179, September 15, 1979.

139. Ibid.

140. NVOI, "The Afghan Problem—An Excuse to Divert Public Opinion," FBIS, *SAS*, 82-175, September 9, 1982.

141. FBIS, *SAS*, 82-169, August 31, 1982.

142. FBIS, *SAS*, 82-166, August 26, 1982.

143. NVOI, "The People Are Defending the Democratic Government of Afghanistan," FBIS, *SAS*, 82-155, August 11, 1982. Also FBIS, *SAS*, 82-116, June 16, 1982.

144. FBIS, *SAS,* 82-110, June 8, 1980; FBIS, *SAS,* 82-123, June 25, 1982. "Continuations of the War Are but the Extension of the Enemy's External Policy," FBIS, *SAS,* 82-160, August 18, 1982. See also FBIS, *SAS,* 82-138, July 10, 1982.

145. According to American military officers who had gone to Kapkan base to free the Americans held captive there, the officer in charge of the Mashad troops sent to Kapkan talked about his training with the Palestinians and "having fought alongside Arafat." Colonel T. E. Schaefer and Captain Johnson to DIA (Secret), no. 2635, March 2, 1979.

146. U. S. Embassy, Tehran, to the Secretary of State, 5491 (Secret), May 27, 1979.

147. In August 1979, Entezam told John Stemple that he was convinced that George Habash had been in Khuzistan three times since the Shah's overthrow and was financing local opposition to the new government. Secretary of State to the Tehran Embassy, no. 3941 (Secret), August 1979.

148. U. S. Embassy, Tehran, to the Secretary of State, no. 5491, May 27, 1979.

149. According to an American briefing to Iranian officials "By the end of September [1979], senior members of the Iraqi Government had become convinced that Iranian policy was to actively pursue its claims to Bahrayn" (which had been abandoned by the Shah). CIA Station officer, Tehran, to the Director, no. 543216 (Secret), November 1, 1979. In June 1979, Tehran radio's Arabic program called on Iraqis: "People of Iraq: it is time for you to unite and work as one man to topple the regime of tyrants . . . what is required of you today is to sacrifice yourselves and your property in the Jihad to establish the role of divine justice." FBIS, *MENA,* June 20, 1979, p. R-14.

150. Entezam had told American officials that Qutbzadeh made broadcast policy without checking with the government. U. S. Embassy, Tehran to the Secretary of State, no. 6378 (Confidential), June 19, 1979. See also a similar report to the Embassy by government spokesman Sadiq Tabatabai, U. S. Embassy, Tehran, to the Secretary of State, no. 7064/1, July 8, 1979. Yazdi was quoted several times as calling for an end to the "propaganda war" between Iran and Iraq. FBIS, *MENA,* July 16, 1979, p. 1.

151. U. S. Embassy, Tehran, to the Secretary of State, no. 12065 (Secret), March 20, 1979. The embassy believed that the Shi'ites of Southern Lebanon "might give us a handle to counter" the Palestinian "hold over the Islamic Movement" in Iran.

152. According to Pakistani officials, Khomeini's anger at Pakistan was particularly due to the fact that the Pakistani president was the last head of state to visit the Shah, and his belief that close ties existed between the Pakistani regime and the Shah. Interview in Islamabad, January 1982.

153. Speech, March 21, 1980, in *Islam and Revolution,* p. 286.

154. There have also been periods of cooperation. For background discussion of Iraq-Iran relations, see Stephen R. Grummon, *The Iran-Iraq War—Islam Embattled,* Washington Papers, no. 92 (New York: Praeger, 1982).

155. Prior to the invasion, Iraq declared the 1975 treaty between the two countries as null and void. It declared its war aims to force Iran: (1) to recognize Iraqi sovereignty over Shatt-al-Arab; (2) to refrain from interfering in Iraqi internal affairs (as well as the internal affairs of other states in the region); and (3) to return the Abu Musa and the Greater and the Lesser Tunb islands occupied by the Shah to the United Arab Emirates. FBIS, *MENA,* September 29, 1980, p. E-3.

156. Prime Minister Ali Rajai declared, "God wants us to share together with the nation of Iraq, in the honor of toppling Saddam and his executioner regime." FBIS, *SAS,* September 23, p. I-7. Hojat-al-Islam Musavi-Khoeini expressed similar sentiment when he said that Saddam Hussein had prepared the ground for Iran to "save the Iraqi people." FBIS, *SAS,* August 9, 1982, p. I-13.

157. FBIS, *SAS,* September 23, 1980, p. I-3.

158. Broadcast by Ad-Dáwah party to Iraq, called on Iraqis to overthrow Saddam Hussein: "Today is yours, the hour is yours and the time for revenge has come. . . . His corrupt regime is on the verge of collapse and it needs someone to topple it." FBIS, *SAS,* July 30, 1982.

159. For the 1982 pilgrimage, Khomeini had appointed Musavi-Khoeini, the cleric who had led the students occupying the American embassy, as the leader of the Iranian pilgrims. He tried to organize demonstrations in Saudi Arabia.

160. Interviews in Pakistan, January 1982. In response to Iraqi protests, Pakistan reportedly told Baghdad they could have similar access if they needed it.

161. Improvement in relations with these two CENTO allies has angered Moscow and Soviet allies in Iran. See FBIS, *SAS,* 82-064, April 12, 1982; April 9, 1982; April 15, 1982; April 23, 1982; May 11, 1982; May 15, 1982; May 19, 1982; May 21, 1982; and July 22, 1982.

162. In interviews with us in early 1982, Afghan and Pakistani fundamentalists complained about this point.

163. FBIS, *SAS,* March 23, 1982.

164. On the employment of the Palestinian irredentism to consolidate the legitimacy of their regimes and define their national identities by other regional leaders, see Charles Cremeans, *The Arabs and the World—Nasser's Arab Nationalist Policy* (New York: Praeger, 1963) and Hatim Nuseibeh, *The Ideas of Arab Nationalism* (Ithaca, N. Y.: Cornell University Press, 1956).

165. FBIS, *SAS,* March 23, 1982.

INDEX

cultural revolution, 116; as a totalitarian leader, 121; criticizes the courts, 122; and land reform, 127, 219n73; and the Kurds, 133–36; tolerance for Tudeh Party, 139–40; distrusts the army, 141; and Islamic internationalism, 147–50; on Israel, 154; on U.S. embassy, 166; and conditions for release of hostages, 166–67; attacks the Soviet Union, 174; on Soviets and Afghanistan, 176; attacks Gulf monarchies, 180; and "export of revolution," 182–85

Kissinger, Henry, 171

Komeleh, 134

Kurdish Democratic Party (KDP), 133–134; banning of, 134

Kurdistan, 134

Kurds, and Islamic government, 133–34

Lahoti, Ayatollah Hassan, 108

Lari, Sayid Mujtaba Rukni Musawi, 94–95

Leiden, Carl, 56

Lembert, Eugen, 63

Lerner, Daniel, 4, 12

Lewis, Bernard, 4

Libya, 28, 184

Liberation Movement of Iran (LMI), 156, 157, 158

Lin Biao, 10

Luckmann, Thomas, 75

Madani, Ayatollah Assatollah, 137

Mainstream development theory, see Development theory

Majlis, see Islamic Assembly; Islamic Consultative Assembly

Man, Marxism, and Islam (Shari'ati), 41

Mardom, 139, 140

Marxism and Other Western Fallacies (Shari'ati), 41

Marxist model of development, 10; see also Dependence theory

Maududi, Maulana, 33

Millennialist movements, see Chiliastic movements

Millspaugh, Arthur, 55

Minorities, and Islamic government, 132–38

Modernists, see Islamic modernists

Modernity, routes to, 69–73, 198n77

Modernization: mainstream views of, 2–6; the leftist version of, 6–12

Moinfar, Ali, 113

Monthly Review, 20

Moore, Barrington, 62; and political constellations, 69; and Iranian case, 69–71; and revolutionary change, 70–71; and revolution from above, 72

Mossadeq, Mohammad, 105; U.S. opposition to, 48; supported by Azerbaijanis, 136

Muhammad, and revolution, 51

Muhammad Reza Shah Pahlavi, see Shah of Iran

Mujahedeen-e-Khalq: as Islamic modernists, 31; as target of violence, 122, 123; estimates of executions, 124; and takeover, 191

Muntaziri, Ayatollah Hussein Ali, 142

Musa, Salama, 96

Muslim authors, on the West, 86, 88–89

Muslim People's Republican Party (MPRP), 136–37

Muslims, and the question of identity, 89–90

Muslim Unity Party, 135

Mustazafin Foundation, 126

Naas, C. W., 160, 164

Naficy, Hamid, 78

Najar, Baldev Raj, 194n22

National Council of Resistance, 134, 139

National Freedom Movement of Iran (NFMI), 105

National Front, 48

National Iranian Oil Company, 105

National Voice of Iran (NVOI), 170, 171, 172, 174, 176

Neo-Marxists: and development theory, 6; and emergence of Islamic Republic, 12

Nirumand, Bahman, 17, 97

Nkrumah, Kwame, 64

Nonalignment, 152

Nourie, Ayatollah Yahya, 166